KEEPING US SAFE:
SECRET INTELLIGENCE
AND HOMELAND SECURITY

KEEPING US SAFE:
SECRET INTELLIGENCE
AND HOMELAND SECURITY

ARTHUR S. HULNICK

 **PRAEGER**

Westport, Connecticut
London

This manuscript was submitted to the CIA, which had no objection to its publication, although its review does not confirm the accuracy of the information nor constitute an endorsement of the author's views.

Library of Congress Cataloging-in-Publication Data

Hulnick, Arthur S., 1935–
    Keeping us safe : secret intelligence and homeland security / Arthur S. Hulnick.
      p. cm.
    Includes bibliographical references and index.
    ISBN 0–275–98150–9 (alk. paper)
    1. Intelligence service—United States. 2. Internal security—United States.
   3. National security—United States. I. Title
JK468.I6H86   2004
363.32'0973—dc22   2004049565

British Library Cataloguing in Publication Data is available.

Library of Congress Catalog Card Number: 2004049565
ISBN: 0–275–98150–9

First published in 2004

Praeger Publishers, 88 Post Road West, Westport, CT 06881
An imprint of Greenwood Publishing Group, Inc.
www.praeger.com

Printed in the United States of America

The paper used in this book complies with the Permanent Paper Standard issued by the National Information Standards Organization (Z39.48-1984).

10 9 8 7 6 5 4 3 2 1

For Oliver

Contents

Acknowledgments

I owe a debt of gratitude to many people for assisting me and encouraging me in the writing of this book. First, thanks to Heather Staines, Senior Editor at Greenwood Publishing Group, who not only asked me to write this book, but who was instrumental in bringing my first book to publication several years ago. The research and writing on this latest project led to the creation of a new course at Boston University on intelligence and homeland security, one of the first in the nation. I appreciate the encouragement of my Department Chairman Erik Goldstein, the willingness of Dean Jeffrey Henderson of BU's College of Arts and Sciences to approve something so new and untested, and the suppport of Associate Dean Susan Jackson in bringing the course into the curriculum. The results were all one might have hoped.

I was aided a great deal in the research for this book by a team of willing and eager graduate students, who quickly pitched in to dig up some of the more obscure data. I wish to thank Emily Thompson, Greg Joachim, Fadi Petro, Dave Diaz, Jim Enos, and Kara Bombach, all of whom gave willingly of their time.

I wish to thank Richard Valcourt, friend, colleague, and literary agent, who made sure that the proposal for the book was translated into an actual project. Richard's work as Editor-in-Chief of the International Journal of Intelligence and CounterIntelligence has helped make the study of intelligence issues a reality at colleges and universities both here and abroad.

I am grateful for the good work done on the manuscript by Judy Ludowitz and her associates at Shepherd, Inc. The original editing on the first draft was ably handled by my daughter Larisa Pazmino, who also edited my first book. This time her good work was complicated by her son Oliver, who demanded a lot more of his mother's time than I did. In dedicating this book to Oliver, I hope that the world in which he grows up is free of the kinds of terrorism I write about here.

Thanks go to my wife Eileen, whose infinite patience and encouragement was most welcome and needed. I was also given support by my daughter Sandra Borgerson, who took the time from her work as a neonatal intensive care nurse and nurse practitioner, in the interest of keeping me on track. All of this assistance and backing kept me focused when it would have been much easier to become swept up in events and avoid coming to closure on this project.

Preface

Just a few days before Christmas, 2003, just as this manuscript was to be sent to the editor, the Bush administration and the Department of Homeland Security raised the threat level for the fourth time since 9/11 to Orange-meaning increased security for travelers, ports, key elements of the U.S. infrastructure, and major cities. People seemed to take the warning of an increased possibility of a terrorist attack on the United States in stride. There was no panic, and most people seemed to go about their business as usual. Was al Qaeda really at work to strike at the United States? The increase in the alert level was based on a high volume of terrorist communication around the world, even though the terrorists knew that U.S. intelligence was listening to what they were saying and writing.

Most observers expect another terrorist strike within the United States, but no one knows where the terrorists will hit us or when. While intelligence seems good enough to detect an increased threat level in general, the system has not yet perfected the sophisticated tools needed to give specific warning. How such tools might be developed is one of the key subjects of this book.

There seemed to be no good reason to delay publication of this book. To wait for the terrorists to strike again or for the other issues and decisions anticipated in the months to come to be resolved may have delayed publication indefinitely.

In some respects, if there is another terrorist strike, it will be a test of the systems that have been put in place since 9/11—another subject of this book. Will our bolstered intelligence and security systems stop the bad guys before they strike? Or, will they somehow break through the barriers we have created at great expense since 9/11? My hope is that, whatever happens, this book will make clear the issues at stake in protecting the homeland. Readers should be able to understand how our systems work and the difficulties involved in operating them.

There are no real secrets in this book. If there were, I would not have been able to write it. I am obligated to protect the secrets I learned in my career in intelligence forever, and as readers can see, I have submitted this manuscript to the CIA so that they could determine that I did not reveal sensitive information. The opinions and evaluations of intelligence and homeland security contained in the book are mine, or belong to the sources I have cited. I have learned, however, from long experience in intelligence work, that much can be learned from open sources. Unfortunately, al Qaeda operatives can learn the same things if they know where to look and how to interpret the material.

One sensible development in the latest increase in security was the admission by several officials that raising the threat level to Orange from Yellow, from significant to high threat, was really intended for security professionals and not for the general public. Much of the security applied at this level would not be visible to the public at all, but would take place behind the scenes. Will it be foolproof? Of course not. But, if enhanced security forces terrorists to postpone or call off their operations, so much the better. Just like the homeowner who hopes his security lights and alarm system will cause a burglar to go somewhere else, security against terrorism might force al Qaeda or other groups to seek easier targets. Stopping them altogether is a much more difficult proposition. Still, we must try to do so, and how we do it is the subject of much of this book.

At the time of this writing, the Supreme Court is slated to rule on the constitutionality of the Bush administration's efforts to detain foreign combatants or U.S. citizens without giving them access to lawyers or the courts. Have we given up our freedoms in the name of security? Or, has the administration gone beyond the intent of Congress and the limits of the Constitution? Should intelligence be used to prosecute criminals—something that used to be forbidden in the interest of protecting intelligence sources and methods—or must we permit potential terrorists to go free if the government can't or won't permit intelligence sources to appear at trial. The courts have rejected the administration's claim that jurists have no role to play in dealing with terrorism.

Another event for which I could not wait to publish this book was the final report of the Independent Commission on 9/11 headed by former New Jersey governor Tom Kean. The report may reinforce what I have written or contradict some of my judgments. Whatever the outcome, I hope these publications spur a dialogue to help improve our intelligence and security systems, rather than disappear onto library shelves once their revelations pass from media attention.

Unfortunately, the Independent Commission let it be known—even before its final report was released—that it would assign blame for what went wrong on 9/11, but this could be very destructive. Those who take the brunt of the criticism cannot be expected to resume their tasks with increased vigor and enthusiasm. The blame lies with the terrorists who murdered almost three thousand of our people.

We should not forget that intelligence professionals worked unceasingly to prevent the 9/11 disaster and came quite close to uncovering the plot. Similarly, first responders, including police and firefighters in New York and Washington, were able to rescue, evacuate, or otherwise save about 55,000 potential victims on 9/11. If it were not for the heroic work of the first responders, the death toll would have been far higher. They deserve gratitude, not condemnation.

In 2005, yet another independent commission will report on the alleged intelligence failure in Iraq. This new group, headed by former Virginia senator Charles Robb, will make recommendations for improving our intelligence system. This, too, should energize a dialogue about reform and renewal, but waiting for all these reports and studies might only delay changes that probably should come sooner rather than later.

The resignation of George Tenet as director of Central Intelligence, announced in early June, 2004, may make reforms a bit easier, since he was one of the key figures defending the existing intelligence system. Tenet said that he had resigned for personal reasons to spend more time with his family, but the media—as he had predicted—put all kinds of spin on his departure. All the good work he had done in rebuilding morale and competence at the Central Intelligence Agency had been quickly forgotten in the wake of 9/11 and questions about the role of intelligence in Iraq.

Intelligence and homeland security are not static issues, but are changing every day in the face of new threats. I hope this book is helpful to readers as they ponder these changes and observe the responses of their government.

Arthur S. Hulnick
Boston, Massachusetts
8 June 2004

List of Acronyms
and Initialisms

ASIS	American Society for Industrial Security
ATF	Bureau of Alcohol, Tobacco, Firearms and Explosives
ATTF	Antiterrorism Task Forces
BTS	Border and Transportation Security
CATIC	Chinese National Aerotechnology Import and Export Corporation
CBP	Bureau of Customs and Border Protection
CDC	Center for Disease Control and Prevention
CFO	Chief Financial Officer
CI	Counterintelligence
CIA	Central Intelligence Agency
CIG	Central Intelligence Group
COMINT	Communications intelligence
COO	Chief Operating Officer
CREEP	Committee to Reelect the President
CSIS	Canadian Security Intelligence Service
CSO	Chief Security Officer
CTC	Counterterrorist Center
C-TPAT	Customs-Trade Partnership Against Terrorism
DARPA	Defense Advanced Research Projects Agency
DCI	Director of Central Intelligence
DDCI	Deputy Director of Central Intelligence
DDI	Deputy Director of Intelligence (CIA)

DDO	Deputy Director of Operations (CIA)
DDP	Deputy Director of Plans (CIA)
DEA	Drug Enforcement Administration
DHS	Department of Homeland Security
DI	Directorate of Intelligence (CIA)
DIA	Defense Intelligence Agency
DIO	Defense Intelligence Officer
DNI	Director of National Intelligence
DO	Directorate of Operations (CIA)
DoD	Department of Defense
DSS	Defense Security Service
ELF	Earth Liberation Front
ELINT	Electronic intelligence
FAA	Federal Aviation Administration
FBI	Federal Bureau of Investigation
FBIS	Foreign Broadcast Information Service
FEMA	Federal Emergency Management Agency
FISA	Foreign Intelligence Surveillance Act
FLQ	Front for the Liberation of Quebec
Gestapo	Nazi Secret State Police
HSC	Homeland Security Council
HSOC	Homeland Security Operations Center
HUMINT	Human intelligence
IAIP	Information Analysis and Infrastructure Protection
IC	Intelligence Community
ICE	Bureau of Immigration and Customs Enforcement
INR	Bureau of Intelligence and Research
INS	Immigration and Naturalization Service
IRA	Irish Republican Army
ISI	Interservices Intelligence Directorate
JETRO	Japanese External Trade Organization
JIC	Joint Intelligence Committee
JSOC	Joint Special Operations Command
JTTF	Joint Terrorism Task Force
KHAD	Afghan Intelligence
MASINT	Other Military Intelligence Sensors
MI-5	British Security Service
MI-6	The British equivalent of the CIA
MSS	Ministry of State Security
NEDSS	National Electronic Disease Surveillance System
NFIB	National Foreign Intelligence Board
NFIP	National Foreign Intelligence Program
NGA	National Geospatial Intelligence Agency
NGO	Nongovernmental Organizations

NIA	National Intelligence Authority
NIC	National Intelligence Council
NIE	National Intelligence Estimate
NIMA	National Imagery and Mapping Agency
NIO	National Intelligence Officer
NIPE	National Intelligence Programs Evaluation Staff
NOC	Nonofficial cover
NORAD	North American Aerospace Defense Command
NORTHCOM	Northern Command
NRO	National Reconnaissance Office
NSA	National Security Agency
NSC	National Security Council
ODP	Office of Domestic Preparedness
OIPR	Office of Intelligence Policy and Review
OSINT	Open Source Intelligence
OSS	Office of Strategic Services
PCC	Policy Coordinating Committees
PDB	President's Daily Brief
PDF	Panamanian Defense Force
PRC	Peoples Republic of China
R&A	Research and Analysis
RCMP	Royal Canadian Mounted Police
RISSNET	Regional Information Sharing System Network
SARS	Severe Acute Respiratory Syndrome
SCI	Special Compartmented Intelligence
Seals	Sea-Air-Land teams
SEVIS	Student and Exchange Visitor Information System
SIGINT	Signals intelligence
SIRC	Security Intelligence Review Committee
SNIE	Special National Intelligence Estimates
TI	Texas Instruments
TRAC	University Transactional Records Access Clearinghouse
TSA	Transportation Security Administration
TTIC	Terrorist Threat Integration Center
UAV	Unmanned Aerial Vehicle
USIB	U.S. Intelligence Board
WMD	Weapons of Mass Destruction

What Went Wrong

The terrorist attacks on New York City and Washington on September 11, 2001 were the most traumatic and gut-wrenching events many of us have ever experienced. Almost three years later, we have not fully recovered from the first attack on a major U.S. city since the British sacked Washington in the War of 1812. For those of us who remember the Japanese sneak attack on Pearl Harbor in 1941, the terrorist attack was worse because we could watch it happen. The Pearl Harbor attack was a distant event for most of us, reported in the press, of course, and in scratchy radio broadcasts, but 9/11 was right there on TV or in smoky skies. The silence in the air that followed, broken only by the roar of fighter jets overhead, was an eerie reminder of what had happened.

In the days that followed, shock and anger began to focus on the U.S. Intelligence Community (IC), a loose conglomerate of agencies dedicated, among other things, to preventing surprise. It had apparently failed in the worst possible way, permitting a band of 19 terrorists to enter the United States, hijack four airliners almost at the same time, and ram two of them into the World Trade Towers in New York and one into the Pentagon in Washington with devastating effect. Only the heroism of passengers on the fourth airliner kept it from striking its likely target, the Capitol building in Washington. How could the CIA, the FBI, and the others have failed to pick up the trail of the terrorists?

In subsequent months, angry rhetoric from members of Congress, scathing articles in the press, and little response from senior intelligence officials only increased the level of condemnation of the IC. Cries went out for heads to roll, especially those of George Tenet, the director of Central Intelligence (DCI) and Robert Mueller, the new director of the Federal Bureau of Investigation (FBI). Eventually, the U.S. Congress mounted an investigation of the intelligence failure to find out what went wrong and why. As evidence piled up, it became clear that the failure was caused by a variety of factors, some of which might have been overcome by better teamwork, more effective information-sharing, and a more rigorous system for "connecting the dots."

The subsequent public hearings and open testimony revealed a number of problems. It was not clear, however, even with better luck, that the terrorist attack could have been prevented. The congressional hearings illustrated how little some senior members seemed to understand about the intelligence process they were supposed to be overseeing. Some members appeared to be out for blood. Who could forget Michigan Democratic Senator Carl Levin badgering DCI Tenet to identify the individual responsible for failing to read a cable from the field, as if the senator was prepared to have him or her flogged in public.

In 2003, the Congressional Joint Inquiry was made public and almost all of its 850 pages were declassified.[1] A second independent inquiry, chaired by former Republican Governor Tom Kean of New Jersey, either made public or forced the White House to reveal a great deal of additional, previously classified information, including a report from the highly sensitive President's Daily Brief (PDB), a top secret publication whose circulation is limited to a handful of readers. The Kean Commission was supposed to be bi-partisan, with an equal number of Democrats and Republicans, and was orginally slated to be headed by former national security adviser Dr. Henry Kissinger. After controversy erupted over Kissinger's nomination to head the commission, he resigned and the baton was passed to Mr. Kean, a far more moderate and quietly effective choice. His deputy, former Democratic Congressman Lee Hamilton, was equally well received in the spirit of bi-partisanship.

Although the commission began its work in a rather low-key way, its aggressive effort to hold open testimony by President George W. Bush's national security adviser Dr. Condoleeza Rice led to controversy. At first the White House balked, but public pressure forced her testimony, which was widely covered by the national media. It focused attention on the commission and its work and led to some partisan wrangling among the commission members. Later, both President Bush and Vice-President Cheney met with the commission in a private session. The commission's final report, due out in July, 2004, is expected to lay blame for the intelligence failure, as well as recommend some rather controversial changes in government intelligence policy and operations.

Both the independent commission study and the Congressional Joint Inquiry took advantage of hindsight to see how the terrorists might have been stopped. Looking back at the data, it's easy to see how mistakes were made, but this does not explain what it must have been like for intelligence professionals to try to unearth fragmented bits and pieces of information, frustrated by inflexible bureaucracies, hamstrung by legal restrictions, and thwarted by turf battles. Nonetheless, enough material has surfaced so intelligence managers, policy officials, and the public can learn what went wrong and why.

AN INFLEXIBLE SYSTEM

Even if we don't have the full story about what went wrong or why, over time enough material has surfaced to make it possible for those of us who are intelligence veterans to fill in some of the blanks where information remains secret. It is not a pretty picture. Animosity between agencies, bureaucratic rivalries, clashing cultures, risk-avoidance behaviors, reduced resources, as well as a lack of critical data all contributed to the IC's inability to find, track, and stop the terrorists. A system designed to fight the cold war was simply not flexible enough for new enemies and different threats. The system had never been called on to defend our homeland before, and it should have come as no great surprise that it couldn't when the chips were down.

At the same time, it must be remembered that we were facing a clever, devious, secretive terrorist group that was well financed and led. According to Khalid Shaikh Mohammed—one of the masterminds in al Qaeda, Osama bin Laden's terrorist organization, who was captured in March, 2003, in Pakistan—the terrorists spent five years putting the plot together.[2] They apparently planned an even more extensive attack, but lacked the resources and personnel to pull it off. A lack of resources hindered the U.S. intelligence system as well, as funding and personnel cuts, especially in overseas components, took a toll on the capabilities of many of the agencies.

Fortunately, the U.S. Intelligence Community (IC) can be fixed, but it's going to require some rethinking of the entire system. Previous efforts to overhaul the process have failed consistently because of turf problems and a lack of will on the part of both the president and the legislature. Intelligence professionals and those who have spent time observing the process, either from the inside or on the sidelines, recognize some of the problems but have failed to agree on the solutions. We cannot wait any longer, however, because our enemies will certainly take advantage of our failure to act.

PAST EXPERIENCE

In looking back at the development of the intelligence system, it is not surprising that some of our current difficulties stem from past experience. The IC that we have today was constructed out of systems that proved effective in World War II. In the dual-front war we fought against Germany and Japan, U.S. intelligence grew from scattered small units able only to analyze open sources to much more capable organizations prepared for fighting war. Relatively tiny intercept and codebreaking units expanded during the war to become effective weapons against our enemies. The navy units that broke the Japanese codes enabled Admiral Chester Nimitz to deal Japan a decisive blow at the Battle of Midway in June 1942, a scant six months after the surprise attack on Pearl Harbor. Japan never recovered from that defeat, although it fought on until 1945.

SUCCESS QUICKLY FORGOTTEN

This experience illustrates nicely one of the greatest problems in intelligence: that failure is heralded and success is quickly forgotten. Everyone alive then or who has studied World War II remembers clearly that the Japanese attack on Pearl Harbor was probably the worst U.S. intelligence failure of the twentieth century, while few can recall that Nimitz's defeat of Admiral Yamamoto's battle fleet at Midway was perhaps one of the greatest victories for intelligence ever.

Clandestine operations in Europe by the Office of Strategic Services (OSS) laid the groundwork for the invasion of North Africa and the subsequent defeat of Field Marshall Erwin Rommel's Afrika Korps. Secret agents recruited guerrilla fighters and saboteurs for the eventual Allied invasion of France in 1944, while a major deception operation fooled the Germans into thinking that the Normandy invasion was the precursor to an even larger landing at Calais, forcing the Wehrmacht to keep major forces out of action until it was too late to stop the Allied forces from moving on Germany.

Developments in aerial photography made targeted strategic bombing possible, while the establishment of analytic units to process and evaluate bits and pieces of information on an all-source basis became an effective technique for Allied forces. When it became clear that our former ally, the Soviet Union, would become our new enemy, all these intelligence elements were reconstituted in the post–World War II period and trained on the USSR and the other Communist states. The transition was a relatively easy one, marred only by then-FBI director J. Edgar Hoover's abortive efforts to stop the creation of a Central Intelligence Agency so that the FBI could be the intelligence arm of government. Hoover never forgot that he had been outfoxed, a legacy that might have contributed to current troubles, although the real problem is much broader.

THE NEW CIA

The new CIA, established in 1947, reflected the plans drawn earlier by Major General William "Wild Bill" Donovan, who had led the OSS in World War II. Its structure was, in part, influenced by the intelligence failure at Pearl Harbor, where different units had failed to share intelligence data, and where crisis warnings were not transmitted to military commanders on a timely basis. Sound familiar?

In addition to gathering and analyzing intelligence from all sources, the CIA was to carry out "such other activities related to intelligence as the president and National Security Council might from time to time direct," a mandate, however vague, for covert action. In 1954, General James "Jimmy" Doolittle, the hero of the first air raid on Tokyo in 1942, wrote that we were facing an "implacable enemy" whose goal was world domination. Under those circumstances, we were playing a game without rules and we would have to be more devious and clever than our enemy if we were to be successful. Donovan added that the American people would just have to accept this "abhorrent philosophy."

Little by little, other agencies were created to carry out intelligence operations. In 1952, the National Security Agency (NSA) was pulled together out of the military service intercept and codebreaking agencies and in 1961, the Defense Intelligence Agency (DIA) was established to provide support for military operations and strategic planning. At about the same time, the National Reconnaissance Office (NRO) was set up to manage intelligence satellite operations. Unlike the other agencies, no public announcement about the NRO was made and its operations were supposed to be secret, although many knew of its existence.[3]

THE ROLE OF THE DIRECTOR OF CENTRAL INTELLIGENCE

In theory, the director of Central Intelligence (DCI) was supposed to coordinate the activities of all these agencies, plus those of the intelligence units in the State, Treasury, and Justice Departments, including the counterintelligence arm of the FBI. In reality, the DCI was not given any authority to control them. The DCI had real authority only over the CIA. Many studies of the American intelligence system, the latest produced in 1996, have recognized that giving the DCI responsibility without authority is unworkable and needs to be fixed, but nothing has been done. Since most of the system belongs to the secretary of defense, the DCI has little leverage. That problem, detailed yet again in the post–9/11 investigations, remains today. The situation is complicated by the fact that there are now 15 agencies in the U.S. Intelligence Community and the DCI still controls only one of them.

The DCI does have a few assets that give the office a bit more power than it had originally. The DCI has budget authority that enables him to set priorities and some spending levels. More importantly, the DCI, as director of the CIA, is the only agency head in the system who has direct access to the president. He controls the only agency that is authorized to conduct clandestine operations, including covert action, although that power has been eroding as the Defense Department moves into this area. Finally, the DCI has visibility and can speak for the IC, a dubious honor when things go wrong, but a little boost when the DCI can claim some sort of victory. Given the mandates of homeland security, as well as the need to remain vigilant in other trouble areas, such as in the case of rogue states, low-level conflict, or weapons proliferation, the entire convoluted, byzantine, and bureaucratic intelligence system begs for overhaul.

This system worked well enough during the cold war, in part because there were a great many informal working groups and committees in which the substantive agencies were represented. Sharing intelligence at the working level was the norm rather than the exception. Analysts at the CIA, DIA, or in the State Department often compared notes and in writing for national-level intelligence publications, were required to "coordinate" or share their judgments before articles were cleared for circulation to policy makers.

INFORMATION SHARING

In the mid-1980s, a series of centers were created to formalize information sharing. Each agency was to be represented in these centers, which were targeted against enemy spies, narcotics trafficking and crime, as well as terrorism. These appeared to work very well, although now we know better. At the time, however, this seemed a good system for connecting the dots, as each agency brought to the center the relevant intelligence the others needed.

The IC had a national-level analysis component as well. The National Intelligence Council, created by DCI William Colby in 1975, is made up of senior officers—called National Intelligence Officers (NIOs)—drawn from the intelligence system, from policy offices, and from academe. These officials were to oversee the production of National Intelligence Estimates to forecast the future and to write interagency in-depth studies. This arrangement had been set up to replace the Board of National Estimates, which dated back to the Donovan era.

In the 1970s, DCI Admiral Stansfield Turner created a management component to help him run the IC. This group, with some personnel drawn from the intelligence agencies and others recruited from outside, was supposed to oversee budget management, plan for the future, and evaluate the effectiveness of the system. Called at first the Intelligence Community Staff and later the Community Management Staff, it was something of a fiction, in that it only worked when the agencies wanted to cooperate with it. It enabled the DCI to claim that he was running the IC as well as the CIA, but most Washington insiders knew how the game was being played.

Intelligence work was made easier during the cold war by the fact that we knew what to watch. The Communist enemy was right in front of us and much of the analysis, perhaps as much as 80 percent of the data, could be taken from open sources. The other 20 percent came from agents recruited and handled by the CIA's Clandestine Service, from intercepts of communications, or from satellite-based overhead imagery. Some lesser enemies, such as North Korea or Iran under the Ayatollahs—so-called closed societies—were tougher targets, but there was enough intelligence available to piece together what was happening.

FAILURE FRONT PAGE NEWS

Of course, there were occasional failures, but for the most part, the IC system did keep policy officials up to speed on world events. Nonetheless, the failure tended to become well publicized while success remained hidden so that it could be repeated. Thus, knowing only of failure, observers of the intelligence system were quick to condemn it when things went wrong. The media were not interested in success, but failure was front-page news. For those people who paid attention to such things, it appeared that the IC was prone to screw-ups when in fact they were quite rare.

After 9/11, some commentators assembled a long list of alleged failures dating back to the 1940s in order to make it appear that the CIA was an agency that could do nothing right. This was especially unfair because the CIA could not fight back. Even the FBI, which for decades had been the darling of the press and the public, came in for its share of criticism. Of course there were mistakes, but the tone and substance of the media complaints, picked up quickly by other critics including some members of Congress, showed how little they understood about intelligence or the intelligence process.

It would have been unreasonable to expect the intelligence system to be fault-free, given the fact that the intelligence process deals with a high level of uncertainty and risk. An examination of some of the most famous—or infamous—failures shows that a variety of things can go wrong in intelligence, whether it involves fallible humans or sophisticated but complex machinery. Of course, these failures can only be studied in hindsight, which only confirms the belief that whatever went wrong should have been caught.

There are several key failures that have provided significant lessons to both students and practitioners of intelligence. In 1950, everyone was surprised when North Korea attacked South Korea. The CIA's analysis indicated that Kim Il Sung's Communist dictatorship had the capability to attack the South, but did not suggest that it had the will to do so. Now we know that Kim had conferred with his Russian allies to obtain Stalin's consent before launching the strike, but the CIA had no assets in either the USSR or North Korea that might have revealed this. Neither did we have the kinds of technical intercept or photo sensors in those days that would have seen or heard preparations for war.

In the aftermath of the Korean War, Walter Bedell Smith, who had been General Dwight Eisenhower's chief of staff in World War II, was brought in as DCI to "fix" the system. Of course, his first move was to reorganize the CIA. Bureaucratic reorganization or restructuring is often seen as the best remedy for failure, but it only ensures that the same mistakes will not be made twice; the system will inevitably make new mistakes instead.

A CLASSIC MISTAKE

The Yom Kippur War in 1973 is often cited as a classic case of intelligence failure and it was one that could have been avoided. It was such a blow to Israeli intelligence that former professionals and academics in Israel still agonize over it. All the signs and data, all the spies and technical sensors, pointed toward an Egyptian raid into Israeli-occupied Sinai by crossing the Suez Canal. Both Israeli and U.S. analysts, however, had concluded that the Arab States would never invade Israel because they would be sure to lose. This false assumption led both Mossad and the CIA to misread the intelligence inputs until it was almost too late. It was a classic case of self-deception, one of the great errors that sometimes creeps into intelligence analysis. It would have been a real disaster if Israel has lost the 1973 war, but since they did not, neither the Israeli Mossad nor the CIA made major changes, although no one has forgotten the lessons learned.

More recently, the CIA was severely castigated for failing to detect a nuclear test in India, even though the Indian prime minister had made a public announcement that he intended to authorize it. If the CIA had been able to pinpoint the test and the Clinton administration had made a strong protest to India demanding that the test be stopped, would the Indian government have caved in? Probably not. This was a case of intelligence embarrassment as well as failure. The president and the Congress were so annoyed that they called in retired navy admiral David Jeremiah to find out what happened. His conclusions pointed to a lack of resources as well as a lack of smarts. He also noted that the Indian government had tried hard to cover up the test and this deception had fooled the CIA.

There are times when failure is so egregious that even professionals cringe and throw up their hands. This was certainly the case of the U.S. attack on the Chinese Embassy in Belgrade during the attempt to drive Slobodan Milosevic from power in 1999. Apparently, the CIA was supposed to nominate a target for an attack by a B-2 Stealth bomber, which would undertake the mission by flying from the United States to Serbia, attacking the target, then returning to the bomber's home base in Missouri. The CIA chose what it thought was a Serbian headquarters in Belgrade, but it turned out that the target had moved and the building had been turned into an embassy for the Peoples Republic of China. Using a precision guided bomb, the B-2 hit its target right on the nose, but the outcry was loud indeed when it soon became clear that the attack was aimed at the wrong building.

Of course, an investigation ensued. How could such a mistake have been made? Belgrade was a city quite open to everyone and there was a U.S. embassy there. Couldn't someone have just gone to see where the target building was? It turned out that an analyst at the CIA did indeed know that the target was the wrong one, but by the time the analyst discovered what was happening, it was too late to stop the mission. To this day, the Chinese government believes that this "intelligence failure" was actually intended to hit the Chinese and not the Serbs at all.

FOREIGN SPIES

Intelligence failure does not always involve errors in collection or analysis. Sometimes the failure involves a foreign spy who has penetrated our system. Why are we so surprised to learn that we are vulnerable in this regard? After all, we expect to be able to penetrate hostile intelligence and governmental systems by recruiting or attracting traitors from the other side. We should not be shocked to learn that Americans are willing to betray their country in the same way that others do. We are astonished when we find out that John Walker, a former navy warrant officer, passed secrets to the USSR over a period of 18 years, or that Aldrich Ames managed to spy for the Russians for 9 years as a mole in the CIA.

Of course, most spies—ours or theirs—do it for the money, even when they profess that they were driven by ideology. Ana Montes, a senior analyst in the Defense Intelligence Agency, became a spy for Cuba because she believed the U.S. government was treating Fidel Castro's regime unfairly. Her dedication to this ideal apparently enabled her to pass the polygraph tests she took and elude security procedures for years. Ames was tripped up by the polygraph, but supervisors mistakenly let him go instead of checking into his responses.

Fortunately, dedicated security and counterintelligence professionals have managed to catch those few Americans who sold out to our adversaries during the cold war, at least the ones we know about. The real danger to our system is that there may be more penetrations we have not found. That's why good security procedures, effective compartmentation, and the use of the "need-to-know" principle still dominates intelligence. We should not be shocked when a spy is caught; we should be grateful that the spy was stopped before more damage was done.

SUCCESS IGNORED

Sometimes, the intelligence system is accused of failure when in fact it has not failed at all. This was certainly the case in regard to predicting the collapse of the USSR and World Communism. A careful study of the documents released to the public shows that the IC was more right than wrong about developments in the USSR and its allies all through the cold war, but especially when the system began to collapse.[4]

During the heat of the cold war, when George H. W. Bush was DCI, the IC set up an exercise permitting an outside team to review the same documents as a group of inside analysts to see where each would come down. Prior to this exercise, hard-liners both within and outside the administration had accused the CIA of being "soft" on the USSR and undervaluing the strategic strength of the main enemy. The A-Team/B-Team exercise, as it was called, had mixed results. Mostly the two teams agreed, although not on everything. These differences in interpretation lasted throughout the rest of the cold war.

Clearly, the IC could see that President Gorbachev was losing his battle to reform the USSR and Communism and that his position was precarious. Looking back, now that information about what was once a closed society has been made available in the West, we know that IC judgments about Soviet military strength may have, if anything, overvalued the military capability of the USSR while missing some of the severe weaknesses in the Communist economic system. Nonetheless, policy makers in Washington could hardly argue that they had been kept in the dark. Still, in writing about 9/11, some commentators continued to accuse the IC of missing the boat on the collapse of Communism.

SIGNALS AND NOISE

What we learn from these examples is that intelligence can fail in a variety of ways and that might help explain what happened before 9/11. Sometimes the system fails to collect the right information, or it collects so much information that the collectors cannot sort out the wheat from the chaff, or as Roberta Wohlstetter has written in a postmortem on Pearl Harbor, collectors cannot separate the signals from the noise.[5] According to James Bamford, who has written two landmark books on the secretive National Security Agency (NSA), the agency that collects signals and communications intelligence may collect millions of signals in an hour.[6]

To obtain intelligence, NSA analysts use various data-mining techniques and filters to sort out what they hope are the signals from the noise, capture the meaningful messages, decipher them if they are encrypted, and translate them from whatever language or dialect of language spoken. This is an incredibly difficult and complex process, especially when the speakers are using odd and obscure languages such as dialects of Dari or Pashto. After 9/11, the press revealed that two messages were captured on the day before the attacks, but were not translated until afterward. These messages provided no specifics about 9/11 but only suggested that something was up. Just finding these two messages among the millions of inputs is quite remarkable, and was probably made a bit easier after 9/11 when NSA had a clearer vision of what to look for. Hindsight always makes the intelligence process look easy.

After 9/11, the CIA was accused of failing to put enough of its clandestine service officers in the field, although penetrating terrorist cells is extremely difficult and dangerous. One outspoken former case officer, the CIA's term for its agent handlers, claimed that field officers spent all their time hanging around the embassies to which they were assigned, and another claimed that the CIA's internal bureaucracy had become stodgy and risk-averse. These claims were quickly erased after 9/11 when CIA officers turned up on the front lines in Afghanistan and later in other parts of the Middle East in the search for members of Osama bin Laden's al Qaeda network.

New aspects of the war on terrorism were revealed, according to press reports, when the CIA was able to track and attack a key al Qaeda leader in Yemen.[7] He and his companions were killed by a missile launched from a remotely piloted vehicle. This, too, was remarkable, since the Predator drone had to find one car carrying the terrorist in a barren stretch of desert. Immediately, the cry went up that the CIA was carrying out assassinations, a tactic that was banned by a series of Presidential Executive Orders issued by Presidents Ford, Carter, and Reagan. In fact, both Presidents Clinton and George W. Bush had signed findings making the attack on the terrorists acceptable in the war on al Qaeda, demonstrating that there are mixed views on how the United States should fight such a war. Does the American public want to stop terrorism by any means, or only if we don't get our hands dirty? This question has yet to be resolved.

INTERNAL SECURITY

The same is true for internal security. The American public, at least to the extent that such things can be measured, wants to be protected, and yet is concerned that the protection may jeopardize civil rights, legal practice, and privacy. The trust and confidence that Americans had for the FBI, the heart of our federal security establishment, has been badly damaged. J. Edgar Hoover, the founder and long-time leader of the FBI in its heyday, must be spinning in his grave. For years, Hoover had gone to great lengths to protect and burnish the image of the Bureau, supporting radio and TV shows that showed his agency in a positive light.[8]

After Hoover's death, however, a number of cases tarnished this image, starting with an effort by Hoover's successor, L. Patrick Gray, to enmesh the CIA as well as the FBI in a cover-up of the Watergate affair. In more recent times, alleged FBI misconduct in raids on the Branch Davidian compound in Waco, Texas, and in a hostage rescue situation in Ruby Ridge in 1993 heaped negative publicity on the Bureau.

While Judge William Webster had led the FBI with great care and skill, his successor, Judge William Sessions, was hardly a model of honesty and good management. Sessions brought discredit on the FBI for his erratic personal conduct, and for allowing his wife to use FBI resources for her private convenience. Sessions's behavior was an embarrassment to his subordinates and eventually led to his dismissal by President Clinton. Sessions was the first FBI director ever to be forced from office for misconduct and it took the personal intervention of President Clinton before Sessions would pack his belongings and leave his office.[9]

The final blow to FBI pride and prestige came with the arrest in early 2001 of Robert Hanssen, a career FBI agent who turned out to be a mole, a spy for the Soviets and later the Russians. The Hanssen case was even more bizarre than previous spy cases because Hanssen was so adept at avoiding detection right in the middle of the key agency aimed at catching foreign intelligence agents at work. Coupled with sexual adventures, financial dealings, and manipulations of the FBI's antiquated computer systems, Hanssen really made the Bureau look bad. No one paid much attention to the fact that a sophisticated U.S. intelligence penetration of the Russian security service had yielded the information to pinpoint Hanssen.[10]

MISSED OPPORTUNITIES

These kinds of negative experiences only added to the outcry against the Bureau after 9/11. In the investigations mounted after the terrorist attack, the FBI seemed to be the agency most responsible for failing to penetrate the terrorist plot that was going on right under its nose. The most damning allegations and complaints came from working-level FBI agents themselves, who revealed that their efforts to go after suspicious Middle Eastern men enrolled in flight schools were rejected by their bosses at FBI headquarters, who saw no probable cause to try to obtain warrants under the Foreign Intelligence Surveillance Act (FISA) to put some of the 9/11 hijackers under closer scrutiny. The erstwhile pilots had committed no crimes, at least not yet.

We know now that this reluctance to develop intelligence, rather than pursue criminals, lies at the heart of the FBI's problems before 9/11. But, again we see this all quite clearly in hindsight. We also know that the systems set up to provide intelligence sharing among agencies broke down before 9/11. In 1985, Judge Webster, who had moved from the FBI after nine years of solid leadership to take over the CIA in the aftermath of the Iran-Contra affair, proposed the development of fusion centers to go after foreign spies, narcotics traffickers, and terrorists. The Counterterrorist Center (CTC) was supposed to bring together officers from all the intelligence agencies and the FBI to share unevaluated data—usually called raw intelligence—as well as analysis on all aspects of terrorism. What started as a small group eventually grew significantly as problems with terrorism expanded.

HOT ON THE TRAIL

We know about some of this because Cofer Black, the head of the CTC at the time of 9/11, laid out some the group's history and problems during public testimony in congressional hearings. Black argued that the CTC was trying to operate with limited resources against targets that were elusive and difficult to pinpoint. His testimony was supported by his boss, DCI George Tenet, and Air Force Lieutenant General Michael Hayden, the director of the still super-secret National Security Agency. They all made clear that the CTC and the intelligence services were hot on the trail of the al Qaeda terrorists, and were getting closer to them when Tenet issued his intelligence warning in July 2001 that a major terrorist strike on a U.S. target was in the works.

But close was not good enough. As Dale Watson, a former senior FBI official said, it was like being a hockey goalie who saves 49 shots out of 50, but misses one and his team loses by one goal. It seems clear that Watson did not mean to trivialize the terrible devastation of 9/11, but rather point out the frustration of those in the national security system about what had happened. One senior intelligence official and an old friend told me that it was "maddening" to have come so close to "getting it." In fact, after 9/11, as intelligence professionals went back over the data and connected some of the pieces that had been missing before 9/11, the reasons for missing these connections became only too real. It was certainly not the total breakdown of the system claimed by some journalists and critics, but it wasn't success either.

The various commissions that have studied the 9/11 failure all seem to agree that there was no "smoking gun," or no particular piece of information that was missed, or single action not taken that would have meant the difference between success and failure. Nonetheless, a number of things went wrong within the intelligence agencies and in the FBI that were inexcusable. The CTC at the CIA, which was supposed to be a clearing house for all information related to terrorism, clearly was not. Intelligence agencies have a tendency not to share particularly sensitive intelligence data with their counterparts in order to protect sources and methods, to be sure, but sometimes they withhold data because having the sensitive material gives them power and the ability to one-up the other agencies. It sounds childish, but it is a fact of life.

CRITICAL ERRORS?

Some critics argued that the CIA could have penetrated the Taliban militia in Afghanistan before 9/11. After all, John Walker Lindh, the 20-year-old American who fought for the Taliban was able to join up and claimed that he once even met Osama bin Laden. He admitted, however, that he knew nothing about the plans for the terrorist attack on the United States and it seems unlikely that bin Laden would have trusted him with information even if Walker Lindh had tried to learn it. Surely, an agent run by the CIA might have been able to do what Walker Lindh did, but to what purpose?

Another outspoken critic of the CIA, a former operations officer named Ruel Marc Gerecht, who occasionally writes under the pen-name Edward Shirley, slammed the CIA operatives overseas for spending too much time on the diplomatic circuit and not being aggressive about recruiting sources. Gerecht thought too many CIA officers were working liaison with foreign intelligence services and faulted them for not seeking out the hard targets. There is considerable value, however, in liaisons with foreign services. For example, two of the 9/11 terrorist team, Khalid al-Midhar and Nawaf al-Hazmi, were identified to the CIA by the Malaysian Security Service because they had attended an alleged al Qaeda meeting in Kuala Lumpur.[11] Unfortunately, the CIA held on to the information until after the two had already entered the United States. The Joint Inquiry refers to them as hijackers, but they were only two Saudi students coming to the United States for training until 9/11. Strangely, they had used their real names and authentic documentation to reach the United States. They would have been impossible to identify after 9/11 if they had used false identities and paperwork.

If the FBI had known about them and tracked them to San Diego, where they were enrolled in flight school, and had obtained permission to interview them, would the two have revealed the plot? It seems unlikely. The erstwhile hijackers might not have known the details about the plan, or they might have had a cover story to explain what they were doing. Under the FISA rules as they existed before 9/11, the FBI would have had no probable cause to put them under further scrutiny.

FBI field agents were particularly frustrated at being unable to follow through on their suspicions that Middle Eastern men in other parts of the country were taking flight training and were up to no good. They might not have unearthed the full details of the 9/11 plot, but they might have been able to connect the pilots undergoing training with each other, and with ties to al Qaeda. Once again, however, the FISA rules got in the way.

BREAKING THE PLOT

In one case, an FBI field agent in Phoenix, Arizona, asked his bosses to consider checking out what appeared to be a pattern of Middle Eastern men enrolling in flight schools around the country. While the agent had no idea why they were doing this, it seemed unusual and worth checking. FBI headquarters turned down his request because the men had committed no crimes. Neither was there a reason to ask for a warrant under the Foreign Intelligence Surveillance Act because there was no indication that the men were acting as agents of a foreign power. Clearly, the FBI bosses were thinking in law enforcement terms and not as intelligence collectors.

The second opportunity came with the arrest in August 2001 of Zacarias Moussaoui, a French citizen of Middle Eastern origin, who was taking flight training in Minneapolis. Moussaoui was detained by the Immigration and Naturalization Service (INS) after an FBI agent became suspicious of his activities. Once again, the FBI found no probable cause to seek a warrant under FISA, but an investigation undertaken after 9/11 showed that Moussaoui may well have planned to be one of the hijackers and he was soon dubbed the "twentieth hijacker" by the press.

Moussaoui, of course, denied knowing anything about the plot, but his bizarre behavior in court made him appear crazy enough to carry out a suicide mission. Later, a senior al Qaeda official arrested in the Middle East confirmed that the erstwhile pilot was considered too unstable to be part of the operation. Nonetheless, if the search of Moussaoui's things had taken place before 9/11, some clues to the operation might have been obtained. Although his arrest was reported to the Intelligence Community and the FAA, there was apparently no indication that he might be a potential hijacker.

Even if the FBI or CIA had gotten closer to the plot, it's very possible, if the terrorists were using standard rules of clandestine procedure, that only a few of the 19 hijackers knew exactly what was to happen on 9/11. The more operatives who knew about a plot, the more likely it was to be revealed. Of course we will never know because all of them died in the attacks, but if only the leader of each team knew what was to happen, then getting closer to the hijackers would not necessarily have broken the entire plan. Some of the hijackers may have thought the planes and passengers were to be used as hostages as in previous airline hijackings.

It's also possible that Mohammed Atta, one of the pilot hijackers, identified as the chief of the hijacking operation, did not make the final decision to carry out the attack until just a few days before 9/11 when he could be certain that the weather would be clear enough for the amateur pilots to hit their targets. They might not have been able to handle the planes in really rough conditions. If that was the case, then there would have been no way for intelligence agencies to pick up the timing of the operation in the few days between the decision and the operation, unless the terrorists blabbed everything over an open phone line.

UNIMAGINATIVE ANALYSTS

Intelligence analysts were unimaginative, it seems, in considering the possibility that terrorists might use passenger airliners as cruise missiles. The conventional wisdom at the time suggested that terrorists might use small private planes for such a mission, but not a fully loaded 767. In 1995, a report surfaced suggesting that terrorists might try to fly a plane into the Eiffel Tower in Paris, but when nothing happened, apparently the report was tossed into a hold file and forgotten.

Then, incoming intelligence data in 1998 suggested that terrorists might try to attack the World Trade Center in New York by hijacking a plane in Europe, but it seemed likely that such an effort could be stopped well before the aircraft reached the United States. Even if one analyst had possessed the imagination to envision a terrorist mission using a commercial airliner, it is doubtful that the analyst would have been able to convince the intelligence managers to circulate such a judgment.

This is exactly what happened before the Iraqi invasion of Kuwait in 1991. The National Intelligence Officer for Warning on the National Intelligence Council had figured out Saddam Hussein's move into Kuwait two weeks before Saddam was about to do it, but he was unable to convince either his bosses or policy officials that he knew what he was talking about until just before the invasion. At the time, the late acknowledgment of warning was thought to be an intelligence failure, too, but we know now that it was not.

In 1998, DCI George Tenet declared "war on al Qaeda," but no resources went to support the battles. Budgets were tight and even though CIA recruiting was beefed up, the agency was not attracting the kinds of people it would have needed to increase its operations in the Middle East. Nonetheless, as more and more information about al Qaeda began to come in, it became clear that a major operation targeted against the United States or Israel was in the works. Most analysts seemed to think that the attack would come overseas; after all, that had been the pattern. In 1998, U.S. Embassies in Kenya and Tanzania were attacked and in 2000, the USS *Cole* was hit in a Yemeni port. While it is true that terrorists had hit the World Trade Center in 1993, this was seen as an anomaly. The terrorists in that case were quickly rounded up and jailed and the event was seemingly forgotten.[12]

STRATEGIC WARNING

In July 2001, DCI Tenet issued a strategic warning that a terrorist plot was afoot, but he could not tell exactly when or where it would occur. This warning was repeated in the President's Daily Brief of August 6, 2001, but like so many of the warnings, it could not give enough specific detail to enable the president to take action. Security officials seemed to be reluctant to take action based on the strategic warning. This is not surprising in the private sector where tightening up security costs money, but surely government officials could have taken notice. Unfortunately, as in many cases of intelligence failure, part of the blame rests with the policy officials who took no action even though warnings had been issued.

For years, terrorists had tried to hijack airliners, but little was done to beef up airport security. The Israeli airline El Al did it, but that was an exception. After Libyan terrorists brought down a Pan Am airliner over Scotland using a bomb hidden in luggage, it should have been obvious that closer scrutiny of passengers and restrictions on what could be kept in carry-on baggage was needed. But such steps would have required expensive security procedures and perhaps flight delays. No airline wanted to spend the money, since they were responsible for checking passengers.

The airlines did take steps to lock cockpit doors, but did not harden them in such a way that would have made them secure. Airline crews were trained to go along with attempts to hijack aircraft because terrorists were thought to have political motives. In most cases, all this meant was an unscheduled stop while negotiations were undertaken to free passengers and isolate the terrorists. In one case, a CIA station chief was actually able to talk a hijacker out of the cockpit of an airliner while it sat on the runway. The use of air marshals, especially in the 1970s when aircraft were sometimes hijacked to Cuba, was eventually discontinued as the threat seemed to diminish.

AIRLINE SECURITY

The great fear before 9/11 was that terrorists would use firearms to hijack planes, bypassing security by having confederates, posing as food service workers or airline maintenance personnel, hide the weapons on the planes before take-off. Yet, we know now that little was done to check out ramp workers or others who had access to airliners before flight. After 9/11, when the crackdown finally took place, some workers turned out to be undocumented aliens, or workers with false papers and criminal histories. Fortunately, none seemed to be tied to al Qaeda.

The private firms that provided gate security for the airlines were also negligent in checking out the people who were supposed to search passengers and their carry-on luggage. Some of the checkers spoke little English, were undocumented aliens, and had had little training. The rules they followed were vague and even before 9/11, journalists checking out security at airports would manage to sneak weapons past the checkers. The FAA was fairly lax about what could be considered a weapon.

We know now that box cutters were used as the weapon of choice by the 9/11 hijackers because those kinds of knives were permitted by FAA regulations. This, too, was a fatal error. We wouldn't know even that much if it wasn't for the heroic passengers and crew who used cell phones to tell families and airline officials what was happening on the hijacked airliners. The hijackers broke some other rules as well and no one blew the whistle. They bought one-way tickets for cash and had no luggage. This was supposed to give gate agents clues to summon security for further checks, but nothing was done.

After 9/11, a new Transportation Security Administration (TSA) was created to establish better security at airports and airlines, but it was too late. Nonetheless, the effort had some real benefits. The airlines, which had been paying for the various private firms that ran security before 9/11, were relieved of that burden. Security checks became standardized and a lot more effective. Over the Thanksgiving holiday weekend in 2002, thousands of knives, guns, bats, and other potential weapons were found and confiscated. By the end of 2002, commercial airports had installed equipment to scan all checked baggage for explosives. This did not create significant delays and gave travelers an additional sense of security.

THE NEW DEPARTMENT

This has not solved all the security problems related to air transportation, but it is a good start. Much remains to be done in regard to consistent checks on food service workers, baggage handlers, and others who have access to aircraft while parked at the gates. While new procedures have tightened security for air travelers, many other parts of our society remain vulnerable. In order to deal with the overall problem of homeland security, the George W. Bush administration signed into law the Homeland Security Act at the end of 2002. This created the new Department of Homeland Security (DHS), made up of about 160,000 federal workers from 22 separate agencies, with a planned budget of about $38 billion for its first full year of operation, about the same level as the U.S. Intelligence Community. The DHS came into existence officially in March, 2003, although many of its components began working on security issues as soon as the law was passed.

The plan for the Department of Homeland Security (DHS) included the creation of an intelligence unit. This was not well fleshed out in the original legislation, but it's hard to argue that the new organization could function without good intelligence. The intelligence function was supposed to be incorporated into the information and infrastructure section of the department. A veteran military officer, retired Marine Lieutenant General Frank Libuti, who had been working on security issues in New York City, was named to serve as undersecretary for that component, but the intelligence function itself was not spelled out. At the same time, the other intelligence and security agencies set up liaison units with the new organization.

STUDIES OF 9/11

By the time the Joint Congressional Inquiry on 9/11 was officially revealed to the public in 2003, there was little in the report that had not already been learned from prior testimony and leaks. The group did make a number of recommendations for changes in the way the Intelligence Community was structured and managed. The press leaped on one as the lead idea, that of creating a cabinet-level director of National Intelligence, but like so many ideas that have surfaced over the years, it did not appear that quick action would be taken.

Despite signals from the White House that controversial legislation, such as that needed to overhaul the American intelligence system, would have to wait as politicians began to focus on the 2004 elections, Democrats in the House of Representatives initiated legislation to create a Director of National Intelligence (DNI). Perhaps they did this just to go on record to show that they were paying attention to the various studies on the subject. Since no comparable legislation surfaced in the Senate, the legislation did not appear to have sparked wide-spread support. An equally controversial issue, that of creating some sort of domestic intelligence agency, will certainly be debated in years to come, with uncertain results. Both topics are worth closer scrutiny in the following pages.

Understanding the role that intelligence can play in foreign and homeland security is important for both practitioners and observers. Whether one agrees with the condemnation of intelligence for failure on 9/11, or understands why it might not have been able to work better, it's time to look forward and see what can be done to make our intelligence system better prepared to prevent future attacks on our country and our people.

Understanding the Enemy

In order to defend the homeland against terrorism as well as the other threats that plague us, we need to identify and understand exactly who these enemies are. This process is called threat analysis and is a major function of intelligence. We cannot defend everything all the time; the resources required would be prohibitive. In addition, total defense would destroy the very freedoms and way of life we are trying to protect. Therefore, we need to decide where we are most vulnerable and we can't do that until we know our enemies.

The Department of Homeland Security was supposed to create an intelligence unit that would perform threat analysis as well as a warning system to prevent surprise. This unit was supposed to be supported by the Intelligence Community (IC), which would provide the data for analysis and warning. The IC has been doing such work for many years, but it has focused on foreign enemies rather than threats to domestic security. Instead of creating its own threat analysis unit, Homeland Security has been relying on the IC-based Terrorist Threat Integration Center (TTIC) to provide the intelligence DHS needs.

Meanwhile, our enemies are at work trying to figure out ways to attack us. We already know a great deal about our adversaries and they are not just terrorists. If we are going to defend the homeland and create a vast new bureaucracy to do it, then we ought to stop the other threats to our society as well, including global organized crime, technology theft, espionage, and subversion.

This idea has already been kicked around a bit with somewhat negative results. Some would say that these other problems are best left to law enforcement and should not be the focus of the Department of Homeland Security's intelligence unit, but these critics are missing an important point. Many of these threats are interrelated. Terrorists may use crime and narcotics sales to fund their operations, leading to what has been labeled "narco-terrorism." Global crime syndicates may be funneling money to terrorists, but even if they didn't, their operations certainly threaten the security of the nation. Technology theft, sometimes called industrial espionage, is robbing the country of billions in lost revenue.

ESPIONAGE AT HOME

We have certainly been the victims of espionage at home. This was made evident during the cold war when spies working on behalf of the Soviets, the Chinese, or the Israelis were caught stealing our national defense secrets. Larry Wu-tai Chin, John Walker, Aldrich Ames, Jonathan Pollard, and Robert Hanssen were among the most publicized spies who gave away defense or intelligence data, but there were several others. Some spies were "walk-ins," who sought out the Russians, or the Israelis, while others, such as Larry Chin, a translator for the Foreign Broadcast Information Service, or Bin Wu, a Chinese agent who stole industrial secrets, were recruited abroad and sent here as secret agents. More recently, the government revealed that three Americans had been arrested in 2003 at the Guantanamo Naval Base in Cuba on charges of spying for Syria.[1]

Countering espionage has always required a combination of intelligence and law enforcement. While the problem has usually focused on operations of hostile—and sometimes friendly—intelligence services, we need to be concerned about the possibility that terrorists will use the same techniques to penetrate Homeland Security and learn about our plans as well as our vulnerabilities. While we have not faced a serious threat in the past from subversives, despite occasional bouts of paranoia over Communism, we need to be alert to the possibility that our own citizens or residents are plotting against the government. After all, the terrorist attack on Oklahoma City was not the work of al Qaeda, but rather a manifestation of hatred among some of our own people over our system of government.

While a good case can be made for protecting the nation against the other threats to security at home, despite the nay-sayers, no one argues about protecting against terrorism. This is not a new danger, but for many years the threat of terrorism manifested itself abroad. Americans were targets for much of the cold war and some conservatives believed that our adversary, the Soviet Union, was behind many of the attacks against U.S. targets. In fact, one of the first tasks of the Intelligence Community under the Reagan administration was to produce a National Intelligence Estimate on the role of the USSR in world terrorism. This project created something of a storm inside the IC; the first draft of the estimate was rejected by DCI Bill Casey as not well focused and too soft on the Soviets.

CIA professionals immediately thought that this was an effort to politicize the intelligence process by producing what the White House wanted to hear. Casey countered that Mr. Reagan wanted to know exactly what role, if any, the Soviets were playing in international terrorism and the estimate had failed to deliver. The second draft was more specific and concluded that, while the Soviet Union and its allies were indeed providing training, equipment, documentation, safe haven, and other support, the Kremlin was not directing world terrorism. The terrorists were managing that quite well on their own.

STATE-SPONSORED TERRORISM

Towards the end of the cold war, the emphasis shifted from Soviet-backed terrorism to a more general category of state-sponsored terrorism. The White House accused several countries, including Iraq, Iran, Syria, Libya, and North Korea of giving direct aid and guidance to terrorists. These countries were branded as "rogue" states that did not follow the norms of international law and practice. This was made clear when forensic evidence showed that Libyan intelligence agents had been directly responsible for planting a bomb on a Pan American Airlines flight 103 in December 1988.[2]

In the aftermath of 9/11, the Taliban regime in Afghanistan was quickly revealed as the sponsor of Osama bin Laden's al Qaeda operations, providing training and support as well as safe haven. The George W. Bush administration wasted no time in declaring the Taliban and its leader Mullah Omar our enemy and that particular rogue regime was brought down by an alliance of anti-Taliban Afghans, with considerable help from the United States. While Afghanistan's neighbor Pakistan was certainly not a rogue state, its government was unable to stop bin Laden and his followers from taking refuge along the border regions after the fall of the Taliban.

THE *MUJAHIDEEN*

Some writers about Osama bin Laden claimed that he was a creature of the U.S. effort to oust the Soviets from Afghanistan during the cold war. There is no doubt that the United States sponsored a coalition of Afghan war lords in the fight to oust the Soviets and their puppet regime, led by the former head of the KHAD Afghan intelligence service, Najibullah, from power.[3] This loose coalition, known as the *mujahideen*, was supported by ISI, the Pakistani intelligence service, and the entire campaign was orchestrated by the CIA. Osama bin Laden and his followers

were reportedly one of the tribal groups in the coalition and were supposed to have received training and equipment from the United States.
Once the Soviets decided to pull out of Afghanistan in 1989, the CIA predicted that Najibullah's pro-Soviet regime would collapse and one of
the tribal leaders would gain power, presumably to the benefit of the
United States.

As it turned out, Najib was able to stay in power for a while because the
mujahideen coalition fell apart in a struggle for control. When Najib finally
was ousted in 1992, a new group called the Taliban, a band of extremist
Muslims whose beliefs mirrored those of the Wahabi sect in Saudi Arabia,
swept into Afghanistan to fill the power vacuum Najib's fall created.
Wahabis believe in a strict and rather ancient interpretation of the Koran
that calls for severe restrictions on a variety of social issues, including ban-
ning women from any activity outside the household, and restrictions on
the entire population based on the Sharia laws. Once the Taliban took
power in Kabul and most of the countryside, bin Laden and his followers
returned to Afghanistan in 1996.

THE STINGER MISSILES

One of the problems created during the struggle to oust the Soviets from
Afghanistan was the delivery to the *mujahideen* of the U.S.-built Stinger
antiaircraft missiles. These are shoulder-fired missiles that one person can
use to bring down an aircraft. The Stinger is much more accurate and
effective than similar heat-seeking weapons built by the Soviets and copied
throughout the Third World. The Stingers were credited with driving the
Soviet forces out of Afghanistan, but they were quickly circulated among
tribesmen after the conflict.

We have to assume that bin Laden and his people have at least some
kinds of shoulder-fired anti-aircraft missiles, either the Stinger or the
Soviet versions, and might use them against civilian airliners. In fact, in
2002, two missiles, apparently Soviet-built Strelas, were fired at an Israeli
airliner in Mombasa, Kenya, but missed. The missiles did not lock on to
the heat from the airliner's engines, as they were supposed to do. The
attack was coordinated with the suicide bombing of an Israeli-owned
resort hotel in Mombasa, a typical al Qaeda–style attack.

KINDRED SPIRITS

Bin Laden and al Qaeda have found kindred spirits throughout the
extremist Islamic world. After the collapse of the Taliban, bin Laden was
able to move to Pakistan where he received aid and comfort from tribal
groups along the Afghan border and perhaps from some sympathizers
within the Pakistani intelligence service. Later, after the U.S.-led invasion

of Iraq in 2003, followers of bin Laden and other Muslim extremists began to flow into Iraq to carry out terrorist attacks on coalition forces. This is similiar to what happened in Afghanistan where foreign fighters, primarily Arab speakers, came to the country to fight with Mullah Omar and the Taliban. These foreign fighters are the people who are being held at the U.S. prison camp in Guantanamo. According to press reports, as of April, 2004, there were 600 detainees in Guantanamo, half of whom could be released if their home countries were willing to take them back. 147 detainees had been released and 6 were designated to stand trial before a military tribunal. The rest were being held subject to a decision by the U.S. Supreme Court as to whether or not the prisoners could be held without trial.

BIN LADEN'S TRACK RECORD

Bin Laden's hands were all over the 9/11 attack, even before he admitted in a television interview that he had directed the operation. Bin Laden claimed credit as well for the first effort to bring down the World Trade Center in 1993, although the ring leaders of that terrorist attack were not so clearly tied to him when they were tracked down and jailed. At the time, they were thought to be "ad-hoc" terrorists and not part of bin Laden's network.[4] Now we know better. He also claimed responsibility for other attacks on the United States overseas, including the bombings of the U.S. embassies in Kenya and Tanzania, and the attack on the U.S. Navy destroyer USS *Cole* in Yemen.

In 2002, bin Laden seemed to be behind the attack on a French oil tanker, also in Yemen, along with the failed missile attack on an Israeli airliner in Mombasa, Kenya. Since 9/11, however, bin Laden has not been able to launch another attack within the United States, although U.S. intelligence seems to think he plans to do so. And when it comes to extremist Islamic groups, bin Laden is not alone.

The U.S. government has credible evidence that other terrorists groups were receiving assistance from foreign regimes, including the Palestinian-based Hamas, which obtains considerable support from Syria, and Hezbollah, the Shia terrorist organization that takes its backing from Iran. If noted U.S. journalist and terrorism expert Steven Emerson is correct, many terrorist groups are gaining considerable support within the United States, not from the administration of course, but from sympathizers who have raised money, recruited personnel, and shipped equipment to terrorists.[5] While Emerson points out that much of this support has gone to the Middle East, he also notes that a consistent source of funding for the Irish Republican Army (IRA), which has had an active terrorist component for many years, comes from the Boston area's sympathetic, ethnically Irish population.

WHY TERRORISM?

Many writers have tried to explain why terrorism has become so prevalent in the modern world, but there are no consistent themes or explanations. So far, even terrorists cannot agree with each other and no terrorist central command or organization has developed.[6] Each terrorist group has its own agenda, and while the rhetoric was sometimes similar, the actions were not. Just as it is incorrect to consider all Latin American countries to be similar just because they have a common language, or all African countries to be similar because they occupy parts of the same land mass, so is it incorrect to lump all terrorist groups together. Each must be studied on its own but evidence is beginning to mount suggesting that Islamic militants in the various groups are beginning to establish connections, based on logistical and financial requirements.[7] In fact, some observers believe that terrorists have turned their crusades into businesses, earning money from followers and from their criminal activities, so that terrorism has become self-perpetuating.

Definitions of terrorism range widely and some observers have noted that we can't fight back against terrorism unless we can agree on what it is. So far, we have not found common ground in defining terrorism, although many have tried. Paul Pillar, a CIA officer and former deputy director of the Counterterrorist Center (CTC), cites the accepted U.S. government definition, which states that terrorism is, "premeditated, politically motivated violence, perpetrated against non-combatant targets by sub-national groups or clandestine agents, usually intended to influence an audience."[8] Today we might question whether or not radical Islamists are politically motivated, but the rest of the definition fits well enough.

The violence in terrorism may be random, such as on 9/11 where the terrorists sought to kill as many people as possible, or directed against specific targets or particular individuals, such as in the kidnappings of former Italian Prime Minister Aldo Moro or U.S. Brigadier General Dozier by the Red Brigades in Italy in the 1980s. Terrorists in such organizations as the Red Brigades, the Red Army Faction, or the Baader-Meinhof gang in West Germany all argued that they had to resort to terrorism because the political system repressed them and forced them to resort to violence.

Terry Nichols and Timothy McVeigh claimed that their attack on the Murrah Building in Oklahoma City in 1995 was driven by anger at the U.S. government for its handling of the Waco affair and the general notion among right-wing militants that the Federal government was trying to suppress them. The attack on the Murrah Building was driven more by rage than by politics. At first, al Qaeda's motivations in attacking the United States both at home and abroad seemed to be driven by rage, but now we know that it is more than anger. It is the belief among Osama bin Laden's followers that the United States is an infidel nation, given to disgusting practices and a wicked lifestyle, and therefore it is an abomination that must be destroyed.

DEEP ROOTS

This condemnation of what bin Laden sometimes calls the "crusader-Jewish alliance" has deep roots in Islam, dating back more than ten centuries. In fact, some of bin Laden's rhetoric does not sound all that much different from Saladin's condemnation of the crusader knights who came to take Jerusalem back from the Muslims in the twelfth century.[9] Violence by Islamic exremists is particularly disturbing because of its reliance on the suicide bomber, fanatics, some of whom believe that by killing themselves and taking others with them, they will become martyrs and guarantee an after-life filled with pleasures unavailable in their current existence. Other suicide bombers, as best we can tell, are driven by rage. Of course, bin Laden and other Islamic terrorist leaders do not seem willing to achieve martyrdom for themselves, but are quite willing to ask their followers to die for their cause.

Understanding the motivation and behavior of terrorists is not so simple. During the war against Iraq in 2003, Syrian clerics called for Iraqis to mount "martyrdom operations" and some did try to do so.[10] In studying what motivates terrorists to commit suicide, the CIA reportedly concluded that "there does not appear to be a single terrorist personality." In studies of terrorists, it appears that a terrorist is committed to the few persons in his or her cell much in the same way that soldiers are bonded into the basic military unit. A retired U.S. Air Force general noted that if you asked a soldier why he is willing to die, he will say it's to support his buddies.[11] Terrorists apparently have the same mind set.

The U.S.-led war on terrorism, now in its third year, has hurt bin Laden's organization by managing to capture or kill several of his key lieutenants. Included in this round-up were Khalid Shaikh Mohammed, the mastermind behind the attacks on the World Trade Center in 1993 as well as the 9/11 plot, Ramzi bin Al-Shib, and Abu Zubaydah. They have apparently provided useful intelligence about al Qaeda to their interrogators.[12] Since the arrests of his key leaders, bin Laden has probably given his followers free reign to carry out terrorist operations without seeking his direct approval. Estimates of al Qaeda strength vary widely because it's not clear who actually is a member or just a follower. Some reports indicate there may be as many as several thousand Islamist radicals who consider themselves part of the organization, scattered around the world.

OTHER ISLAMIC GROUPS

Several other Islamist terrorist groups have a different agenda from the al Qaeda group, although we tend to lump them all together. The second most dangerous from the U.S. perspective is Hezbollah (Party of God), the Shia terrorist group that emerged after the overthrow of the Shah of Iran in 1979. Hezbollah has been blamed for several attacks on U.S. military targets, including the destruction of the U.S. Embassy in Beirut, in which several key CIA officers were killed. Hezbollah was also responsible for the suicide attack on the marine barracks in Lebanon, and the bombing of the Khobar Towers in Saudi Arabia. Hezbollah was the force behind the kidnappings of Americans in the Middle East, including the CIA Chief of Station in Beirut William Buckley, and the hijacking of a TWA flight in 1985 in which a U.S. serviceman was killed.[13]

According to recent press reports, Hezbollah may have cells in as many as sixty countries, although no one knows for sure. The organization has been led for many years by Sheik Hassan Nasrallah and receives support from both Iran and Syria. Nasrallah claims that Hezbollah is focused only on the Arab-Israeli dispute and has no other agenda, but its attacks on U.S. targets abroad over the years tell a different story. Another key figure in Hezbollah, Imad Mugniyeh, is supposed to be the leader who perfected the role of the suicide bomber, a technique that has been used by other groups as well. In fact, the Tamil Tigers terrorist organization in Sri Lanka claims that it was the group that perfected the suicide bomber technique, a dubious claim to fame.[14]

Because they are Shia Muslims, Hezbollah had no discernible relationship with Osama bin Laden, whose followers are Sunni radicals. This may be one of the key reasons why no "Terrorist International," to use Paul Pillar's terminology, has developed among the radical Islamic groups. This may be changing, however, at least outside the Middle East. Hezbollah has never tried to pull off an attack against a domestic U.S. target, but according to Steven Emerson, it has been active among U.S. Shia believers in raising money and perhaps recruits for action against Israel. Far worse, it has struck in the Americas.

Hezbollah was behind two attacks on Jewish targets in Argentina and has set up a training site in the remote area where the borders of Argentina, Brazil, and Paraguay come together.[15] There may be some interchange or cooperation between Hezbollah and al Qaeda in this area. It is too far away from the United States to provide the kind of easy access that can be made from a Canadian base, as some potential and actual terrorists have managed, but the South American site could certainly be used to target U.S. and other targets in the southern cone.

The third important radical Islamic group is based in Indonesia, which has the largest Muslim population in the world. Jamaah Islamiyah, as the terrorist group is called, has been active for many years and was responsible for the attack on a night club on the resort island of Bali in 2002. Apparently, the terrorists thought that they would be able to kill a significant number of Americans with a suicide bomb, but the victims were mostly Australian or Indonesian. Some reports suggest a close tie between Jamaah Islamiyah and al Qaeda.

One of the most aggressive terrorist groups in the Middle East is Hamas, a Palestinian-derived organization, whose main target has been the State of Israel. Hamas comes from a long line of anti-Israeli terrorist groups including Fatah and Black September, the gang that kidnapped Israeli athletes at the 1972 Olympics in Munich. Hamas has been active in fund-raising in the United States but has not pulled off an attack here so far. Hamas receives most of its support from Syria and from Palestinians themselves in what they see as a war against the Jewish state.

HOMEGROWN TERRORISTS

While these fanatic Islamic terrorist groups all talk about attacking the United States itself, only al Qaeda has done it. But other terrorists have carried out operations in the United States and they have nothing to do with Islamic radicals, or with other foreign powers, or foreign nongovernmental organizations (NGOs). They are homegrown terrorists and are just as deadly and frightening as the Islamists. Some have an institutional base, while others seem to be lone actors. In any effort at protecting the homeland, they must be part of the security equation.

The bombing of the Murrah Building in Oklahoma City in 1995 was the work of at least two right-wing extremists and demonstrates the need to treat extremist groups in the United States as more than criminals. The existence of these groups and their potential for terrorism cannot be overlooked. They seem to be stimulated by talk-radio shows around the country, where radio hosts—in the interest of maintaining market share and larger audiences—play up the evils perpetrated by the federal government. The FBI has been quite successful over the years in penetrating such groups, but federal agents were unable to unearth the McVeigh-Nichols plot. So far, no credible evidence has emerged that the right wing is plotting more terrorist violence, but good homeland intelligence might give authorities the kinds of warning they need to protect against domestically based extremist operations.

Bruce Hoffman, a terrorism expert, has written extensively about what he describes as the fundamentalist Christian right.[16] He sees them as racist, anti-Semitic, and fervently opposed to anything that smacks of gun control. He accuses them of sedition and plotting against the federal government and reports that such elements, in loose coalitions, are spread around the United States. Jessica Stern, a lecturer at Harvard university and another expert on terrorism, actually visited prisons where some American right-wing extremists were incarcerated to find out more about their motivations.[17] Clearly, these terrorists are as fanatic as their Middle Eastern counterparts, but unlike bin Laden's people, they are here.

Equally fanatic are terrorists who seek to stop abortions by murdering the doctors who perform such procedures. Although they seem to think of themselves as "saviours" of the unborn, they use many of the same violent methods as other terrorists, bombing clinics and shooting their victims. Their explanations for their motivations, as related by Jessica Stern, sound even more irrational than those coming from al Qaeda.[18]

The role of intelligence in dealing with such groups is clear. The United States cannot afford to have this kind of activity swept under the rug. It cannot wait for another attack on the federal government, as took place in Oklahoma. The government needs to do exactly what the extremist groups are complaining about. While the free speech of these groups is protected by the very government they hate, sedition or terrorism is not. They must be tracked and their plots must be broken. This is as much an intelligence problem as a matter for law enforcement.

Another threat to homeland security has grown up around die-hard environmentalists who style themselves as "ecoterrorists." So far, their operations have been relatively low-level, and mostly aimed at destruction of property rather than at random violence. They are terrorists, nonetheless. Styling themselves the Earth Liberation Front (ELF), they have freed laboratory animals only to see them die after their release, they have burned down housing developments, and they have even turned children's toys into vehicles for their antiestablishment messages. They have begun circulating propaganda attacking owners of large sport utility vehicles because these truck-like giants pollute and use excessive amounts of fuel. In 2003, at one auto dealership, about fifty SUVs were destroyed by the ELF. These ecoterrorists, although they seem to be relatively harmless so far, may very well resort to real violence to reinforce their messages and cannot be overlooked.

AGRO-TERRORISM

Law enforcement and private security officials have become increasingly concerned about agro-terrorism and threats to the U.S. food and water supply. This could take place at a number of different levels, from attempts to poison animal feed stocks to efforts to put poison chemicals in reservoirs or water treatment plants. In fact, followers of an Indian swami in Washington state some years ago did plant salmonella bacteria in salad bars in order to demonstrate their power. There have been other cases of terrorists, usually lone actors, who have poisoned products on the shelf such as Tylenol, leading to the development of those devilishly hard-to-open protective covers and seals on so many products in the modern marketplace. However inconvenient, these measures have at least reduced the vulnerability of packaged food and drugs to terrorist tampering.

Meanwhile, the food industry is fighting back against efforts to further protect the food supply, arguing that the costs, which the private sector has to bear, far outweigh any security benefits from increased regulation and scrutiny.[19] Department of Homeland Security Secretary Tom Ridge announced in March 2003 that he was making food security a key part of his defensive effort against terrorism, but only some of the key agencies belong to DHS. The Food and Drug Adminstration and its Center for Food Safety remain part of the Department of Health and Human Services, while the Customs inspectors who work to protect against tampering with food imports are part of Homeland Security.

THE LONE TERRORIST

An insidious kind of terrorist is the lone bomber who seeks to murder not because of a political agenda or religious rage, but for the thrill of killing and causing fear and panic among the general population. This was high-lighted in 2002 when an American named John Muhammad, along with a foreign-born teen-age accomplice John Malvo, carried out sniper attacks on random human targets across the country. The two were allegedly involved in more than a dozen separate sniper shootings in which many of the vic-tims died. People in the Washington, DC area, where most of the attacks took place, became afraid to go outside to shop or go to school, and typical police methods at first seemed unable to track down the terrorists.

Profilers believed the sniper was a white male and probably part of a right-wing conspiracy. Muhammad and Malvo were black and acted alone. Eyewitnesses gave conflicting information to police about the vehi-cle the sniper used and his appearance. Finally, an intelligence surveillance aircraft from the Army was put to use to try to find the snipers, who were eventually nabbed when a truck driver spotted the two at a rest stop. Muhammad was just the latest example of the lone terrorist and the case demonstrates how hard it is, using either police or intelligence methods, to track down down such a figure. After all, no one has been able to find the person who sent anthrax through the mail to a firm in Florida and to law-makers on Capitol Hill.

WEAPONS OF MASS DESTRUCTION

So far, terrorists have used easily available materials to carry out their operations. Suicide bombers have put together traditional kinds of bombs for their work, either using explosives such as semtex or creating their own explosives with diesel fuel and fertilizer, as McVeigh and Nichols used in Oklahoma City. The 9/11 hijackers needed nothing more than box cutters and the threat of a bomb to hijack four airliners. What everyone fears is that terrorists will begin to use weapons of mass destruction (WMD) to carry out their attacks. The possibilities are truly frightening and were highlighted in January 2003 when the British and French internal security services discovered a terror cell of Algerians in London that was trying to make ricin, the toxic nerve agent, that is produced from commonly available castor beans.

Ricin was used by the Bulgarian intelligence service during the cold war in several assassination operations in which a poison pellet was injected into the victim using an umbrella with a special injector tip. We know about this because French doctors who treated one of the victims recovered the pellet that contained the traces of ricin. Another attempt to use WMD took place in Japan when operatives of the Aum Shinrikyo cult released highly toxic sarin gas in the Tokyo subway, killing 12 and injuring hundreds.

In the wake of 9/11, there was much discussion about the possibility that terrorists might use a so-called dirty bomb to attack the United States. A dirty bomb is made up of a conventional explosive wrapped with radioactive material so that the detonation produces a radioactive cloud that could render an area uninhabitable, in addition to killing victims through radiation poisoning if not through the explosion itself. In 2002, the United States arrested Jose Padilla, whom the FBI thought was planning to make such a bomb, based on materials that were found with him. This kind of bomb would be a low-tech alternative to a real nuclear weapon, which requires a much higher level of technology and the availability of weapons-grade fissionable material to construct. Padilla was declared an enemy combatant and jailed in a military prison.

According to a study undertaken by the Monterey Institute of International Studies in 2002, there are "thousands of lost and abandoned radioactive devices" scattered around the world that would provide enough material for a dirty bomb.[20] Some radioactive material, such as cesium-137 or cobalt-60 are contained in commercial applications, such as medical diagnostic tools, or even small amounts in home smoke detectors, according to the study. It's not clear how much of the radioactive material would be needed to make the dirty bomb, but a few ounces might be enough to cause property damage and perhaps a few casualties. Certainly, the use of such a bomb would cause panic.

Alternatively, terrorists might try to acquire a suitcase bomb. These were small nuclear devices that were man-portable and were developed by both the United States and Russians during the cold war. If they still exist, they are supposed to be tightly controlled and secured. The great fear among Western observers is that the former Soviet nuclear arsenal is not well guarded and, given the precarious state of the Russian economy and the growth of organized crime groups in Russia, a criminal group might try to steal a suitcase-size weapon—or weapons-grade plutonium or uranium—and sell the stuff to a terrorist group. Although there have been reports of sales of tiny amounts of radioactive weapons material, so far, no major theft has occurred and security has been tightened.

OTHER WEAPONS

Terrorist followers of bin Laden have clearly considered other kinds of biological or chemical weapons, based on material that was found in Afghanistan after al Qaeda was chased out, but they have not attempted to use them so far. The lone terrorist who circulated anthrax spores is really the exception, but the case illustrates how easy it is to create fear and panic with limited resources. The same is true of the Washington area snipers, who used a legally available assault rifle to terrorize a significant area of the country. Despite the fact that terrorists have generally relied on readily available weaponry rather than more sophisticated methods, the use of a weapon of mass destruction cannot be ruled out. Therefore, first responders—usually police, firefighters, or medical teams—have to be prepared for the worst.

One weapon terrorists can use against the homeland is the electronic one, that is cyber-terrorism. It is enough of a problem that the White House retained an official to keep an eye on cyber-terrorism outside the new Homeland Security Department, while the private sector has taken steps to build firewalls and other measures to control possible attacks. Press reports in early 2003 suggested that Iraq might use cyber-weapons to disrupt communications, or spread computer viruses to infect computer systems to combat the United States in the war. If Iraq could do it, it seems reasonable to suppose that Islamic or other terrorists could, too. As it turned out, Iraq did not use cyber-weapons in the war with the United States.

In January 2003, American and Pakistani investigators arrested a Pakistani citizen who had used the Internet to acquire $3 million in computer equipment from the United States without ever having set foot in the country. The con man advertised computer equipment for sale on Internet sites for eBay and Yahoo, and when buyers submitted credit card numbers, the Pakistani entrepreneur used the credit card numbers to buy actual equipment, which he had shipped to Singapore, then forwarded to Dubai where he had an office for the purpose.[21] Ironically, the story appeared on the same day that the *New York Times* reported on several Pakistanis, working in the United States, who were summarily deported for overstaying visas or other seemingly minor issues.

The point here is that increasingly sophisticated computer hackers bent on destruction or crime in the United States do not have to be physically located in this country to carry out their operations. The *Times* reporter noted that the investigation into the Pakistani con man's activities took several years to complete and required technical computer sophistication at least equal to that of the criminal. Most of the tracing took place in the United States, although it required the Pakistani police finally to arrest the man. The incident also points out that Internet surveillance technology has kept pace with erstwhile hackers, whether they are terrorists or common thieves.

OTHER THREATS

The debate on whether or not to include other threats besides terrorism in homeland security continues, but evidence is mounting that there are connections between terrorists, criminal groups, narcotics dealers, and both legal and illegal financial institutions. In addition, technology theft could be a way for terrorists to obtain new systems for their own purposes, but given the billions of dollars that are lost to industrial espionage each year, this becomes a security issue all by itself. Add to that the more traditional kinds of espionage to steal government secrets and it seems unavoidable that any homeland security system has to take into acount all of these threats to national security.

The reach of global crime into the heartland of the United States was a threat long before anyone had heard of Osama bin Laden. After all, the FBI and other law enforcement agencies had been combating organized crime groups since the 1920s. The services organized crime can provide to terrorists within the United States include smuggling illegal aliens and weapons into the country, kidnapping, and illegal financial transactions, such as money laundering and counterfeiting. So far, there is no evidence that the various organized crime organizations—such as the Italian mafias, Russian crime families, Chinese Triads, or a host of others—have become involved with al Qaeda or other terrorist groups, but it would be good to know if this changes.

Many of the organizations involved in tracking global organized crime, such as the FBI, are not part of the Department of Homeland Security (DHS), but the Secret Service, which is still responsible for protecting against counterfeiting, and the former U.S. Customs Service, responsible for dealing with smuggling, are DHS components. The Coast Guard is part of the new department as well, creating at least one tie to the existing U.S. Intelligence Community. Coast Guard Intelligence is one of the 15 agencies that are now part of the IC. Thus, DHS will be involved with these other issues in any case.

NARCOTICS AND OTHER CRIMES

Federal agents are already investigating narcotics rings to see if there are ties to terrorists. When Osama bin Laden was based in Afghanistan, drug money helped finance his operations. In December, 2002, the *Los Angeles Times* reported that Federal agents, presumably from the Drug Enforcement

Administration (DEA), were tracking some forty cases where it appeared that the proceeds of illegal narcotics sales might have been diverted to terrorists.[22] In November, 2002, according to the report, three men tried to trade a half-ton of heroin and five tons of hashish for four Stinger shoulder-fired anti-aircraft missiles, which were then to be shipped to al Qaeda. The traders were arrested by the FBI. Neither the FBI nor the DEA are part of the DHS, but they are in a good position to track deals between drug dealers and terrorists. According to the *LA Times*, the DEA has more than 360 agents in 56 countries

Earlier in 2002, the DEA discovered significant evidence that a methamphetamine ring in the United States may have sent millions of dollars from drug sales to Hezbollah in Lebanon. The *LA Times* also noted that Colombian paramilitary groups had tried to swap $5 million in drugs and cash for weapons. The deal was negotiated in Panama. One DEA agent reportedly said that it seemed clear to him that drug dealers were willing to support extremists or anyone else who had the money.

Counterfeiting is a potentially useful weapon for terrorists, according to Paul Kaihla, a reporter for the online publication *Business 2.0*.[23] Kaihla notes that counterfeiting has gone well beyond making copies of U.S. currency, although new printers and scanners make that kind of crime much easier than it used to be. Forgers are making credit cards, passports, and other documents that will pass all but the closest scrutiny. A collusion of terrorists and organized crime means that terrorists have new means to raise funds, disrupt commerce, and perhaps gain illegal entry into the United States. According to Kaihla's investigation, much of this criminal activity is centered in the Middle East, with Hezbollah operatives operating quite openly in Lebanon. Other centers of activity are reportedly in Syria, Iran, and Turkey.

COUNTERING ESPIONAGE

The traditional problem of countering espionage, mentioned earlier, really deserves more attention than it has been getting in regard to homeland security. Politicians and intelligence professionals alike seem to have forgotten the threat that espionage poses to government security, and to private industry as well. Throughout the cold war, friends and enemies tried to steal U.S. governmental secrets and American technology. Current members of Congress seem to have forgotten the outrage unleashed on Capitol Hill when spies were caught inside the CIA, NSA, or DIA. Until the alleged intelligence failure on 9/11, failure to uncover spies had been one of the major complaints about America's intelligence system. Yet, in the debates and discussions about creating the Department of Homeland Security, the issue of espionage was not raised.

If friends and adversaries are willing to mount espionage operations against the United States, why should we believe that terrorists won't do the same thing? In most industrialized countries, countering espionage is one of the main tasks of the internal security service. The danger of espionage, while not life-threatening in the same way as terrorism, is still a major threat to homeland security and will be discussed in more detail in the next chapter.

THE SECURITY CYCLE

Threat analysis is the first step in what has become known as the "security cycle," a series of steps to detect threats, uncover security gaps, plan security programs, and implement the plans. The security cycle is not as widely known or as thoroughly taught as the intelligence cycle, which is part of the instruction in most intelligence services and in courses about intelligence. Threat analysis is critical because no security system can protect against every conceivable threat. It would be too costly and would likely dilute defensive measures. Once the threats have been identified, however, security planners can see where security gaps exist in defensive plans. This second step in the security cycle is what most security professionals call the security audit, an effort to uncover vulnerabilities or gaps in any plan to protect against the recognized threats. Clearly, the U.S. homeland is vulnerable to many of the threats identified here, despite the creation of DHS.

Late in 2002, a study undertaken by former U.S. Senators Gary Hart and Warren Rudman listed many of these gaps in homeland security.[24] The American insurance industry has also been looking around to try to judge vulnerabilities and potential targets for attack so it can determine how to assess the cost of insuring the private sector. The government is essentially self-insured at national, state, and local levels, so much of the focus of these studies has been on privately owned sectors of the nation's infrastructure, about 85 percent of the total.

The United States is vulnerable to terrorism, and to many of the other threats, because we are a huge open society. We bridle at security regulations that impede freedom of movement, or attack privacy. We object to notions such as national identity cards or any other efforts by the government to keep track of us. This was made clear in the outcry that arose after the public learned that the Pentagon had undertaken a study to see what could be done to track Americans and foreigners alike in the United States using electronic data collection. The reaction immediately caused members of Congress to try to delay the program until open hearings could be held to find out if the study was designed to violate individual privacy. Eventually, the protests were so loud that the study was cancelled.

CONTROLS ON FOREIGNERS

Efforts to increase controls on foreigners legally residing in the United States, especially people from Middle-Eastern or South Asian countries, raised concerns as well. The Bush Administration said that the crackdown was designed to root out people who were here illegally, who had over-stayed their visas, or who had submitted false information in order to get here. All but three of the 9/11 hijackers were in the United States quite legally, so if they had been forced to report to the Immigration Service to be fingerprinted, as many Middle Easterners have been, apparently noth-ing would have happened to most of them. The three others had expired visas and action would be taken these days to deport them. Before 9/11, they might have faced no consequences.

The crackdown on Middle Eastern men after 9/11 began to take on the flavor of the ill-conceived and unwarranted removal of persons of Japan-ese descent in World War II from their homes on the West Coast to con-centration camps east of the mountains. They lost jobs, homes, and practi-cally everything they had. The same thing seems to be happening in this latest racist crackdown. As far as we can tell, no terrorists have been uncovered. In fact, the Hart-Rudman report notes that ill-conceived restrictions on individual liberties, especially in regard to people of Middle Eastern descent or those who follow Islam, could hurt the United States far more than the terrorists did.

In January 2003, the FBI told 56 of its field offices to run a census of Islamic mosques in their areas, again raising concerns about racism and profiling. If, however, Steve Emerson is correct about fund-raising among U.S. Muslims for radical Islamic groups abroad, then learning more about this issue ought be a high priority. A professional intelligence service would not broadcast so publicly its targets in order to protect sources and methods, a skill the FBI should understand.

The former Immigration and Naturalization Service came in for a lot of criticism in early 2003 when studies revealed that the INS was unable to track students who have come into the United States on student visas but then either did not report to the schools they were supposed to attend or left after a short period of study. Apparently, three of the 9/11 hijackers entered the United States on student visas. The INS, now part of DHS as the Bureau of Immigration and Customs Enforcement, instituted an elec-tronic system, called the Student and Exchange Visitor Information System (SEVIS) to track students, but it requires the schools that the students are attending to provide data on each student—something the schools have only limited resources to manage.[25] According to investigative reporters, thousands of students with visas may well be in the United States illegally after using the visas to gain entry. The SEVIS system will not be able to track those who "disappeared" before the system was implemented.

General Accounting Office investigators told members of Congress in January, 2003 that they were able to enter the United States using false names and forged identity documents, despite the supposed tightening of border controls.[26] Coupled with all the other problems that surfaced in regard to the INS, the Department of Homeland Security, which has inherited the immigration agency, will be hard-pressed to fix the system to make sure that only those people who are supposed to be in the United States actually gain entry.

These problems suggest that a determined individual, intent on gaining entry into the United States, can probably do it. It would require patience and a knowledge of the systems and its weak points, but these have been well publicized. The danger is that terrorists can still enter the United States either legally or using forged documents and then disappear into the population, perhaps to set up sleeper cells. Such cells, usually no more than four or five people, wait for the opportunity to strike, or for directions from some terrorist leader to activate them.

OTHER VULNERABILITIES

While the United States has undertaken a massive and expensive overhaul of security in regard to air transportation, other parts of the transportation sector remain vulnerable. Before the beginning of the war against Iraq in 2003, trains, busses, and ferries were largely without security controls, as were bridges and highways. When the war began and the threat level was raised to Orange or high, state and local governments took on the task of protecting those parts of the infrastructure, although at considerable cost. Retired Coast Guard Admiral James Loy, the head of the Transportation Security Administration (TSA) said in TV interviews that he planned to implement security controls on container and other heavy shipping into the United States. Early steps included a method to put electronic control mechanisms on the containers at their port of origin so inspectors could monitor tampering when the containers arrived in the United States, since searching them would be prohibitive.

There is, however a downside to the massive restructuring of airport security. According to a report issued by the Justice Department, immigration screeners are apparently unable to handle the volume of foreign travelers who come through U.S. airports and may be missing illegals or alien smuggling.[27] Some officials in the immigration system blamed lobbying by airlines to keep security checks from interfering with the smooth passage of foreign travelers. Nonetheless, security checks have been strengthened at the more than a thousand border crossing points between the United States and Canada. In the past, many of these border points were not staffed at all. It was not clear whether or not the improvements on the ground led to deficiencies at the airports, but the DHS responded to the Justice report by promising to tighten up at airports.

We are vulnerable at home because we are part of a global infrastructure system, much of which is based abroad. The Hart-Rudman report points out that we can't protect the homeland infrastructure unless the United States pursues protective measures overseas. So far, the provisions in Homeland Security legislation to link DHS efforts with those of other U.S. agencies whose main focus is the foreign environment, remain to be implemented. This is especially true in regard to intelligence, despite the fact that the planned intelligence unit within DHS will be part of the U.S. Intelligence Community. While each of the intelligence agencies reportedly has established a unit for Homeland Security, it's not yet clear how the agencies and DHS will work together.

THE ROLE OF THE MILITARY

Hart-Rudman suggests that the National Guard should be brought into the Homeland Security system in order to help deal with any kind of catastrophic attack on the homeland, but the report points out that, at this point, the Guard is neither equipped nor trained for such functions. This raises yet another issue, that of the use of military forces in general to defend the homeland. The Northern Command has been established, at least as a headquarters, to carry out such operations, but has yet been called upon to do so. According to press reports, Northern Command has practiced the technique that would be required to shoot down civilian airliners, although they have never actually had to carry out an attack. Some observers have questioned what the proper role of the military should be in homeland defense. These questions have been raised because the Posse Commitatus Act of 1887 proscribes the military from any role in law enforcement in the United States.

This issue came up during the reign of terror caused by the sniper attacks in the Washington, DC area in 2002. At one point, when the U.S. Army reconnaissance aircraft was used to try to patrol the area to look for the snipers, some thought this violated the nineteenth-century law. Since most elements of U.S. intelligence belong to the Department of Defense and are staffed, at least in part with military personnel, the entire issue of the role of the military, especially its intelligence units, deserves careful review and will be dealt with in a subsequent chapter.

GUN CONTROL

While the United States works to stem terrorist access to weapons of mass destruction, the nation continues to be vulnerable to the proliferation of small arms—handguns, assault rifles, grenades, and rocket launchers— that have been the most common weapon of our enemies.[28] U.S. policy, under the George W. Bush administration, and well supported by the National Rifle Association, a powerful lobbying group, has been to withhold support for any measures designed to rein in traffic in such weapons. Apparently, gun owners in the United States fear that any clamp-down on illegal weapons traffic abroad will affect their ability to obtain such weapons at home. The result is that the weapons are readily available to terrorists, both at home and overseas.

In fact, more and more countries are manufacturing small arms and they have become increasingly available at low prices. Ted Dishman, a reporter for *USA Today*, notes that knock-off copies of the AK-47, the world's most popular assault rifle, can be purchased for as little as $150 in Egypt. Just before 9/11, the United States voted against a UN measure that would have stopped the transfer of shoulder-fired anti-aircraft missiles to terrorists, guerrillas, and criminals. Even though such a weapon was used against an Israeli airliner in Kenya, and airline security officials are concerned about the possibility of these rockets being used against American commercial aircraft, the U.S. policy on this issue has not changed. Nonetheless, the U.S. government is studying the costs and methodologies of installing protective devices against anti-aircraft missiles on commercial airliners, similar to systems that are already in place on military aircraft.

Control of small arms and similar weapons has been the purview of the Bureau of Alcohol, Tobacco, Firearms, and Explosives (ATF), a part of the Treasury Department, until it was moved to the Justice Department in 2003.[29] It has never been clear why the ATF was not put into DHS, but perhaps the gun lobby had something to do with it. ATF will put more effort into control of illegal firearms and explosives, according to a spokesperson for the agency, but it is not clear how, or if, it will cooperate with Homeland Security officials.

TERRORISTS AND CYBERSPACE

Another serious vulnerability lies in our increasing dependence on cyberspace to carry out commercial activity as well as communications. In January, 2003, a computer "worm," a form of electronic virus, slowed Internet communications worldwide for a period over a weekend, until patches and other defensive measures could bring the system back up to speed. The work originated in Hong Kong, but other details were sketchy. Was this a lone hacker trying to see what damage he or she could do? Or was this a form of terrorism? Law enforcement officials were trying to pin this down, but some admitted that cyber-criminals were ahead of the electronic game, since the criminals probably have better equipment and more advanced skills than the investigators.[30]

Terrorist groups have learned to take advantage of the Internet to advertise themselves and their philosophy, as well as to communicate with their followers. It may be a useful way for them to recruit new adherents, or send signals to activate sleeper cells. Of course, this is one way for intelligence organizations to track terrorists, so the vulnerability cuts both ways.

Many private firms are reluctant to report cases of cyber-crime because it makes the firm's security look bad. Besides, many of the crimes are carried out by insiders within the company and since their tools are virtual, not real, they are difficult to catch, never mind prosecute. In one case, two accountants for Cisco Systems broke into the company's computer system and issued themselves $8 million in stock before they were caught. There have been several cases where bank employees have siphoned off funds, presumably to personal accounts, and some have apparently gotten away with the theft. Since the U.S. Secret Service remains responsible for tracking some of these crimes, the involvement of DHS in fighting cyber-crime is inevitable.

ATTACKS ON THE ENVIRONMENT

In order to try to detect attacks on the environment, the Bush Administration began deploying monitors to detect anthrax, smallpox, or other harmful substances if they are released unto the atmosphere.[31] The system is called Bio-Watch and uses existing air quality monitors to detect the pathogens if they are spread using an aerosol system. It would not, however, have detected the anthrax spores spread by mail shortly after 9/11. The Federal government is also looking at ways to keep track of diseases that might have been spread by terrorism through the establishment of a communications network among health care workers.

DHS, the intelligence agencies, and other parts of government are not the only ones worried about vulnerabilities. The U.S. insurance industry has been making a concerted effort to try to determine where and how the United States is vulnerable to terrorism and other threats so that premiums and costs can be estimated. Most of this has not been made public because no one wants to give terrorists a shopping list. While we can assume that al Qaeda has operatives within the United States scouting out potential targets, we can't assume that foreign terrorists will see the vulnerabilities in quite the same way as Americans do. Intelligence analysts studying the problem have to be careful about mirror-imaging, the tendency to believe that all humans think like we do and would therefore do what we would do in similar circumstances. This can lead to intelligence failure.

While the threat of terrorism in the United States continues and we worry about the extent of our vulnerabilities to surprise attack, other problems related to homeland security might be more manageable, but they ought not to be ignored. Especially important is the threat of espionage and technology theft. This is something that has a long history in the United States and should be on the homeland security agenda, although it has not been given much attention in the more pressing fear of terrorism. It's a subject well worth exploring in depth in the next chapter.

The Threat of Espionage

In April 2003, the FBI announced that it had arrested a Chinese-American woman whom the FBI claimed was a double agent spying both for the United States and for the Chinese Ministry of State Security, one of China's two main intelligence services.[1] As the story unfolded, it appeared to be more than just a simple case of espionage. The agent, Katrina Leung, a naturalized American citizen, had been an active fund-raiser for the Republican Party, a well-known socialite in San Francisco, and the mistress of at least two senior FBI officials, neither of whom knew that his colleague was also bedding Ms. Leung. Although the FBI had suspicions about Ms. Leung for years, nothing was done to stop her and she was able to send secret documents, most of which she obtained from her FBI lovers, to her Chinese masters. Even Robert Mueller, director of the FBI, admitted that it was a "sad day for the FBI" coming as it did only a few years after the celebrated espionage case involving FBI agent Robert Hanssen, who spied for the Russians.

Espionage, the theft of secrets from one's enemies, adversaries or, competitors is as old as recorded history. Sun Tzu, the Chinese military philosopher wrote about the use of spies about 2,500 years ago, and spy stories appear on Babylonian tablets, in Egyptian writings, and in the Bible. One writer described it as the "second oldest profession."[2] Espionage figures sporadically throughout American history, but as so often in the world of intelligence, we only learn about it when the spy gets caught.

People rarely die because of espionage and it does not seem as frightening or destructive as terrorism. Yet, it threatens U.S. security at home and abroad so countering espionage ought to be part of any system of homeland security.

The roots of espionage against the United States date back to the Revolutionary War when Dr. Benjamin Church, the surgeon general of the Army, was caught passing secrets to the British.[3] It was Church who told British General Gage where to find the cannon and ammunition the Colonials had hidden in Lexington and Concord. Church was betrayed when his mistress passed his encrypted message, intended for his British cohorts, to an American she mistakenly thought was a Tory sympathizer. When the message was deciphered, the Revolutionaries realized what had happened, but also discovered that the Continental Congress had failed to pass a law against espionage. All they could do was send Church back to England, but his ship sank and he was lost at sea. Soon after, a law on spies was passed enabling General George Washington to have Major John Andre, the British officer who handled Major General Benedict Arnold's defection, hanged for spying. If Washington's covert operation to kidnap Arnold from behind British lines had worked, Arnold would likely have suffered the same fate.

During the Civil War, Southern sympathizers and members of the government who intended to leave to join the Confederacy stole government secrets as they departed Washington. One spy who caused considerable damage was Rose Greenhow, a Southern sympathizer, who ran a boarding house in Washington. Mrs. Greenhow learned of the plan to send the Union Army to Centerville, Virginia, to take control of the railroad junction in the town and thus cut off supplies to the rebel states. Mrs. Greenhow sent news of the secret plans to General P. G. T. Beauregard, the Confederate commander, and the Union Army, under Major General Irwin McDowell, was sent fleeing back to Washington when the Confederates knew where to strike.[4]

Mrs. Greenhow was nabbed by Alan Pinkerton, a former railroad detective, who had come to Washington after uncovering a plot to kidnap President-elect Lincoln before his inauguration. Pinkerton created what he called the Secret Service, a kind of counterintelligence and internal security unit, and went after other spies and Confederate sympathizers in the capital. When Pinkerton became General McClellan's intelligence chief, Lafayette Baker took over the task and turned the service into a vigilante unit. His badge read "Death to Traitors," and his technique was decidedly draconian.[5]

A NEW SECRET SERVICE

After the Civil War, the Secret Service, under more enlightened management, devoted itself to pursuing counterfeiters, still one of its major tasks, and the threat of foreign spies was soon forgotten. Interest in countering espionage did not revive until the United States began to inch closer to involvement in World War I. Although President Woodrow Wilson tried to keep America out of the war, the growing threat of German espionage and sabotage was making it difficult for the United States to remain neutral. In January, 1917, a German saboteur blew up the ammunition and weapons depot on Black Tom Island in New York Harbor, breaking windows all over Manhattan, destroying part of the facilities at Ellis Island, and sending shrapnel into the Statue of Liberty. Wilson then called on the Secret Service to root out German spies.[6]

It turned out that there was a German spy ring, headed by Dr. Heinrich Alpert, operating in New York. The ring was working in conjunction with another group, headed by Baron von Rintelen, who was run, in turn by the German Ambassador himself, Count von Bernsdorf.[7] Ironically, German policy at that point in the war was aimed at keeping the United States out of Europe, but the revelation that Germans were spying and sabotaging ships and weapons depots only spurred Wilson's resolve to come in on the side of the British.

While the Secret Service was working to wrap up German espionage operations, another government agency, the Bureau of Investigation, also began to take on a counterintelligence role. The bureau was part of the Justice Department and when the Congress passed an Espionage Act in 1917, as the United States entered the war, this group of special agents, much to the chagrin of the Secret Service, began to take over counterintelligence operations.[8] In 1919, Attorney General A. Mitchell Palmer, fearful that the Bolshevik Revolution might spur subversion in the United States, gave the role of stopping Communism in the United States to the bureau. It later became the Federal Bureau of Investigation (FBI) and its new chief, J. Edgar Hoover, began his lifelong campaign to make the FBI the lead agency in protecting the United States against espionage and crime.

AXIS SPYING IN THE UNITED STATES

Prior to World War II, both Germany and Japan ran espionage operations in the United States. The two Axis Powers were preparing for the possibility that the United States might enter a war involving the European or Asian powers, despite professions of neutrality on the part of American politicians. The Japanese used secret agents to gather information about U.S. interests in the Pacific, focused especially on the U.S. naval facilities in Hawaii, but after the attack on Pearl Harbor, the Japanese agents were rounded up by the FBI.

Germany set up spy rings in the eastern United States well before the U.S. entry into World War II, taking advantage of Nazi sympathizers. In one quite clever operation, an American working as a German agent was able to steal the plans for the top secret Norden bombsight, a device designed for high-altitude strategic bombers.[9] A German officer, operating undercover, was able to sneak the plans, hidden in a specially prepared umbrella, back to Germany. The operation did not benefit the Nazis, however, because they never built the kinds of high-altitude bombers for which the bombsight was most useful. Germany tried again to infiltrate spies and saboteurs into the United States, dropping some by submarine along the eastern coast, but they, too, were quickly captured.

SOVIET PENETRATIONS

We did not know it at the time, but in the 1930s, the Soviet Union began a campaign to recruit agents to penetrate Western governments, including the United States. This effort was managed by the NKVD, the Soviet intelligence and security service and aided by the GRU, the intelligence arm of the Soviet General Staff. These operations only became known after World War II when intercepts of Soviet communications revealed the identities of the spies and the nature of their work.[10] The United States could not have picked this up earlier because we had no foreign intelligence service before World War II, and only very limited communications intercept capability.

Soviet efforts to penetrate the U.S. government during the cold war did not yield much, despite claims by Senator Joseph McCarthy that the government was "riddled" with Soviet spies. Nonetheless, this led to increasingly tough background checks for prospective U.S. government employees, all of whom had to swear that they had no intention of betraying or overthrowing the government. Of course, any real enemy agent would have been quick to take the oath.

SOVIET TECHNOLOGY THEFT

During the war, the Soviets began to focus on obtaining technology through espionage. Soviet agents, including Ethel and Julius Rosenberg, who were couriers and atomic scientist Alan Nunn May penetrated the top secret Manhattan Project organized in the United States to build nuclear weapons. The Soviets had learned about the project from one of its British agents, John Cairncross, who was Executive Secretary to the British project leader. Cairncross was one of the infamous "Five," British agents who worked for the Soviets, including Kim Philby and Anthony Blunt. The secrets the Soviets obtained through espionage aided them in constructing their own nuclear weapons much earlier than Western analysts had expected.

The Soviets acquired and copied other technologies as well. U.S. bombers and transports that landed or were interned in the USSR in World War II were copied faithfully, along with their electronic systems. Even cars and trucks were taken from U.S. designs. The ubiquitous Soviet GAZ jeep was mechanically identical to its U.S. counterpart as were a variety of other vehicles. During my air force assignment in Korea, I had occasion to drive a Soviet copy of an International Harvester light truck, which had been captured during the war from the Chinese. It was a faithful replica of the American product, right down to the dashboard.

When the KGB, the Committee for State Security, was created in 1953 after Stalin's death, a unit for technological theft was set up and continues to operate as part of the Russian SVR intelligence service. Later in the cold war, the theft of U.S. technology increased, as the Soviets recruited the sister intelligence services of the Eastern European states to help out. Technology theft became one of the specialties of the Polish intelligence service, something we learned when a senior Polish intelligence officer was arrested by the FBI as he was trying to obtain secret information from an electronics specialist on the West Coast. The result of technology theft was ominous. U.S. designs were appearing in Soviet-guided missiles, submarines, and other weapons systems to be used against us in the event of war. As the Soviet economy deteriorated, the need for foreign technology only increased. The Soviets could not afford to buy the technology, but even if they could, there were severe restrictions on what could be sold to them. Thus, they had no choice except industrial espionage.

SOVIET SPY CASES

One traditional way to gather information about a hostile government is to penetrate its intelligence services to learn about an adversary's plans, capabilities, and intentions. The Soviets had only limited success in this area, but the spy cases that hit the front pages of the press made it appear that the U.S. intelligence services were thoroughly penetrated. In fact, the cases were rare, but each received considerable publicity. Most of these cases were developed by the KGB or GRU right here in the United States.

As is true in most counterintelligence cases, the Americans who spied for the Soviets were volunteers who sought out KGB or GRU officers to offer themselves and their secrets for cold hard cash. One of the first of these "walk-ins" was John Walker, a navy warrant officer, who in 1967 simply visited the Soviet Embassy, located in the former Pullman Mansion on 16th Street in Washington and said he wanted to sell communications secrets. He was paid promptly and began a career as a traitor that lasted about seventeen years and earned him more than a million dollars.[11]

Walker and the network he created passed communications codes to the Soviets that allowed them to read top secret navy traffic. This might have left the navy extremely vulnerable if a war with Soviets had ever taken place. It enabled the Soviets to pass information to their North Vietnamese allies about air strikes during the Vietnam War. The Walker case was probably one of the most damaging in modern U.S. history. Walker was betrayed by his former wife, who had to convince FBI agents, who were turned off by her frequent drunken phone calls, that her ex-husband was really a Soviet agent. For his part, Walker had become increasingly sloppy and greedy, helping the FBI track him down. To the Soviets, of course, the Walker case was a major victory in the cold war.

In 1994, the nation was shocked to learn that Aldrich Ames, a mid-level CIA officer, had been caught passing secrets to the Russians and had been doing so for 9 years.[12] Ames had begun his career as a traitor by offering to spy for the Soviets, using his contacts in the Soviet embassy to make the offer. Ames claimed that his motivation was strictly greed and not ideology. Ames was adept enough to hide his tracks, at first, and work around at least two polygraph tests, while betraying FBI and CIA Soviet agents, traitors in turn to the Soviet Motherland. Only the determined counter-intelligence work of CIA officer Paul Redmond and his team, along with colleagues in the FBI, prevented Ames from doing more damage. Ames, like Walker, became sloppy and greedy, flaunting the money he received from the Soviets. He'll spend the rest of his life in prison.

Robert Hanssen, a career FBI agent, was the most recent of the Soviet/Russian agents to be caught spying. His case is even more bizarre in many ways than the Ames case because he never revealed his true identity to his KGB handlers, used the money he received for sexual exploits and home renovations, and was caught after 22 years as a spy. An American penetration of the Russian system was well paid to turn Hanssen in. The U.S. agent found a plastic bag with Hanssen's fingerprints and turned them over to the FBI. Neither Hanssen nor Ames knew about the other, a tribute to KGB compartmentation.[13]

OTHER SPIES

Spies do not always turn traitor just for the money, although that is the usual motivation. Spy handlers try to pay their agents, even if they are volunteers, to maintain control over them. For example, Israel used money to keep U.S. Naval Intelligence analyst Jonathan Pollard on the string, even though Pollard had agreed to turn over U.S. secrets because of his love for Israel. Pollard had pressed himself on the Israelis in 1985 because he believed that the U.S. was withholding key intelligence data from Israel. Pollard was ill-equipped and poorly trained in the art of clandestine operations, requesting classified material at work to which he was not supposed to have access. He was soon pinpointed and caught by the FBI. When Pollard sought asylum at the Israeli Embassy in Washington, security guards turned him away. Pollard has been in jail ever since his capture, although the Israeli government has tried several times to have him released.[14]

Another traitor who spied for ideals was Ana Montes, a senior analyst in the Defense Intelligence Agency (DIA), who became an agent for Fidel

Castro because she disagreed with the U.S. economic boycott of Cuba. Montes turned over a great deal of intelligence from her own agency and others with which she worked, but the extent of the damage has not and might never be made public. Montes was arrested in 1999, but apparently was under suspicion for several years before that. As in so many other spy cases, Montes agreed to participate in a thorough damage assessment in return for a plea bargain.

NOT THE WHOLE STORY

These cases are not the whole story. Over the years since the end of World War II, there have been dozens of others. While some Americans did their dirty work overseas, most were willing to cooperate with hostile or friendly intelligence services right here at home. And these are the cases we know about because the spies were caught. Are there others out there spying for Osama bin Laden, or North Korea's Kim Jong Il, or American right-wing militias? We don't know for certain, but two cases have surfaced that illustrate why countering espionage ought to be part of any effort at homeland security.

Ali Mohamed was an officer in the Egyptian Army who had reached the rank of major before he was cashiered. Ali was enough of a professional to have earned a chance to attend training with U.S. forces at Fort Bragg, North Carolina, but during the early 1980s, Ali had also joined the Islamic Jihad. When he left the Egyptian Army, Ali came to the United States and enlisted in the army, apparently as a method of earning U.S. citizenship. Ali began to smuggle classified documents for terrorists, including passing them to El-Sayid Nosair, who was implicated in the 1993 bombing of the World Trade Center in New York and the assasination of pro-Israeli activist Meir Kahane. After leaving the U.S. Army in 1989, Ali became a training officer for al Qaeda specializing in intelligence methods, and in training Osama bin Laden's bodyguards.[15]

In the second case, a Washington State National Guard intelligence officer admitted that he had stolen secret and top secret documents over a nine-year period and apparently was planning to deliver them to a right-wing militia unit. Some of the files contained data on weapons of mass destruction. Investigators were reportedly unable to track down all the documents, some of which were delivered to contacts in other parts of the United States.[16]

THE COST OF ESPIONAGE

The losses of government secrets are hard to measure in terms of monetary cost, but the loss of technology can be calculated and it's expensive indeed. Most of the cost estimates come from organizations such as the American Society for Industrial Security (ASIS) or the U.S. insurance industry and these groups put the losses from technology theft and industrial espionage in the billions. For example, ASIS estimates, based on surveys of industry, that U.S. losses from industrial espionage in the 1996–1997 period amounted to $44 billion. In 1998, the National Counterintelligence Center estimated that U.S. firms lost $600 million in sales and 9,500 jobs over a 14-year period.[17]

The Defense Security Service (DSS) issues periodic reports on foreign efforts to steal secrets from U.S. defense contractors. The FBI keeps track as well.[18] In 1999, former FBI Director Louis Freeh told reporters that 23 countries were trying to steal U.S. trade secrets and that the losses amounted to about $2 billion a month.[19] Again, much of what we know about technology theft and industrial espionage comes from cases where the spies were caught. Many companies would prefer that no one know that they have been victims of espionage, but defense contractors do have to report what they know, even if the espionage is unsuccessful.

Two enterprising journalists have compiled some of the industrial espionage cases into books, while other material has emerged from cases brought against corporate spies under the Economic Espionage Act (EEA) of 1996. This law made industrial espionage a federal crime. Prior to 1996, technology and trade secret theft were largely prosecuted under individual state laws, except where the espionage was aimed at U.S. defense contractors. The DSS and its predecessor agencies as well as the FBI always had jurisdiction in those cases. Now the FBI is the lead agency in all industrial espionage cases brought under the EEA. In other, more rare cases, wire fraud or organized crime statutes come into play, but the FBI remains the agency of first response.

While the DSS reports do not specify which countries have tried to obtain U.S. defense technology, we can see at least some of the details of what's going on. In 1997, 37 countries tried to gather defense technology. By 2001, this number had doubled and included a great many countries whose economies and technologies had reached an advanced stage. Information systems, sensors and lasers, and armaments were among the targets. The methodologies for collection ranged from requests for information, to acquisition of technology companies, to "inappropriate conduct" during foreign visits to U.S. companies. The DSS does not mention espionage in its unclassified report, but one can assume that that threat might be included in inappropriate conduct.

Most of the intelligence collecting was done either through government sponsored or affiliated collectors, or through commercial entities. In many countries, commercial companies have either government support or encouragement for intelligence collection. While the DSS, like the FBI, never identifies the countries involved, the report does show that technology collectors come primarily from Europe, Asia, and the Middle East. It's not hard to guess which countries might be trying to obtain embargoed or restricted technologies.

The DSS notes that an increasingly popular target for intelligence collection is unmanned aerial vehicle (UAV) technology such as the United States uses in the Predator or Global Hawk aircraft. The DSS reports that 31 different countries tried to acquire information about UAVs in 2001. One popular methodology came from overseas students who claimed that they needed the information for their research. The DSS is less specific about other techniques used to try to obtain information but the methodologies are well known.

COLLECTION METHODS

One of the most effective intelligence gathering methods foreign intelligence services and their agents use centers around attendance at technical meetings, conventions, and expositions where U.S. defense contractors show off their wares to the public, to each other, and to government officials. Typically, intelligence collectors visit the booths, gather up whatever brochures or information the contractors hand out, engage the technicians in conversation, exchange cards, and see what they can learn through casual conversation. Some company representatives may seem more willing to talk than others, so the more gregarious people are singled out for special attention, including invitations to lunch, dinner, or drinks.

Using a technique called elicitation, the intelligence collectors try to see what they can learn by steering casual conversations onto more substantive issues. Elicitation requires that the collectors do their homework and learn the jargon of the industry against which they are trying to gather data. Government targets tend to use acronyms as well—the DSS reports are full of them—so this requires more memorization. The collector must prepare for the chance encounter as well as the planned contact by preparing questions ahead of time. The elicitation technique is based on the notion that people prefer to talk about themselves rather than listen to others, so the collector has to encourage the contact to talk, rather than try to match experiences and stories.

Ideally, the collectors will have sent enough people to a trade show or conference that they can divide up and gather data where they can. Then, they return to a hotel room to share what they have gathered and try to see what each collector has learned. Finally, they might write a report, summarizing their findings, or identifying gaps in their knowledge so they can go after the specific pieces of information they might have missed. This methodology requires practice and is probably taught in most intelligence training programs, including our own.

The DSS restricts its reporting to material it obtains from defense contractors. In 2001, the DSS received 717 reports of suspicious contacts of various kinds, but these are the unclassified ones that can be included in a report released to the public. Based on what we know about foreign industrial espionage in the United States, this may just be the tip of the iceberg. Reviewing the cases, it seems clear that the theft of U.S. technology and industrial secrets is a serious threat to homeland security and is perpetrated by friends and adversaries alike.

INDUSTRIAL ESPIONAGE CASES

In December 2002, the U.S. Attorney's Office for the Northern District of California revealed that two men had been indicted for economic espionage, possession of stolen trade secrets, transportation of stolen property and conspiracy. They were accused of trying to steal the secrets from four Silicon Valley companies, two of which had once employed them. One of the two was a U.S. citizen, the other a resident alien, but both were born in China. They were arrested as they were trying to return to China with their stolen data. Although the Chinese government was not mentioned in the indictment, the supporting data shows that it was the likely beneficiary of the espionage.[20] This was just another in the series of industrial espionage cases in which the Peoples Republic of China (PRC) was involved.

We know a fair amount about Chinese industrial espionage because of information that surfaced during the 1999 investigation into allegations that Wen Ho Lee, a Taiwanese national, U.S. citizen, and nuclear scientist had passed nuclear secrets to the PRC. Other data has come from defectors and trade partners. Of course, the Chinese government has denied allegations of espionage and claimed that the W-88 nuclear warhead it was supposed to have stolen from the United States was actually designed based on open source material available on the Internet. The case against Lee fell apart after revelations that investigators had mishandled the evidence and even the *New York Times* apologized to its readers for failing to pursue the story in a more evenhanded fashion.[21]

The PRC is one of the few countries that uses two intelligence services for industrial spying. One operates out of the Ministry of State Security (MSS), the agency that ran Ms. Leung, while the other is the intelligence service of the Peoples Liberation Army.[22] It is not always clear which service is running operations in the U.S. but both do so, according to those who know their system well. Another case we know that was run by the MSS is that of Bin Wu, who was an instructor in philosophy at Nanjing University in 1989 when he was approached by the security service. The service pressured Wu to move to the United States with the clear understanding that if he did not agree, his academic career might not go well in China. The MSS even agreed to allow Wu's girlfriend to accompany him to the United States.[23]

The MSS wanted Wu to gather technical data in the United States, a difficult assignment for someone whose education and background were in philosophy. Nonetheless, Wu accepted the assignment, married his girlfriend, and set out for America. The MSS provided a passport and Wu had no trouble obtaining a visa. The MSS thought of Wu as a "fish at the bottom of the ocean," in American parlance, a deep cover agent.[24] Because Wu had a cousin in Norfolk, Virginia, he headed there to work for his cousin.

A DOUBLE AGENT

The MSS sent an intelligence officer, a resident of the United States, to remind Wu of his duties and even sent Wu a Christmas card with instructions for further communications.[25] Wu, nervous about his new responsibilities as an espionage agent, decided to turn himself in to the FBI, and when he told the Bureau his story, the FBI turned him into a double agent. The FBI reportedly told Wu that if he cooperated fully, he would be allowed to remain in the United States and would be paid for his work.

In August 1991, Wu's MSS case officer summoned him to Washington and gave him new requirements for collection, along with $2,000, which Wu later turned over to the FBI. Wu's task for his Chinese masters was to set up a private business venture to purchase underwater cameras and satellite communications equipment and ship them to China. To make the effort profitable, Wu kited the prices he was charging the MSS. He had no trouble buying the materials and shipping them, since none of them were export restricted. The MSS had set up a front company and an accommodation address in Hong Kong to mask the ultimate destination of the equipment, and Wu was able to deliver the goods.

In Fall 1991, Wu was ordered to obtain 1,500 night-vision scopes from a company in Garland, Texas.[26] Wu paid the company $1,500 for each scope and charged the MSS $2,100—a nice profit. These devices were export restricted, so Wu disguised them as optical tubes, which could be exported legally, all with the approval of the FBI—although the FBI later denied this. By October 1992, Wu had successfully shipped 144 scopes to China.

Soon after, the FBI's double-agent case was sabotaged when the U.S. Customs Service raided Wu's company and arrested the hapless spy. Customs had raided Wu's trash after a tip from the company in Texas that had been selling Wu the scopes. Customs had failed to notify the FBI and might not have known that Wu was working for the other agency. Faced with the returning to China and the wrath of the MSS or a jail term in the United States, Wu chose to take the jail sentence in hopes of staying in the United States when his jail term was over. John Fialka, the *Wall Street Journal* reporter who wrote about the case, was able to interview Wu in prison in 1995.[27] When Wu was released from jail in December 2001, he appealed a deportation order based on his belief that he would be executed if he returned to China. According to press reports, Wu's appeal was received favorably by the judge who heard the case, but his deportation order stood. Instead of going back to face his MSS masters in China, however, Wu was reportedly allowed to move to Taiwan where he had a cousin.

THE MCDONELL DOUGLAS CASE

A second technology transfer case involved the McDonnell Douglas Corporation, now part of Boeing. No espionage was involved, but rather an operation to circumvent technology export controls, using legal methods and a bit of subterfuge. In 1993, the Chinese National Aero-Technology Import and Export Corporation (CATIC), apparently a unit closely associated with the Peoples Liberation Army of China, targeted McDonnell Douglas, which was then still independent but in deep financial trouble.[28] Its military transport program was ending and its civilian airliners were no longer competitive with those of Boeing and Airbus Industries. When CATIC engineers came to visit the McDonnell Douglas Plant 85 in Columbus, Ohio, it seemed pretty clear what they wanted.

For McDonnell Douglas, the chance to sell high-tech machinery to China might have been a way to bail out the company and satisfy grumbling stockholders. For CATIC, the equipment they wanted was too big to steal and illegal to export, so they needed to persuade McDonnell Douglas executives to convince the U.S. government to permit the company to move the plant to China. At the time, some aircraft parts were already being assembled in China, but the equipment at Plant 85 could be used to manufacture military aircraft, so the Pentagon opposed any plan to move the plant out of the country.

In March 1994, McDonnell Douglas had convinced the Clinton administration to grant an export license and the company began packing up Plant 85 for the move. After setting up in China, McDonnell Douglas was supposed to monitor the plant to make sure that it was only being used to make civilian aircraft equipment, but John Fialka reports that the plant ended up constructing parts for cruise and ballistic missiles. Unfortunately for the American firm, moving Plant 85 to China did not save it and it was ultimately bought out by Boeing. In November 2001, the U.S. Commerce Department concluded, after a six-year investigation, that McDonnell Douglas had violated an agreement to keep the plant out of the hands of the Chinese military and fined Boeing $2.1 million. Ironically, McDonnell Douglas officials had sparked the investigation themselves in 1996 when they discovered the Chinese switch to military hardware.[29]

According to one source, the Chinese actually operate a training program for industrial espionage in Nanjing.[30] The source, who attended the training program, told an interviewer that he had run across fellow

Chinese graduates who were employed in the U.S. private sector as well as in the U.S. government. While Chinese industrial espionage might not be unexpected given the prickly relations between Washington and Beijing, other countries—many ostensibly our friends—are also involved in trade secret theft. Some business managers in the United States have said that we need not worry because U.S. experts can invent things faster than others can steal them, but the cases we know about are not reassuring.

JAPANESE ESPIONAGE

Even Japan, which seems to have an edge on the United States in many areas of cutting-edge technology, has sponsored industrial espionage, although the Japanese government always denies the charges. In the most recent case, the FBI arrested two Japanese scientists who had been working at a private laboratory in Cleveland, Ohio, and charged them under the Economic Espionage Act. Both were Japanese citizens with U.S. residency permits and had systematically stolen material related to their research on Alzheimer's disease. They had shipped the data and biological materials to a Japanese lab, whose funding came from the Japanese government. The two then sabotaged what remained of their research materials left in Cleveland before attempting to depart the country.[31]

Earlier examples of Japanese industrial espionage date back to the 1970s. In 1977, Japanese agents operating out of their consulate in San Francisco recruited an employee working for Fairchild Semiconductor and ordered him to steal confidential research, including computer developments and corporate plans.[32] Fairchild discovered that 160,000 documents were missing. Although Fairchild thought they had the agent pinpointed, he was never actually caught. In 1986, Fujitsu, apparently helped by the documents the agent had obtained, made a bid to buy Fairchild, but Casper Weinberger, Secretary of Defense in the Reagan administration, rejected the sale because Fairchild was a key supplier of semiconductors to U.S. defense industries. Weinberger could not permit a foreign supplier to control the market.

In a second case in 1980, Hitachi, with the backing of the Japanese government, found an agent to steal copies of IBM's design books for a new mainframe computer.[33] The agent, a former IBM employee, was a kind of industrial defector who steals secrets from his employer and then tries to peddle them to competitor firms. In this particular case, the buyer was another U.S. businessman who saw the chance to sell the IBM secrets to Hitachi. As it turned out, the FBI stumbled across the case while trying to track down Soviet industrial espionage. The Bureau had asked IBM to cooperate in tracking the Soviets and they were quite willing to do so, unaware of the loss of their design books. When IBM managers realized that the books were missing, they asked the FBI to step in and a sting operation was mounted that turned up the thieves and their ties to the Japanese government. The FBI was so proud of the way it had handled the case, it made a training video out of the recordings of the sting.

Hitachi settled the case out of court, but ironically the U.S. Social Security Administration, probably unaware of the espionage case, later selected Hitachi computers over IBM. Then, in 2002, Hitachi and IBM joined forces in a joint venture to combine disk drive units and announced that they would collaborate to develop data storage systems.[34] Perhaps a new generation of managers in both companies had forgotten the espionage case.

Japan has never had the kind of centralized foreign intelligence organization common to many industrialized countries. Instead, after World War II, Japan concentrated on collecting economic and technological intelligence through its economic and trade ministry, and an operating element called the Japanese External Trade Organization (JETRO). The Japanese were able to do this, in part, because the United States was committed to defending Japan against foreign enemies. Its postwar constitution prevented Japan from becoming involved in international conflicts where foreign intelligence is necessary. Thus, Japan could concentrate on acquiring economic data and technology, a task they continue to pursue.

FRENCH OPERATIONS

France is another friendly country that has mounted industrial espionage operations in the United States from time to time, although most French efforts seem to be concentrated against U.S. targets in Europe. After the French foreign intelligence service, the DGSE, was reorganized in 1982, its leaders made public statements admitting that France carried out industrial espionage to help make French firms competitive in world markets. Pierre Marion went so far as to certify that the DGSE had bugged hotel rooms and even the passenger cabins of the French models of the Concorde supersonic airliner, although he did not say what, if anything, might have been learned that way.[35]

Beginning in 1986, in what was supposed to be a four-year operation, the DGSE reportedly managed to recruit a penetration of the Defense Advanced Research Projects Agency (DARPA), the Pentagon's technological research arm.[36] The aim was to steal the secrets of stealth technology, such as is used on the U.S. Air Force F-117 Stealth fighter. There is no evidence, however, that France has adopted the technology for its own aircraft.

In 1987, the DGSE targeted three U.S. corporations for industrial espionage, including IBM, Corning Glass, and Texas Instruments.[37] Apparently, the French managed to recruit agents in all three companies, but only Texas Instruments (TI) suffered serious loss. According to Peter Schweizer, the CIA picked up information about the operations from sources in France and alerted the companies, whose security officers had already become aware of the French operations. One way the French picked up information on TI was through a time-honored technique called "dumpster diving" or "garbology," stealing information from trash. It was the same method used by the FBI to pinpoint Aldrich Ames, and as long as the trash is out on public property for pick-up, it is perfectly legal. When it is still in possession of the company, then dumpster-diving is theft.

The operation against TI was run by the French consul in Houston, Texas, Bernard Guillet. Texas Instruments should have been wary of the French because they had planted a mole in the company once before in 1976. In that case, Bull, the French chip maker, sued TI for patent infringement. Disclosure revealed that the technique Bull claimed was being used illegally by TI was, in fact, stolen by the French mole inside TI and the lawsuit was quickly dropped. The FBI arrested Guillet in the later case, but he apparently had diplomatic immunity and escaped prosecution.[38]

Ironically, in 1995, the French expelled several CIA officials who had been working with the DGSE's sister service, the internal security service DST, claiming that the CIA was trying to steal French economic data. Journalists who covered the story believed the CIA personnel were ousted for domestic political reasons, since they would have been well known to the government. One of the key officials involved in expelling the CIA officers was the same Bernard Guillet who had been arrested in the TI case, so revenge may have been part of the motivation in this case.[39]

In 1988, French operatives tried to steal information from Boeing about their new 747-400 airliner in Seattle. The DGSE set themselves up near Sea-Tac airport, which overlooks the Boeing test site and used high-tech electronics to intercept signals from the test aircraft. The French then used the information they had acquired in developing the Airbus 340, a competitor to Boeing's new plane. Finally, the CIA discovered that the French intended to target Hughes Aerospace when it put up a display at the Paris Air Show. The company was alerted and withdrew from the show before it could become another victim of French intelligence.[40]

Despite these setbacks in its operations, French intelligence managers continue to insist that industrial espionage is a legitimate function of an intelligence service and aiding the competitiveness of French firms in world markets is a worthwhile use of the service. On that basis, French industrial espionage is likely to continue and U.S. firms should be aware of the threat.

ISRAELI SPYING

Perhaps no friendly nation has been more active in industrial espionage in the United States and elsewhere than Israel, not surprising considering the country's size, its limited resources, and the threats from its Arab neighbors. Despite massive U.S. aid to Israel, especially in defense technology, the Israelis have used their formidable intelligence resources to acquire material they could not invent or buy on their own. In the 1980s, the key Israeli organization devoted to technology theft was LAKAM, the Scientific Affairs Liaison Bureau, the same organization that had run Jonathan Pollard.[41] LAKAM was reportedly founded in 1957 and among its early exploits was the theft of Mirage fighter technology from France in 1971. After Rafi Eitan, an experienced intelligence professional, took over LAKAM in 1981, it became even more aggressive.

Eitan had become well known as one of the masterminds behind the kidnapping of Nazi war criminal Adolph Eichmann, one of the leaders of the extermination program under Hitler. Eichmann was snatched from the streets of Buenos Aires, Argentina, to stand trial and execution in Israel. Eitan was also instrumental in a daring operation in 1968 to steal enriched uranium from a plant in Pennsylvania in order to start up Israel's nuclear weapons development.[42] It was Eitan who had convinced a skeptical Israeli government to take up Jonathan Pollard's offer to become an Israeli agent and it was Eitan who, at about the same time, recruited U.S. Assistant Secretary of Defense Melvin Paisley to pass U.S. defense secrets to Israel.[43]

Melvin Paisley was no ideological agent, but took up spying for the same reason that most do it: greed. He agreed to provide technology to Mazlat, an Israeli company that was developing remotely piloted aircraft for photo reconnaissance. Mazlat had previously had a contract with the U.S. Navy to develop the unmanned aerial vehicle, but the results were disappointing and the Navy dropped Mazlat in 1986. By this time, with the scandal of the Pollard affair, LAKAM had been dissolved and other elements of Israeli intelligence had picked up the Paisley operation. In 1987, probably sensing that he was in trouble, Paisley resigned but agreed to become a consultant to the navy to keep his security clearances. In 1988, the FBI arrested Paisley and discovered, hidden in his house, a treasure trove of secret documents Paisley had taken from the Pentagon.

Another Israeli operation was aimed at Recon Optical, a firm located in Barrington, Illinois. The company had undertaken a new contract with Israel in 1984 to develop photo-reconnaissance cameras for aerial surveillance.[44] Recon Optical's contract was just the latest in a series that dated back to the 1960s. This time, three Israeli Air Force officers were assigned as contract monitors, but their tasks went well beyond supervision and observation. When it became clear that the Israeli officers were secretly shipping Recon Optical proprietary data back to an Israeli firm, Electro-Optical Industries, the CEO of Recon Optical asked for help from the U.S. Justice Department. This was a tough call for Recon Optical because the contract with Israel was one of the largest the firm had.

Unfortunately for the American company, the U.S. State Department intervened when it found out that the Justice Department was about to assign the FBI to the case. The State Department was concerned that

U.S.–Israeli relations would be damaged if the FBI found yet another case of Israeli spying. Nonetheless, Recon Optical took Israel to court and won a settlement of $3 million in 1991, but the case had almost put Recon Optical out of business by the time it was over.[45] As happens in so many of the industrial espionage cases, the cost of fighting the spies in court is more than many firms can bear, especially when they get no assistance from the government.

There are a number of other cases of espionage by foreign intelligence services either to steal government secrets or private ones. Germany, South Korea, and Russia, among other countries, have been caught—as intelligence professionals say—"with their hands in the cookie jar." Perhaps that is why the CIA, in celebrating its fiftieth anniversary, sold a commemorative cookie jar among other souvenirs.

PRIVATE SPYING

Foreign intelligence services are not the only organizations that try to steal industrial secrets and proprietary data. There are many cases of private companies or individuals who have engaged in industrial espionage, but in many of the cases, the spies are incompetent, clumsy, greedy, or so inept that they pose no danger to homeland security. They are merely thieves and ought to be dealt with through a combination of good private security and cooperation with law enforcement.

There was a recent case, for example, in which a kitchen worker at Mastercard's headquarters filmed what he thought were private meetings concerning the credit card company's strategic plans, then offered to sell the video containing the secrets to credit card rival Visa. The erstwhile spy put his true name and address on the envelope of the letter he had written to Visa, however, and was easily caught after security officials at the two companies shared the data and called the FBI. In other industrial espionage cases, the spies have talked too much or failed to cover their tracks. Private security is well equipped to handle such problems, but dealing with highly trained and experienced intelligence operatives may be a different story.

If the French, Japanese, and Israelis can mount clandestine intelligence collection operations in the United States, why should we believe that Osama bin Laden or other terrorist leaders won't try them as well? The basic principles of carrying out such operations are well known all over the world and we must expect that, as the KGB did during the cold war, foreign intelligence services will assist, train, and equip those they support against the United States when such aid assists their own policy goals. The threat from espionage or efforts to curb it do not appear in any of the laws or plans supporting homeland security, but surely that mistake should be corrected.

The Realities of Intelligence Collection

Few functions of government are as misunderstood as those of intelligence, even though scores of books have been written about it, courses have been created in numerous universities, and the government itself has made a reasonable effort to explain the system without compromising secrets. No government is more open about its intelligence system than the United States. Yet, the American public, to the extent such things can be measured, seems woefully ignorant about the intelligence process. Coupled with the misinformation passed around in fictional spy stories in the movies, in novels, and on television, Americans have many bizarre and quite wrong ideas about how the intelligence system really works. It is no wonder, then, that many Americans either fear or ridicule a system purposely designed to protect them.

The intelligence system is often maligned by the press, which tends to put error and scandal above the fold in newspapers and in lead slots on TV. Success is of little interest and stories of intelligence victories are buried on the back pages or relegated to sound bytes. For example, the alleged intelligence failure on 9/11 was front page news, but the CIA's accurate prediction that a virus such as SARS might spread rapidly was buried in the inner pages of several major newspapers.

Reporters tend to hark back to old stories of intelligence failures and cases of abuse as though the same managers and workers who made the errors 30, 40, or even 50 years ago were still leading the intelligence agencies today. Coupled with the kinds of secrecy needed in intelligence to protect sources and methods, perhaps it's no wonder that the public is sometimes misled about intelligence.

Early U.S. presidents put great value on intelligence, especially George Washington, who extolled its virtues and at the same time emphasized the need for secrecy. His letters to subordinates on the subject were preserved and one of them was displayed on a first floor wall at CIA to remind us about our first president's views. The value of intelligence was also cited by other Founding Fathers, such as John Jay and Alexander Hamilton, in the Federalist Papers as they debated the provisions of the proposed U.S. Constitution in 1787.

THE NEED FOR SECRECY

President James Knox Polk defended the need for secrecy in 1846, rejecting a demand from the Congress to produce information about a secret operation mounted by his predecessor John Tyler to convince the people of Maine to accept a U.S.–British agreement defining the Canadian border. The operation involved the circulation of phony maps and disinformation about the proposed treaty, funded in part by the British. Polk noted that no nation on earth was prepared to release information on what we would call today intelligence sources and methods, noting that keeping these items secret was the only way that intelligence success could be repeated.[1]

Several presidents ran secret operations right out of the White House including Thomas Jefferson, who sanctioned the first effort to overthrow a foreign government, James Madison, who sought to use secret agents to wrest Florida from Spanish control, and Theodore Roosevelt, who helped Panamanian revolutionaries break from Colombia in exchange for an agreement to allow the United States to build a canal through the newly independent country. American intelligence, however, was not well prepared for World War II, although its handful of code breakers did manage to intercept Japanese messages before the surprise attack on Pearl Harbor.

President Franklin Roosevelt did understand the need for good intelligence as the United States edged closer to war and turned to his socialite friends to help him set up an intelligence system. He asked William "Wild Bill" Donovan to organize a system that became the Office of Strategic Services (OSS) while Navy code breakers gave Admiral Chester Nimitz the information he needed to defeat the Japanese Navy in the Battle of Midway in 1942. Intelligence played a key role in the invasion of the European continent in 1944 and kept the homeland safe against spies and saboteurs throughout the conflict.

The modern intelligence system we have today in the United States has its roots in World War II, but it remains more or less, a system designed to fight the cold war. It grew from a small operation set up by President

Truman in early 1946 into the conglomerate system we have today. It is a system that clearly begs for change, but efforts to overhaul and restructure the system have not moved very far from where they were more than a decade ago when the cold war ended. Yet, the basic principles behind the system are as valuable today as they were in George Washington's day.

FOUR BASIC ELEMENTS

There are four basic elements to any intelligence system. It must be able to gather information, analyze it, protect the system against enemies, and run secret operations on behalf of the state. An intelligence system must have the ability to gather data from enemies, adversaries, competitors, and even friends—especially when they try to hide the information. Equally important, the intelligence system must be able to analyze the data collected to provide warning of crisis, frequent updates of existing conditions, and forecasts of what is likely to come. Stealing the enemy's secrets is not enough; we must also be able to solve the mysteries of our enemy's intentions. The third process is counterintelligence, stopping our adversaries from doing to us what we are doing to them. Today, counterintelligence has broadened to include stopping other threats such as terrorism, global crime, narcotics flows, and subversion. Finally, intelligence operations may be used to fight an adversary through the use of covert action or even secret military operations, such as those carried out in Afghanistan and Iraq, which—for a change—was given friendly coverage in the media.

We can begin by reviewing the intelligence cycle, the theoretical model that is used in almost all U.S. intelligence training programs, even those in the private sector. It suggests that policy officials, in step one, provide requirements for intelligence to agency managers. In step two, the managers assign collection tasks to the various systems that gather information, including clandestine human source operatives, technical sensor operators, or those gathering open source data. In the third step, analysts evaluate and compare the data, package their conclusions, and in step four, disseminate the conclusions to the policy officials who laid on the requirements in step one so that they can either make decisions or provide more requirements. In my view, this is a flawed representation of what actually happens and it ignores two of the four parts of intelligence: counterintelligence and covert action.

THE REALITY

In reality, policy officials rarely provide requirements for intelligence collection, although they may indicate their general areas of interest and their priorities. In fact, intelligence managers, analysts, as well as collectors themselves are the ones who know the most about what to collect, based on known gaps in the existing data bases, patterns of developments among adversaries, and the general flow of world events. To manage an efficient collection system, the United States has relied for years on a committee system to establish collection goals and targets and assignment of requirements to collection elements. As long as the committees represent all of the various intelligence collection elements, this should be a very workable system and ought to be flexible enough to allow collectors to gather additional information on targets of opportunity even though the specific requirements were not laid down.

The use of committees may sound bureaucratic and stodgy, but the idea is to allow human source, technical, and open source collectors a venue to compare notes, discuss problems, and hash out procedures to make sure that collectors don't all target the same data—except when a bit of redundancy may be useful. The committees should cross agency lines and, in my experience, bringing collection managers together at the working level in this way is a good method for making sure the right targets are not overlooked, and that scarce collection resources are not wasted. Of course, each agency may have its own favorite targets and there can be disagreements over priorities, but the system can work well, as long as the agency representatives have some freedom and flexibility to negotiate on the issues.

MINING DATA

Collection operations require patience, imagination, and talent. A great deal of the data collected is from open sources such as print and electronic media, or from readily available data bases. With the proliferation of Web-based information sources, data collection has been made easier, but at the same time, the Web has increased the amount of worthless, misleading, or ambiguous material that makes up open source intelligence, or OSINT. Collectors have had to develop increasingly sophisticated methods for data mining, sorting the useful data from the vast sea of information. This is a well known problem for any computer user who uses search engines to find information and receives hundreds of thousands of responses, most of which are not really relevant. Multiply this by a thousand and you have some idea of the problem facing intelligence collectors.

In order to help sort data, the U.S. intelligence system has turned to the private sector for help. The CIA has sought to invest in private firms that might be able to develop data-mining techniques through a unit called In-Q-Tel, run outside the agency by a venture capitalist. What little we know about the results of this effort suggest that it is bearing fruit and that new techniques are being used in what some people call "knowledge management."

Most intelligence services around the world typically have had access to the world media through the translation of foreign media sources and the

United States is no exception. In spite of severe budget cuts and reductions in personnel, the Foreign Broadcast Information Service (FBIS) soldiers on, although its products are now primarily available electronically through the U.S. Commerce Department. The advantage of a translation service is that government officials can read media products in English and don't have to be fluent in a host of foreign languages. For those who can manage, however, the proliferation of world press on the Web is certainly helpful.

NEW OPEN SOURCE INTELLIGENCE SOURCES

Intelligence services have been able to take advantage of the growth of what are now known as 24/7 news services that broadcast constantly on TV, whether news is breaking or not. These services, such as CNN, have become a kind of early warning network for intelligence. While their news may not always be accurate and they tend to focus on events where live or filmed visual coverage is available, they are certainly helpful to both collectors and analysts in alerting them to world events. Use of these services is both timely and cost-effective. Even though the United States has a wide-ranging intelligence and warning system set up through major world military commands, CNN or its equivalent is probably playing in all the centers all the time.

Robert D. Steele, a former CIA intelligence officer and military veteran, has argued in two persuasive books that the United States should rely more on open source intelligence than it already does.[2] Most intelligence veterans will probably agree that about 80 percent of the material analysts work with comes from open sources, but there is a downside.[3] Knowing that OSINT is feeding into the intelligence system, adversaries can float disinformation—usually false information wrapped around a nugget of truth—to confuse or mislead analysts. When disinformation is picked up by the media and repeated, intelligence consumers may take false information for truth and find it more convincing than intelligence analysis. This is known in the intelligence world as "blowback." Analysts then find they are fighting an uphill battle to convince policy makers that the news stories they have already heard may be off the mark.

A SECOND FORM OF OPEN SOURCE INTELLIGENCE

A second kind of open source intelligence comes from within the government itself. Much of this material is unclassified, but some might be labeled "For Official Use Only," or classified at a low level to protect sources or the identification of the writer. For many years, intelligence analysts have received data from governmental organizations that are not part of the intelligence community, but have acquired or reported on material that is useful. This data might include memos of conversations, reports from agricultural or labor sources, and debriefings of officials who have traveled abroad. This kind of reporting is particularly important for homeland security because the Department of Homeland Security (DHS) has a limited number of its own intelligence collection resources and has to rely on intelligence units to provide inputs.

According to DHS statements, the new department is receiving its intelligence from the newly created Terrorist Threat Integration Center (TTIC), which was opened in May 2003. Although housed within the CIA temporarily, TTIC is supposed to move to an independent facility, along with the existing CIA and FBI Terrorist Centers, which continue to operate. Since the DHS has only limited intelligence collection resources through its own components, such as the Coast Guard or the Secret Service, it will have to rely on the national intelligence agencies for inputs. This creates several problems.

Clearly, the DHS needs a broader range of intelligence sources than just those focused on terrorism. It will have to have intelligence from the collection services on global crime, narcotics, and espionage. This means that CIA, NSA, and collection elements in the Department of Defense will have to provide data to DHS. This ought to be easy enough to arrange, because it involves intelligence collected abroad. The problem yet to be resolved is that intelligence material from domestic sources, including from DHS units and the FBI, may begin to compromise individual privacy and human and legal rights. It is an issue that has raised the hackles of many citizens, including members of Congress on both sides of the aisle, and requires careful study.

TECHNICAL INTELLIGENCE

Technical intelligence from intercepted communications is a major element in intelligence collection and has always been part of the data-gathering process, although it is more sophisticated and complex today than in the past. The American system considers signals intelligence (SIGINT) to be top secret and takes strong measures to protect the system, but the public has learned a great deal of information about SIGINT over the past 50 years. It has its roots in the nineteenth century when communicators began to use the telegraph for sending messages and spies realized that intercepting the signals by tapping into the wires was possible. Of course, code breaking is an even older method of intercepting messages and goes back at least to ancient Greece.[4]

In 2002, when Secretary of State Colin Powell attempted to convince the UN Security Council that Iraq was building weapons of mass destruction and hiding them from UN weapons inspectors, he used intercepted SIGINT messages to illustrate his points. It was a telling example of how SIGINT is used in intelligence, but it also showed that intercepted communications may be ambiguous, lacking in detail, and subject to a great deal of interpretation. When communications are encrypted and use obscure languages or dialects, the problem of understanding the message becomes even more complicated and subject to false interpretations because of mistranslations, garbles, or missing words.

Of course, our enemies and adversaries know full well that we have the capability to intercept and decipher communications, so they have turned to sophisticated encryption software and other techniques to protect their communications. It has made life a lot more difficult for the U.S. National Security Agency (NSA), which is the agency responsible for most SIGINT collection. In public testimony and in press releases, NSA's leaders have made clear that they understand their need to become more sophisticated in collecting intelligence.[5]

Many NSA breakthroughs, however, seem to have come about because the targets have made mistakes in the use of communications. For example, in the effort to track down accomplices of Osama bin Laden, at least one of the terrorist masterminds, Ramzi bin Al-Shib, was captured because he used a satellite phone from his hiding place in Pakistan. His voice print had become known when he gave an interview to Al Jazeera, the Middle East news outlet, and so when he made an open phone call, intercepts revealed his location. Press stories suggested that Khalid Shaikh Mohammed, another captured senior al Qaeda leader, may have revealed his location through careless use of a cell phone, enabling Pakistani security officials and the FBI to grab him in Pakistan.[6]

SIGNALS INTELLIGENCE IN HOMELAND SECURITY

One of the problems yet to be solved in regard to SIGINT is how it might be used to protect homeland security. According to long-standing laws, rules, and regulations, the NSA is not supposed to intercept communications from U.S. persons—that is, American citizens, legally resident aliens, and U.S. corporations. Unfortunately, these rules have not always been followed, leading to distrust of the U.S. intelligence system in general, and suspicion about NSA in particular. We know quite a bit about this problem because of the work of James Bamford, the enterprising journalist, who wrote two landmark books about NSA, the most secretive of the 15 agencies that make up the U.S. Intelligence Community. We used to joke in Washington that NSA stood for "Never Say Anything" or "No Such Agency" and it remained something of a mystery, before Bamford's exposes, even for those intelligence professionals in other agencies who had the necessary clearances for NSA intelligence.

Bamford's books angered many NSA officials who had been schooled in maintaining the extreme secrecy of the agency, but in recent years, new and more enlightened directors have begin to realize that the NSA's work and responsibilities are generally known to those who care about U.S. intelligence. National Security Agency professionals have begun to identify themselves in public, instead of saying only that they "worked for the government," and NSA has begun to publish unclassified material about its work. Bamford claims that the NSA violated the rules about SIGINT targeted against U.S. citizens and he has good sources to validate his claim.

According to Bamford, the NSA began intercepting communications in the United States as far back as the 1960s, and he blames this in part on the NSA's deputy director, who responded to U.S. Army concerns about antiwar protesters by agreeing to put the names of known protesters on a watch list so that their phone calls could be monitored. Eventually the informal agreement became part of the NSA's regular operations, although the reports were not to be identified as coming from that agency.[7] Some NSA officials apparently protested the domestic surveillance program, but because the NSA was essentially a military organization, there was no way to fight the orders from the top.

THE HUSTON PLAN

In 1970, President Nixon ordered the NSA as well as the Defense Intelligence Agency (DIA) to focus on the antiwar groups referring to them as "revolutionary" and the program became known as the "Huston Plan," named for one of Nixon's White House aides. At the same time, the CIA was told to find out if the protesters were being run or financed by foreign agents. President Nixon had not counted on the attitude of J. Edgar Hoover, who saw any effort at domestic surveillance as encroaching on the FBI.[8] Hoover protested to his boss, Attorney General John Mitchell, who agreed with Hoover and convinced President Nixon to drop the Huston Plan. Despite the cancellation, during the Watergate Scandal, the plan surfaced in the investigation and the NSA's role was revealed.

According to Bamford, the investigations showed that privately owned U.S. communications companies had cooperated with the NSA by providing the agency with magnetic tapes of communications between the United States and foreign countries.[9] Later, during the hearings into allegations of intelligence abuse carried out by Senator Frank Church in 1973, even more information came out. The Church Committee hearings and subsequent legislation led to the creation of the House and Senate Intelligence Oversight Committees and spurred the passage of the Foreign Intelligence Surveillance Act (FISA) to regulate just how and when U.S. intelligence resources could be used against people living in the United States.

Generally, the NSA has restricted its intercepts involving people living in the United States to those who might be agents of a foreign power, including terrorists and spies. Almost all of the work against foreign agents operating in the United States is handled by the FBI, reinforced with the passage of the Patriot Act and new interpretations of the FISA. Meanwhile, the NSA continues to intercept, decipher, and translate SIGINT into usable intelligence. This category of intelligence remains top secret because the NSA does not want its potential targets to know how it manages to focus on them. The NSA's products remain restricted to those who have the appropriate clearances at the Special Compartmented Intelligence (SCI) level and even increased publicity and openness is not likely to change such protection of the NSA's sources and methods.

OTHER METHODS

There are other types of intercepts and collection methods besides those devoted to communications intelligence or COMINT. Electronic intelligence, ELINT, is derived from signals sent by aircraft, ships, rockets, or other machinery. It is usually collected by military ELINT sensors in satellites, special collection aircraft such as the Navy's EP-3 aircraft—which became famous when one was involved in a mid-air collision off the coast of China and was forced to land on Hainan Island—or sensor ships such as the USS Liberty, which was attacked by North Korea. The Iraq War in 2003 highlighted the uses of ELINT in combat, both to collect intelligence and to target the enemy. For example, Iraqi forces had to shut down their antiaircraft radar systems or risk being struck by "smart bombs" that used the radar signal to hone in on the target.

Other military intelligence sensors fall in the category of MASINT, or Measurements and Signatures Intelligence, which is targeted against such esoteric weapons as lasers or particle beam weapons. Measurements and Signatures Intelligence may also be used to sniff out weapons of mass destruction (WMD) including nuclear devices, or chemical and biological weapons. All through the cold war, military units used ELINT and MASINT techniques to keep track of developments among our Communist adversaries. Since the end of the cold war, those sensors have been refocused on states such as Iran or North Korea, which might have the potential to use both missiles and WMD against the United States or its allies. Whether or not such military intelligence sensors could or should be used for homeland security remains a matter for further investigation.

IMAGERY INTELLIGENCE

The second category of technical intelligence collection concerns imagery, including photography, radar imaging, and infrared sensors. The technique of trying to view enemies, capture images of them, and analyze the results dates back to the U.S. Civil War, when both Union and Confederate forces sent observers up hundreds of feet in tethered gas balloons to observe and photograph the battlefield. The heavy plate cameras of those days and the instability of the balloons made this a cumbersome task. When airplanes came along at the beginning of the twentieth century, the task of aerial reconnaissance became a lot easier. The first scout planes in World War I used newly miniaturized cameras and roll film to photograph the enemy, although senior British officers thought that flying behind enemy lines lacked chivalry and at first refused to permit such missions. The Germans had no such compunctions.

Between the World Wars, photographic techniques and aircraft improved to the point that aerial reconnaissance became a regular part of intelligence gathering. When World War II began, all the major powers had the capability to carry out overhead intelligence collection for targeting, for bomb damage assessment, and to establish the enemy's order of battle—its strength in soldiers and equipment—to determine the capability of the enemy. This carried over easily into the cold war, but with certain restrictions. Because the Soviets and their allies as well as the Chinese Communist government restricted their airspace, the United States and Britain were reduced to flying "ferret" missions along the borders of these countries. A number of aircraft and crew were lost on these missions, which could not really see into the heartland of the enemy. Efforts to launch free-floating balloons over the USSR proved equally fruitless and brought back little intelligence.

For their part, the Communists found targets in the United States easy to access, either by having agents fly over them in regular commercial aircraft, or even more simply, by visiting military bases during the open houses held to impress the public with the strength and capability of U.S. forces. In addition, many U.S. magazines, such as *Popular Science* or *Aviation Week*, regularly published details about U.S. military equipment. One good way for Soviet agents to find out about U.S. military hardware was to purchase the plastic model kits sold at hobby shops, which were often developed from military plans, and were usually quite accurate in detail.

THE U-2 AND SR-71

Finally, in the early 1950s, Richard Bissell of the CIA, working with the U.S. Air Force and the Lockheed design bureau, known as the "skunk works," supervised the development of the U-2 reconnaissance aircraft which was designed to fly over restricted territory at an altitude of at least 70,000 feet, too high to be struck by the existing set of antiaircraft guns and missiles used by the USSR or China.[10] At first, this was a huge success and the images revealed, for the first time, that the United States was well ahead of the Soviets in terms of missile and aircraft capability. But, the Soviets soon developed antiaircraft missiles capable of hitting a high-flying U-2 and after Francis Gary Powers was shot down on a U-2 mission over Sverdlovsk, overflights of Soviet territory ceased.

During the next decade, both the United States and the USSR built space systems to put cameras in orbit in order to bring back photography from space-based satellites. This proved to be a lot more effective and safer than trying to send up an air crew for reconnaissance, although the U-2 continued to fly and does to this day. In early 2003, a U-2 bearing the insignia of the UN began inspection flights over Iraq to determine if Saddam Hussein was disarming. The United States also built an even faster and higher-flying aircraft, the SR-71, which was capable of reaching very high altitudes at Mach 3, three times the speed of sound, faster than the missiles that might be sent against it. The SR-71 proved to be too expensive to use on a regular basis and the fleet has been dispatched to air museums around the country. When one SR-71 was sent to Dulles airport to be part of a display, it reportedly flew from Los Angeles to Washington, DC, in little more than one hour.

SPACE RECONNAISSANCE

The cameras used in satellite systems produced very fine images but it sometimes took weeks before the film was sent back to Earth for processing and analysis.[11] In the 1970s, the United States began to develop a near real-time imaging capability using digital photo techniques, which could send highly detailed images back from space to receiver sites in the United States or abroad. While the actual resolution of the imagery remains highly classified, those shots that have been released by the government, from time to time, show that the digital systems are capable of producing imagery with great detail.

Interestingly, space reconnaissance intelligence, which was at one time as highly classified and sensitive as SIGINT, has become quite open and well known, as have details about the U.S. intelligence agencies that run the systems. In addition, commercial companies have launched digital photo satellites and sell the images for relatively little money. This means that any intelligence service or even a terrorist group can now have access to overhead photography that was once available only to a handful of countries. Even the U.S. government itself has become a customer for commercial imagery, but it has arranged to prevent U.S.-owned space imagery from being sold to others in time of crisis. The Russian and French companies that provide similar services, however, are not embargoed.

UNMANNED AERIAL VEHICLES

In recent years, a great deal of interest has been generated in using unmanned aerial vehicles (UAVs) for imagery reconnaissance. These drone aircraft, flown by remote control, can stay aloft for extended periods of time. They fly at relatively low altitudes compared to the U-2, are powered by piston or jet engines, and have become part of the inventory of many countries. The Israelis have been the pioneers in developing UAVs along with the United States. The great advantage of these aircraft is that they can fly over hostile territory without a threat to an air crew, although they are costly enough by themselves. The U.S. Predator UAV has been seen on TV and looks a bit like a regular propeller aircraft but with no cockpit. The U.S. Global Hawk is jet-powered and more expensive to build and fly, but has greater altitude and range.

Unmanned aerial vehicles can become both reconnaissance vehicles and weapons. The Predator was used to fire a missile at terrorists in Yemen, after the plane's camera picked up the image of the terrorists driving in the Yemeni desert. In the Iraq War, UAVs were used for spotting targets and damage assessment, as well as intelligence collection. It seems clear that other countries will soon have the same capabilities, although it might be a bit of a stretch for terrorists groups, unless they can get their hands on a flyable aircraft from the countries that already have UAVs.

Designers have been working on developing tactical UAVs, some as small as a credit card, that could be carried by fighting units to spy on an enemy just over the next hill and send back real-time images. The images sent back by these kinds of UAVs are not designed for lengthy imagery analysis, but rather for tactical views of the opposition. These tactical UAVs were used in the Iraq War; the most popular seemed to be one used by U.S. Marines, which resembled a large model airplane. Unlike flimsy balsa-wood models, however, the Marine UAVs were able to survive a pretty hard crash landing and their handlers could soon have them back in the air for another mission.

MANAGING SPACE RECONNAISSANCE

In the U.S. Intelligence Community, space reconnaissance is managed by two separate agencies: the National Reconnaissance Office (NRO) which operates the satellite systems, and the National Geospatial Intelligence Agency (NGA), the new name for the National Imagery and Mapping Agency (NIMA), for analyzing the images. The NRO used to be a secret agency, but media stories about it have forced the government to make its operations public. The NGA is a conglomerate of former units devoted to photo analysis and is now run by the Defense Department along with the NRO. The UAVs are flown by the military and, according to press reports, by the CIA as well.[12]

Whatever kind of "platform" or system carries the imagery equipment, the images themselves require interpretation, manipulation, and evaluation in order to provide useful intelligence. Just as intelligence collectors turn SIGINT into intelligence by deciphering and translating data, similar kinds of experts must turn the raw images received from sensors into usable reports. This is especially true of overhead images from space, where the camera is looking almost straight down at a target, but even images taken at an angle don't always conform to what the photo interpreter might expect. Thus, the images may be just as ambiguous as an intercepted communication. Photo interpreters are now aided by computer programs, which can turn the overhead images into visual displays that make it appear that the images were taken at ground level rather than from space.

When Secretary of State Colin Powell showed images taken over Iraq to the UN Security Council, the pictures had to be labeled and annotated so that the viewer could understand what was being shown. Even with sharp resolution, some images are degraded by atmospheric conditions, subjects partially hidden by vegetation or other structures, lighting, shadows, and movement. The imagery analyst is aided by the fact that there are certain identifiable characteristics or "signatures" to many targets, such as weapons or manufacturing plants, that can be seen, even if other parts of the images are not so clear, so that the image can be clarified. Imagery analysts may send along their own evaluation of what they see, or think they see, to help other analysts use the imagery to write intelligence for users.

GROUND TRUTH

Besides images taken from space or from UAVs and other aircraft, ground photography can be helpful in identifying or evaluating overhead imagery. This so-called ground truth is obtained openly from print sources, travelers, and other collectors, some of whom may be using "spy cameras" to gather information in places where the open use of a camera might cause trouble. Intelligence agencies have long used cameras hidden in match boxes, briefcases, watches, or other devices to give collectors the tools to capture images on the ground in areas where agents can go only if they know what they are doing. Thurman "Jack" Naylor, a member of the Photo Historical Society of New England, has put together one of the world's largest collections of spy cameras, and other examples are displayed at the National Spy Museum in Washington.

For many years, the CIA managed a huge database of ground images from various sources that could be used to verify or debunk interpretations of overhead imagery. For example, there was a great deal of controversy during the cold war about allegations that the USSR had built a large number of shelters for its senior officials and that these shelters would give the Soviets certain advantages during a nuclear exchange with the United States. While overhead imagery seemed to confirm the existence of these shelters, ground photographs showed that many of them were other structures and had nothing to do with civil defense.

IMAGERY IN HOMELAND SECURITY

The use of imagery in homeland security remains an open issue. During the sniper terrorist campaign in the Washington area in 2002, federal officials asked the U.S. Army, in conjunction with local law enforcement, to provide a low-flying reconnaissance plane to try to determine the location of the snipers. Even if it had been used, it seemed doubtful at the time that the plane's sensors could have picked up two men in a civilian vehicle, unless the plane just happened to be in their vicinity when they fired on a victim. Even then, the circumstances would have had to have been just right to detect the incident. The request raised the issue of whether or not the use of an army plane would violate the nineteenth-century Posse Comitatus statutes restricting the military from engaging in law enforcement.

More likely, imagery intelligence would be useful after a terrorist attack in order to assess the extent of the damage, such as was done after the 9/11 attack in New York. Imagery would also be useful in the event of natural disasters to evaluate problems and determine what, if anything needs to be done to ameliorate the situation. Since the Federal Emergency Management Agency has become a part of the Department of Homeland Security, a system will probably be established to request imagery assistance when it is needed.

While there are legal restrictions on the collection of SIGINT intelligence against U.S. persons, the restrictions on the domestic use of U.S. intelligence imagery resources are a matter of practice rather than law. Space imagery is not capable of conducting surveillance of individuals, but UAVs can and have done this abroad. In order to use national intelligence resources for domestic surveillance, a warrant would have to issued by the Foreign Intelligence Surveillance Court. Local law enforcement has long used helicopters to carry out surveillance in cases where a crime has been committed. Who can forget the images of O. J. Simpson, in his white SUV, fleeing police while the chase was captured on national television.

The use of local resources would seem to be the method of choice for surveillance of terrorists or other criminals. According to the Associated Press, the FBI is using a fleet of about eighty aircraft to stalk suspected terrorists, using infrared night vision equipment and electronic sensors, although the FBI would not reveal the exact capability of the equipment.[13] According to press reports, the Bureau of Customs and Border Protection in the DHS is using aircraft for patrols as well, and may be experimenting with UAVs. The DHS apparently plans to purchase additional patrol aircraft for border surveillance in 2004. This kind of activity is just a more sophisticated method of surveillance and is not really either signals intelligence or imagery intelligence in the traditional sense. There are concerns that such surveillance might stray into the area of unreasonable search and seizure, based on a Supreme Court ruling in 2001, but it seems unlikely that the use of this kind of surveillance in a terrorist case would be ruled out in the current environment.

ESPIONAGE

The third category of intelligence collection, after open source intelligence and technical sensors is what professionals call HUMINT, but others call espionage: the use of secret agents to steal information from enemies, adversaries, competitors, and even occasionally from friends and allies. Espionage has long been the most intriguing and exciting part of intelligence for those who have never done it. The reality is usually a lot less exciting than fiction would have it, but there are times when espionage can be just as dangerous and devious as the best in spy novels. This has been true ever since the Chinese writer Sun Tzu wrote about the use of spies 2,500 years ago.

Espionage figured into U.S. history from its earliest days, but it was not until the creation of the Office of Strategic Services (OSS) in World War II that the United States had an organization with the official mandate to run espionage operations. Before that, most espionage was handled right out of the White House or from the State Department. The military services had tried spying from time to time, but those operations were set up for a specific case, and there was no clandestine intelligence collection organization in the armed services until World War II either. When the cold war began in 1946, the United States took advantage of the war experiences to manage espionage in the military and after 1947, in the new CIA as well.

Today, U.S. espionage operations remain the responsibility of the CIA's Directorate of Operations, often called the Clandestine Service, and the Defense Department's Defense Humint Service, a part of the Defense Intelligence Agency (DIA). The Defense Humint Service was established because the military services wanted an increase in human source collection since the CIA did not collect intelligence against tactical military targets.

During the height of the cold war, there were military units specifically organized for human source collection, but apparently these were eliminated during various periods of downsizing in the Department of Defense (DoD). This left only military attaches to gather human source intelligence, usually involving liaison with the military services of host countries rather than more typical clandestine espionage operations. Now, the Department of Defense seems to want to enhance military HUMINT and rebuild its capability to gather tactical intelligence from human sources.

ESPIONAGE REALITIES

Although much has been written about spying, the truth seems to be overwhelmed by fiction, and therefore many people have the wrong ideas about how clandestine human source collection actually works. Relatively few experienced officers have written about their careers in espionage, perhaps because all of them, whether American or foreign, have a responsibility to protect the secrets of their work, even into retirement. Nonetheless, there is enough material in print to make it possible to describe the general principles of running clandestine HUMINT without compromising the secrets of sources and methods. Almost all intelligence services handle secret agent operations in much the same way, although they may differ in style. Thus, any description of the American system can be applied generally to foreign services as well.

Espionage means using human sources to steal—acquire is the polite term—information from targets who are trying to keep that information secret. The secrets may be about an adversary's defenses, technology, internal politics, or intelligence and security services. Espionage ought to be a weapon of last resort against an enemy and should be used only when other methods of intelligence collection have produced few results or cannot be used. The reason is a simple one: Espionage is illegal throughout the world and puts those engaged in it at risk. Despite its illegality, most nations have come to accept the fact that espionage might be used against them, so they tolerate the presence of foreign intelligence officers on their soil because they may be carrying on similar operations abroad themselves.

We in the United States refer to the intelligence officials who manage espionage operations abroad as case officers, a term apparently derived from British practice. The people the case officers recruit are the agents or spies. The CIA officers are not the agents, although the press often misuses this terminology. While case officers may be at risk overseas, the agents are often the ones who suffer the most danger. For example, the three Iraqis who allegedly fingered Saddam Hussein's hiding place at the beginning of the Iraq War were quickly identified and summarily executed, according to the Iraqi government at the time. When Aldrich Ames and Robert Hanssen identified Soviet officers who were agents for the CIA and FBI, the agents were recalled to Moscow and executed as well.

NOT FOR AMATEURS

Espionage operations are not for amateurs. This is well illustrated by the number of people who have been arrested in the United States for carrying out industrial espionage. Most of these erstwhile operatives had no training and violated the basic rules of running such operations, leading to their capture. True intelligence professionals rarely get caught, so when they do, it becomes a spy scandal of great interest. Most intelligence services subject their clandestine operatives to lengthy training before permitting them to go abroad and require them to prove themselves before taking on hard target operations in sensitive areas.

In recent years, the CIA has been harshly criticized for failing to attract first rate people who have the necessary foreign language skills and area knowledge for its clandestine service. Former operatives have criticized collection managers for bureaucratic stodginess, nit-picking, and failure to allow risky operations.[14] My experience is quite the opposite. During my service overseas, and on visits abroad to CIA stations, I was always impressed with the language skills and area knowledge of my colleagues. They knew a great deal about their targets and were mindful of the cultures, religions, and other characteristics of the people with whom they were working. Some writers have suggested that CIA officers are ignorant of such things, but I believe the ignorance lies with the writers who seem to think that CIA officers are nothing but dumb thugs, who stumble around foreign countries like typical ugly Americans. A more realistic description of CIA officers who serve abroad is contained in CIA Clandestine Service veteran Milton Bearden's book on his intelligence operations.[15]

It is true that the CIA went through a period after the cold war when political leaders in government and even the CIA director questioned the use of sources who had been guilty of human rights abuses or crimes and directed that such sources be terminated. When John Deutch was DCI, during the Clinton administration, he reportedly ordered that anyone serving as a CIA agent whose record was shady should be dropped from the rolls. This was another result of people in power failing to understand the real nature of clandestine human source collection. How could the CIA learn about terrorists, Iraqi dissidents, or North Korean technicians, for example, without recruiting sources who might be a lot like the targets. I suspect that intelligence professionals argued against these restrictions, but lost. After 9/11, the rules were quickly changed back to the way they had been during the cold war.

BEGINNING WITH REQUIREMENTS

Human source collection begins, as do most things in intelligence, with requirements. These are laid on by analysts, collection managers, and even by operatives in the field who can see from other reporting what gaps remain in the database. There has always been some sort of committee in Washington to sort out what should be collected using HUMINT, and to gather requirements for collection from the agencies who do not run their own HUMINT operations but who need the data. These requirements then go out to field stations around the world so that the stations can plan operations against the targets that might be in their areas. Thus, it is quite possible that a station in the Far East might seek to satisfy a requirement for intelligence on an Iraqi or Iranian target because there are appropriate source possibilities there.

Once the field station has received the requirements, case officers begin to seek out potential targets; that is, people who might have access to the necessary information and who might be persuaded to work as agents, gathering the information and giving it to the case officer. This is a time-consuming and labor-intensive process. Many people who have access to the information the case officer seeks are unlikely to cooperate with an agent recruitment, so the case officer has to be patient and perceptive. In reality, much of the clandestine recruiting that goes on overseas is not done directly by the case officer, but rather by a principal agent: a person from the local area who speaks the right languages, understands the customs and traditions, and can move about in the society because he or she looks, dresses, and appears similar to everyone else.

The notion that CIA officers can somehow blend into populations abroad and handle recruitments on their own is the stuff only of fiction. One of my classmates in training, the only African American in the group, said that when he was posted to Africa, he quickly learned that he was considered no different than any other American and could not really blend into the society any more than the rest of us could. Still, CIA officers abroad, as well as attaches and military HUMINT collectors, have to be able to handle local languages and customs to work with a principal agent even if they have no direct contact with the subagents the principal agent recruits and handles.[16] This means the CIA and DIA have to invest time and money in training officers in languages and customs as well as tradecraft: the term used to describe clandestine intelligence collection methods.

THE USE OF COVER

CIA has been severely criticized in recent years because it sends officers overseas under diplomatic cover. There are costs and benefits to such practices. Since espionage is illegal all over the world, having diplomatic status can help protect clandestine operations officers, civilian or military, from harsh treatment by local security services if they get caught. In order to protect the identity of officers engaged in clandestine intelligence collection, both at home and abroad, the CIA has had to develop an elaborate cover system for its operatives. Sometimes, CIA officers overseas are required to maintain a fictional identity, using an alias and back-up documentation, which further complicates intelligence management.

This is even further compounded when the officer is serving abroad under nonofficial cover as a business consultant or employee of a firm doing business overseas. Such officers—called NOCs in the CIA—have to maintain a certain distance from American officials and have to operate in much the same way as principal agents. Their meetings with CIA station officers have to be kept secret and their collection and reporting work has to go on around whatever cover job they do. They lack any kind of diplomatic protection, so running operations in this fashion—as many politicians and CIA critics have encouraged—has significant risks.

The other problem with NOCs is gaining access to sources. Principal agents can gain access because they usually live in the midst of potential sources and, because they are part of the society, they are more likely to be able to approach potential sources; CIA officers under diplomatic cover can gain access to some potentially interesting sources through the international community of which they are a part; NOCs, however, may have to be brought together with potential sources through an "access agent" who can make the proper introductions or arrange the contacts.

NATURAL CAPACITY

Thomas Patrick Carroll, writing in the *Middle East Intelligence Bulletin*, suggests that the CIA should break away from using official cover abroad to something more daring.[17] He proposes that the CIA establish functioning business firms abroad in target countries as a new way of running espionage operations. The companies, according to his scheme, would do actual business, most likely in service industries or light manufacturing, raising capital for the venture from legitimate venture funding sources. The business managers would be the case officers and carry out their operations when they were not engaged in the business of the firm.

This is not a new idea. The CIA has for many years used such companies, called "proprietaries," to support its operations abroad, although most of these companies have provided support services rather than cover for actual operations. The most famous of these was probably Air America during the Vietnam War, but there were many others. The companies could provide various services while protecting the identity of the case officers they supported.

The problem with such proprietaries is that their connection to CIA is hard to hide over time. Carroll's suggestion that the companies do real work is fine, but asking case officers to put in a full week at work and a full week at carrying out espionage operations all at the same time is sure to lead to burnout. It takes time and money to set up such companies and they are not likely to be operational in time to provide the kind of instant collection policy officials want. It is an idea worth exploring in certain limited circumstances, but as a general rule, it's just too hard to do.

WALK-INS

While CIA officers abroad are trained in agent recruitment techniques, in reality, many good agents are walk-ins, volunteers who seek out American intelligence. All through the cold war, potential agents sought to make contact with CIA. One of the most famous was Oleg Penkovsky, a colonel in the Soviet GRU, who provided good intelligence about Soviet missile capabilities before he was caught and executed. Walk-ins might be good agents, but they also might actually be working for the enemy, they may be deranged, or they may know a lot less than they claim. Then the problem for the case officer is to determine whether or not the walk-in is genuine, a provocation, or a fake. Checking out a potential agent thus requires a good deal of care to make sure that he or she is not a pipeline to the bad guys.

Once the agent is on board, the case officer or the principal agent is responsible for training the agent in good tradecraft and secure communications. The agent needs to receive carefully focused requirements so that he or she can produce good intelligence. The case officer has to turn the material provided by the agent into a useful intelligence report geared back to the requirements. Otherwise, officials who receive the agent reports will not understand why they are getting them or what they mean. The case officer has to be careful to report what the agent has said and not what the case officer wished the agent had said, although in the American system, the case officer can add comments, perhaps reflecting on how the agent's report compares to other data.

AGENT REPORTING

The CIA uses collection management officers to help the case officer make a solid intelligence report out of what might have been a long and rambling conversation between the case officer and the agent. These collection management officers are really analysts and they often know a great deal about how to compare agent reporting with other intelligence material. They can assist in evaluating agents to make sure they are productive and not just "paper factories," making up information to earn the money the case officer pays them. This is not usually a great deal of money because the case officer does not want the agent to appear suddenly wealthy in an impoverished society, but giving the agent a stipend does help the case officer to maintain control.

The final step in the clandestine collection process is to make sure that the reports reach the appropriate consumers at the right time and are set up in such a way that they do not compromise the identity of the agent. The CIA uses code names for its agents, as do most intelligence services, while the true name is supposed to be known only to a handful of officers. This is one of the reasons that CIA's Clandestine Service is reluctant to share agent reporting with other U.S. intelligence agencies and puts restrictions on how the agent report may be used. Case officers fear that somehow the true name of the agent will be revealed.

This is one of the problems yet to be solved in providing agent reporting for homeland security. If the Clandestine Service is reluctant to provide sensitive agent reporting to analyst colleagues in the CIA's Directorate of Intelligence, they will be even more restrictive in sending such reports to other members of the Intelligence Community, never mind state and local law enforcement officials.

INFORMANTS AND LIAISON

In addition to running controlled agents, CIA officers overseas pick up lots of information from informants, contacts in the target community, and from liaison with the host security services. The CIA has been slammed for spending too much time in liaison and not enough in running agents, but I can say from personal experience that working with the host intelligence and security services is extremely valuable. Local officials have contacts that the CIA can't always make on their own, and have perspectives on events that will inevitably be different from those in the U.S. Embassy. Information from these informal sources gets back to CIA headquarters through operations channels, but the information may not become intelligence unless headquarters' operations officers share the material with their analyst counterparts. This means that analysts have to be aggressive in establishing good working relationships with Clandestine Service officers, something they may be reluctant to do.

At one point some years ago, an effort was made to have analysts and operations officers co-located in one place to improve the sharing of informal intelligence and the creation of solid requirements. Apparently, that has not worked all that well and may have been abandoned. Security concerns, compartmentation, and need-to-know issues may have hurt the effort to have the analysts and collectors work more closely together. This may be an area where the 9/11 dots were not connected, although no data has yet surfaced to prove this. This was also supposed to be solved through the centers on terrorism, counterintelligence, crime and narcotics, but we have learned that the intelligence sharing at this level was faulty, according to congressional investigators.

HUMAN INTELLIGENCE AGAINST TERRORISM

While the various kinds of HUMINT can work well against traditional kinds of targets such as unfriendly governments, dissident groups, guerrillas, or revolutionaries, they rarely work against terrorists. As Daniel Benjamin and Steven Simon have pointed out, terrorists operate in small cells, use good compartmentation and security, are not usually tempted by money, and rarely defect.[18] Both Benjamin and Simon served as counterterrorism experts in the Clinton White House.

Terrorists are fanatics and very often come from the same tribe or clan, speak a common dialect, and would be quick to kill any of their members who tried to give away secrets to their enemies. Yet, the CIA and the FBI, working with foreign security services in the two years after 9/11, were able to dismantle much of the al Qaeda leadership circle, even though Osama bin Laden and some close associates remained at large. It appears that those who were wrapped up made mistakes in security and got careless in their movements. Essentially, they were tracked down by good police work as well as aggressive intelligence.

INTERROGATION IN HUMAN INTELLIGENCE

This brings up another kind of HUMINT, that which is derived from the interrogation of prisoners. Traditionally, that is more a counterintelligence or law enforcement function rather than HUMINT, but we have learned from press reporting that several key al Qaeda operatives have revealed a great deal of information after being captured in Afghanistan and Pakistan. Interrogation of prisoners can tell intelligence officers a great deal about the background and operational methods of the enemy, but their value drops after their capture, because the enemy will change any ongoing plans, assuming that the captured operatives will reveal what they know.

There is a great deal of misinformation floating around about interrogation and the methods used to extract information from prisoners. Soon after the press reported that key members of al Qaeda had been captured, I received several phone calls from the media wanting to know about the use of "truth serum" and torture in interrogations. They found it hard to believe that there was no such thing as truth serum and that the use of torture in interrogations, besides being illegal and distasteful, is often counterproductive. The proper use of interrogation is a useful tool in intelligence and will be discussed in more depth in a subsequent chapter.

ACCEPTING THE USE OF ESPIONAGE

Carrying out espionage and informal HUMINT abroad has long been accepted as the proper role of both CIA and military intelligence collectors, even though some of the activities are illegal. The rule has been that intelligence officers are only required to obey U.S. laws; breaking foreign statutes is OK. Robert Baer, the former CIA case officer, complained bitterly in his book that the FBI opened an investigation into allegations that he had violated U.S. prohibitions on assassination in trying to run operations to overthrow Saddam Hussein in Iraq.[19] This sends a chilling message to operations officers who are already taking risks abroad when the agency that sends them out to do the work then refuses to defend them. Baer was not convicted, but the same was not true for former CIA officials Clair George and Duane Clarridge, both of whom were indicted for their activities in the Iran-Contra scandal, but later pardoned.

CIA managers and military commanders are responsible for making sure that officers overseas know the rules and are following them. The leaders should make sure that the working troops are protected from the kind of harassment that Baer suffered. To do this, field officers should keep headquarters informed of their activities, which is normal practice, and headquarters officers should take responsibility for their officers abroad. George Tenet understood this quite well when he defended CIA officers in front of congressional probers, who were apparently trying to pin blame for 9/11 on a relatively low-level CIA employee.

COLLECTION AT HOME

The American people have come to accept the fact that CIA and military intelligence officers may break foreign laws in the interest of national security, but they have a much different attitude about the use of intelligence collection here at home. The CIA does indeed collect intelligence in the United States, but only from Americans who have traveled abroad, and who are willing to discuss what they might have learned with CIA officers. The arrangement is strictly voluntary and the identity of those who cooperate is kept confidential. By law, the CIA may not engage in domestic operations and is forbidden from engaging in internal security issues or having police power, except in guarding its facilities. When these proscriptions were violated during the Vietnam War—when CIA resources were used to track antiwar protesters—the outcry was so great that even now journalists continue to cite this experience as if the CIA was somehow still violating the rules.

The CIA is a foreign intelligence service. It has no mandate or resources for intelligence collection at home, nor should it. The same holds true for the other intelligence agencies in the Defense Department. They can, however, provide a great deal of information gathered abroad to assist other government agencies in fighting terrorism, organized crime, espionage, and narcotics flows. This leaves open the question of how the United States should gather intelligence domestically to fight threats to national security. In 2003, Robert Mueller, director of the FBI, argued repeatedly that the FBI ought to be the lead agency in collecting homeland intelligence, but many are not so sure. Tom Ridge, the secretary of Homeland Security, has already said that the DHS will not collect homeland intelligence itself, but will rely on other agencies to do this. It seems clear that these issues need to be resolved if intelligence is going to be effective in guarding the homeland.

Some lawmakers and intelligence pundits have pushed for the creation of a domestic intelligence service, but clearly the kinds of methods used abroad would not be acceptable at home. In many dictatorships, homeland security means having government informants in every apartment complex, in every large business, on sports teams, and in any sizable organization. As it is, people are beginning to complain about the U.S. government's efforts to gather intelligence on private citizens and the Congress quickly killed an initiative in the Pentagon to see how data might be collected on individuals. This is an area worth further investigation in a subsequent chapter.

Intelligence Analysis for Homeland Security

Gathering data is just the first part of the process of creating finished or evaluated intelligence. The second and equally important step is that of analysis, evaluating the data and piecing together an understanding of events. The need for good analysis and the handling of such information came under close scrutiny in 2003 as the George W. Bush administration claimed that intelligence analysis proved that Iraq had weapons of mass destruction, even though the weapons were never found. President Bush also said that intelligence analysis showed that the al Qaeda terrorists had ties to the Saddam Hussein regime in Iraq, even though several senior terrorist leaders denied the claim. Soon after the invasion of Iraq, some members of Congress, the press, and even retired and active intelligence officials accused the Bush administration of distorting and misusing intelligence to support the war.

Secretary of State Colin Powell—who had used the intelligence analysis at the UN to try to enlist the cooperation of members of the UN Security Council in the planned war against Iraq—and Secretary of Defense Donald Rumsfeld were both the targets of a wave of criticism for abusing intelligence. Secretary Powell defended himself by pointing out that he had spent four days at the CIA going over the material and had been selective in using only the intelligence that seemed authoritative. Mr. Rumsfeld was slammed for setting up an independent team of analysts to select out only the data that supported the war effort, although he denied that the team was given a mandate to reach a fixed conclusion. Director of Central Intelligence George Tenet defended the integrity of the analysis process in the case, but this was dismissed as bowing to White House pressure.

Interestingly, British Prime Minister Tony Blair came in for similar criticism that he had politicized intelligence analysis in seeking support in Parliament for joining with the United States in the attack on Saddam Hussein. Although the British have a somewhat more orderly process for intelligence analysis that must go through a joint committee before reaching the prime minister, the British intelligence system—especially MI-6, the foreign intelligence service—was attacked in Parliament and in the press as being no better than a handmaiden to the Blair government.

COMPETITIVE ANALYSIS

One aspect of this dispute that came in for particular attention was the allegation that Secretary of Defense Rumsfeld had assigned at least two of his policy officials to provide an independent review of the intelligence from the IC. This process is called competitive analysis and was performed at least once before in the 1970s when the George H. W. Bush administration sponsored an A-Team/B-Team intelligence review to look at the extent to which the Soviet strategic arsenal threatened the United States.

The A Team was made up of serving intelligence professionals while the B Team, headed by a Harvard professor, consisted of former intelligence professionals and academic hard-liners. While the two teams mostly agreed with each other, in looking at strategic missiles, the two disagreed, with the B Team not surprisingly seeing more of a threat than the A Team. After the cold war, we learned that the B Team had overstated Soviet strength, but it's easy to see errors in hindsight.

Secretary Rumsfeld's current "B Team" was made up of two political appointees with no prior intelligence experience. The unit, entitled the "Counter Terrorism Evaluation Group," reviewed what they claimed were "tons" of raw, unevaluated intelligence reports and concluded that the danger of Saddam Hussein having weapons of mass destruction and ties to al Qaeda were much greater than the rest of the Intelligence Community had stated.[1]

Stuart Cohen, who was the Acting Chairman of the National Intelligence Council (NIC), which supervised the writing and coordination of the National Intelligence Estimate (NIE) on Iraq, wrote a rather detailed defense of the product in the *Washington Post* in November 2003.[2] Although the text of the NIE has not been made public, Cohen's defense was rather unusual, in that intelligence officers rarely defend their analysis in such an open fashion. Cohen argued that the NIE was based on multiple sources, and that there was no pressure from the White House to change, distort, or delete any of its conclusions. Cohen also pointed out that the

Intelligence Community was forced to spend a great deal of time going back over the material, when it could have been focusing on more pressing current issues. Further, he noted, analysts may be intimidated by this process to avoid the kinds of judgments that go beyond "iron-clad evidence." If that were to happen, the nation would be ill-served by an intelligence system increasingly risk-averse.

While it is not likely that the total content of the intelligence analysis will ever be completely revealed, enough has leaked out already to make clear that much of the IC analysis was sufficiently ambiguous to support either side of the issue. President Bush remained adamant, as did members of the National Security Council, that Iraq posed a clear and present danger to the world, while opponents of the administration continued to cry "foul" in the weeks after the war. In order to quell the turmoil over the intelligence on Iraq, President Bush established another independent commission to investigate the issues. Its chairman, former Senator Charles Robb of Virginia, indicated that the commission would need until some time in 2005 to complete its work.

Because intelligence data is often fragmentary, distorted, ambiguous, or wrong, intelligence analysts understandably differ in their interpretation of the material. We may never know for certain whether the intelligence was politicized before the Iraq war, but it has brought attention to a part of intelligence that doesn't usually receive so much scrutiny, compared to espionage or secret operations. In fact, intelligence analysis, and the problems that go with it, have deep roots in American history.

DEEP ROOTS

In 1777, George Washington wrote to General Israel Putnam, one of the heroes of the Battle of Bunker (Breed's) Hill, noting that it might be possible to determine the strength of the British army by extrapolating from a head-count of a fraction of the forces. Later, he wrote to James Lovell "It is by comparing a variety of information, we are frequently enabled to investigate facts, which were so intricate or hidden, that no single clue could have led to the knowledge of them. . . ."[3]

In 1845, President James Knox Polk—knowing full well that Mexico would declare war on the United States if he sent forces south of the Nueces River into disputed territory in the new state of Texas—ordered General Zachary Taylor to move his forces to the Rio Grande, thus forcing Mexico to make good on its declaration.[4] Of course, Polk made it appear that the war was caused by Mexico, but in fact the United States was clearly the aggressor.

At the end of the nineteenth century, President William McKinley—eager for an excuse to drive Spain out of Cuba, its last bastion in the Western Hemisphere—latched on to the sinking of the U.S. Battleship Maine as an act of war, although it was most likely an accident. After McKinley was assassinated by an anarchist, successor Theodore Roosevelt manipulated information to gain support for assisting Panamanian revolutionaries in their break from Colombia to gain access to the isthmus in order to build a canal between the oceans. Even Woodrow Wilson manipulated intelligence to support entering the war against Germany in 1917, after trying for years to keep the United States out of the conflict.

During the cold war, President Lyndon Johnson clearly distorted intelligence, seizing on a supposed attack on a U.S. Navy ship in the Tonkin Gulf off Vietnam to obtain a resolution from Congress authorizing the use of U.S. troops in Southeast Asia. We know now that the attack was a phantom caused by faulty radar and a little panic on the part of the navy. Similarly, President Richard Nixon lied about Watergate including the role of former CIA agents in the scandal and it cost him his presidency.

RESEARCH AND ANALYSIS IN THE OFFICE
OF STRATEGIC SERVICES

America did not have an institutionalized system for intelligence analysis until World War II, when General Donovan created the Research and Analysis (R&A) section of the OSS, bringing together academics, business professionals, and scientists to evaluate incoming intelligence data. Richard Harris Smith, one of the few historians to chronicle the exploits of the OSS, described R&A as "a star-studded academic faculty."[5] Donovan realized quite correctly that intelligence analysis is just as important in understanding an adversary as collecting secrets. In those days, many intelligence services thought analysis meant providing comments on individual agent reports or incoming data, and it appears that some services still do no more than that.

Donovan not only created R&A as a separate division of the OSS, he established as well an elite board of senior advisors, dubbed the "College of Cardinals," which served as the model for CIA's Board of National Estimates in later years.[6] Research and Analysis produced regional studies, weekly intelligence analysis, and other studies, but it did not pull together the kind of tactical intelligence for the military services that would aid in war fighting. That was left to the intelligence units of the army and navy. When President Roosevelt asked Donovan in 1944 for recommendations about how to set up an intelligence service after World War II, Donovan outlined a centralized, civilian-run organization that would include more or less the same capabilities as the OSS, including a research and analysis organization for strategic intelligence. The early history of what became the CIA's Directorate of Intelligence (DI), its research and analysis wing, has been nicely outlined in a CIA publication celebrating the fiftieth anniversary of the DI's creation in 1952.[7]

FOUR BASIC CATEGORIES

Intelligence analysis falls into four basic categories: warning intelligence to alert policy officials that a crisis is coming or has begun; current intelligence to keep consumers up-to-speed on daily developments; basic intelligence to create in-depth studies or create databases for future needs; and estimates of future developments, which are supposed to be forecasts of the future. Intelligence analysis is a critical part of "getting it right," and many intelligence failures can be attributed to errors or poor judgments in analysis, rather than failure to gather sufficient data. Once again, however, it should be noted that intelligence analysis failure often becomes known, while success is usually not newsworthy.

This is well illustrated by an article in the *Atlantic Monthly* written in 2003 by conservative columnist David Brooks, in which he slams CIA intelligence analysis as being neither creative nor well informed.[8] Brooks's criticisms were derived largely from an innovative long-range study produced by the National Intelligence Council—the modern version of Donovan's College of Cardinals—to investigate what the world might look like in 2015.[9] It was a collaborative effort to bring together intelligence professionals from around the Intelligence Community, not just from CIA, as well as outside academics and scholars to think about what a future world might look like. Brooks condemned it as a lengthy bureaucratic exercise, whose scenarios could have been drawn by "any halfway intelligent person . . . after five minutes of thought."

The point of the estimate was to bring intelligence and academe together to develop a dialogue, but Brooks said the study failed to understand passion or emotion. In that sense, he may be correct, in that intelligence analysis is supposed to be reasoned, nonpartisan, nonemotional, and without bias. It is the endgame of the intelligence process since it presents judgments, ideas, and truth to power. Often, it is not what policy officials want to hear, but it is what they ought to know. As we know from the Iraq war experience, however, it can be manipulated when power decides what is truth.

PRODUCER–CONSUMER RELATIONS

For many years, the CIA has studied the various aspects of intelligence analysis, looking for new methodologies, examining producer–consumer relations, studying analytic techniques, and presentational methods. Unfortunately, much of this work, which stretches back over at least twenty-five years, has not been made public, or has appeared in ways that have not triggered the attention of the media. I became enmeshed in it in 1979 when I was asked by then-DCI Stansfield Turner, to spend a year investigating the impact of intelligence on policy. Others have done similar work, some of which has appeared in the unclassified issues of the CIA's *Studies in Intelligence,* or in the outside journals devoted to intelligence issues. In recent years, with the establishment of the Sherman Kent Center for analysis training, more of the dialogue about intelligence analysis has become public.

Although the Department of Homeland Security had not yet established an intelligence analytic unit of its own after it became operational in 2003, it will inevitably have to do so. When it does, it will undoubtedly have to operate in the same fashion as any other intelligence analysis organization, similar to those run for years by the CIA, the DIA, and the State Department. Its focus will be different, because most governmental intelligence analysis has been directed toward foreign issues rather than domestic ones. Nonetheless, it will have to follow the same general pattern as any of the other agencies, or even of those of business intelligence units in the private sector. Unlike the existing intelligence agencies, whose customers are usually senior officials in the executive branch of government, the DHS will have to satisfy the needs of its own disparate units as well as those at the state and local levels.

WARNING AND ALERTING

The DHS has already established a system for warning and alerting key officials about "breaking news." The warning function is supposed to avert surprise by detecting an event even before it happens, based on changes in various indicators. For example, American intelligence during the cold war assumed that any surprise attack on the United States would have to be preceded by buildups in supplies, movements of military units, increases in communications, and signs that our adversaries were holding high-level meetings. These indicators were detected before the Soviet invasion of Prague in 1968 and the invasion of Afghanistan in 1979. Of course, when such indications are not detected, or detected too late, there is great potential for intelligence failure. One of the reasons U.S. intelligence did not detect the 9/11 attack is that there were few indicators to watch.

The United States has a highly developed warning and indications network that has been established over many years. The DHS has become part of this network which includes 24/7 watch centers at all the intelligence agencies, at the White House, the Pentagon, and in the military service headquarters, as well as at all the major military commands worldwide. All have secure communications and computer links and can easily talk with each other at any time. They practice alerting and using the communications systems to make sure that they will function in a crisis. The centers can also serve as a venue for crisis management when policy officials have to come together on an emergency basis.

MANAGING THE CENTER

In order to manage such a center, the various agencies must assemble five dedicated teams of analysts to rotate through the shifts and create a secure facility similar to those at the White House Situation Room, or the Pentagon's Joint Military Intelligence Center. Each team is usually headed by an experienced senior officer who can make decisions about alerting managers to a crisis or how to handle some lower-level situation. I have worked in several different operations centers during my Air Force and CIA assignments and have learned that managers tend to want to run the centers with fewer than five teams; however, studies on the subject, as well as experience, shows that five teams are necessary to account for illness, vacations, and the stress of having to work rotating shifts. This means that such centers are inevitably highly labor-intensive and require a rather large pool of human resources to operate properly.

The methods for running indications and warning centers are widely known, so the DHS has probably received lots of advice about what to do. Since the DHS center will have access to the secure system set up for the intelligence agencies, their operations center personnel will have to be cleared for access to special intelligence, including NSA material, imagery, and CIA reporting. It's possible that the various agencies have been tapped to send people to the DHS center on a temporary basis pending the assignment of permanent employees with clearances.

THREAT LEVELS

Secretary Tom Ridge noted in 2003 that the DHS has to develop a better system for threat warnings to the American public. After 9/11, the Bush administration created a colored five-stage security system in which Red, the highest level, meant a terrorist threat was imminent or underway; while Green, the lowest level meant no danger. The United States has hovered between Yellow, elevated threat level, and Orange, the high level, since 9/11. Each time the level was raised from Yellow to Orange, the DHS had to admit that it had no specific intelligence to justify the increase outside of "increased chatter" from terrorist communications. Many people became skeptical about these warnings and there was an increasing tendency to ignore the changes. Secretary Ridge admitted that the DHS would have to do better and it seems likely that the DHS warning center will be heavily involved in decisions to raise the threat level in the future.

The analysts in warning and alerting centers have quite a task. They must scan media and open sources as they come in, as well as raw intelligence data, to determine what material should be passed forward to policy officials, what should be kept in case something related breaks, and what ought to be ignored. The volume of this material is so great that trying to store anything in electronic databases is best left to others. In his book on fixing the American intelligence system, retired Lieutenant General William Odom, the former director of the NSA and Army Chief of Staff for Intelligence, criticizes CIA analysts for trying to keep raw intelligence from policy officials so the analysts could see everything first.[10] General Odom is quite wrong about this.

It has long been the practice, as General Odom ought to know, that CIA raw reports, as well as those from the other intelligence collection agencies, are distributed to policy agencies at about the same time as they are sent to the intelligence units. If all of this material was sent directly to senior policy officials, they would be inundated with material and would have to have their own staffs sort through it to pick out the key data. Instead, the watch centers perform this function. Although some intelligence managers might have preferred that analysts see the stuff first, in fact, once the spigot is turned on—as Bob Gates, former DCI used to say—it's hard to turn off. Policy offices would be outraged if the intelligence agencies were to cut off the flow of raw intelligence, even though senior officials hardly have time to sort through the mountains of material themselves. Thus, the watch centers can usually determine which office ought to get what material. If senior officials take the time to tell their watch center the nature of their interests and concerns, so much the better.

The DHS can learn from the other policy agencies about how to circulate material down as well as up. The CIA uses its watch center to alert its own officials, but relies on the watch centers at the White House or the State Department to carry the ball, once those centers have been warned or alerted to a breaking situation. The watch centers at the policy agencies then determine who to contact. The DHS watch center carries out the same function, alerting those officials who need to be told, based on a predetermined list. This is particularly important at the DHS because it has so many functions and offices that really have little relationship to the rest of the agency.

DAILY BRIEFS

Warning and alerting intelligence is a critical function, but it is often overshadowed by the daily reporting function common to many organizations both within and outside government. The need to have "all the news" first thing on any business day is so ingrained that it has become a routine function of any intelligence organization. Every military command and every policy office expects to have some sort of intelligence briefing to start the day, along with the coffee and donuts. This is so at the CIA, where members of a special staff put together the President's Daily Brief (PDB) each day. When the President is in the White House, it is common to have the DCI and the FBI director turn up for the morning briefing.

When the President is out of town, the PDB staff arranges for delivery of this very sensitive publication through some secure electronic or courier arrangement.

The PDB is special because it contains material for "The President's Eyes Only," to use the title of Christopher Andrew's book on intelligence, and is only seen by a handful of other senior officials.[11] Not to be outdone, the Bureau of Intelligence and Research (INR) in the Department of State produces the State Morning Summary, also for a select audience, including the White House, and the DIA writes a similar summary for the Secretary of Defense and top Pentagon officials. For years, these publications were actually printed up much like a daily newspaper and delivered using secure delivery systems. With the advent of electronic delivery, it is now possible to deliver daily briefs through the secure Web-like system called Intelink, although it is likely that some senior officials still prefer paper copies, just as many still favor printed newspapers rather than the online versions.

The CIA, DIA, and INR have established offices dedicated to intelligence analysis, where such daily products are put together. Surveys of policy officials have revealed over the years that current intelligence is really the most popular and widely read of all intelligence products. It's not hard to see why. The daily briefs are usually short, easy to read, and take up perhaps only a few minutes of a busy policy official's time. The briefs have short focus, and in today's world, where policy officials rarely have the luxury of long-range planning, current intelligence is the most useful product for them.

NO INTELLIGENCE OFFICE?

At first, the DHS did not plan to establish an intelligence office to produce a homeland security intelligence brief; it planned to rely instead on products from the intelligence agencies, but this is not good enough. The CIA's products, like those from the State Department, have a foreign focus, which is necessary for the DHS but is hardly sufficient. The DIA's products relate to military issues, again with a foreign focus. It seems likely that the Terrorist Threat Integration Center (TTIC)—the multiagency fusion center that will either replace or duplicate the work of the Counterterrorist Center (CTC) run out of CIA—will end up producing a daily brief on terrorism, but the DHS has a broader mandate, so this will again be necessary but not sufficient to satisfy all of its needs. Dealing with this is not complicated nor will it have to be expensive.

The DHS could easily build on its existing 24/7 watch center, creating a small core group of analysts who could produce the kind of daily brief that would be useful for senior DHS policy officials. The core group could be co-located with the operations center in their secure facility and seek to develop the kind of daily brief that would incorporate the foreign and military intelligence coming from the CIA, DIA, and State Department with information about domestic activities that would be drawn from DHS units such as the Directorate of Border and Transportation Security, the Coast Guard, and the Secret Service. The missing element, a domestic intelligence service, does not yet exist. Either this will emerge from a revamped FBI, or from some new organization yet to be established, and will cover threats, trends, and developments relating to internal security issues such as terrorism, crime, narcotics, and espionage. The DHS core analysis group could pull together the daily report from these inputs.

The daily intelligence report has one major drawback. We used to hear complaints at the CIA from consumers who were experts in various fields that the daily intelligence brief did not tell them anything more than they already knew. We had to explain to them that the report was really designed for senior policy officials who tended to be generalists and who needed a quick update on events. Specialists don't need the kind of information in the daily report because they will have already seen the same material as the analysts. Typically, a single item in the daily report might be no more than a paragraph, with perhaps one full-page piece on an item of particular interest. Still, this is usually enough to keep busy decision makers informed. They know that they or their staffs could obtain more detailed intelligence if it were needed.

SEEKING MORE DEPTH

In the 1960s, CIA analyst managers decided that they needed to provide policy consumers with more in-depth analysis. At that time, in addition to the daily report, a weekly publication permitted analysts to draw long-term judgments about events. The new publication was to contain even more detailed analysis, perhaps 10 to 20 pages worth, to delve deeply into an issue. This became increasingly the desired "art-form" for the CIA's Directorate of Intelligence (DI) to the point that in the Reagan administration, when Robert M. Gates became the CIA's deputy director for intelligence (DDI), analysts were expected to write at least two in-depth pieces per year. Soon, policy officials were buried in thousands of these studies, and many of them went unread, except by working-level policy officials and officers at the CIA itself. When I was involved in the production of these memoranda, I canvassed our readers periodically to find out what they did with the studies. Most respondents said that the papers were safely stored in a secure location and would be read if they were needed. I also learned that some of the people on our distribution list were either dead or had long ago moved to some other assignment.

As time went on, the DI learned that it could better serve its customers by producing a few such memos, tailored to the particular needs of a handful of policy consumers, instead of printing up 400 copies that no one read. If the DHS creates an intelligence analysis unit, its analysts may from time to time find that there is a need for longer pieces than can appear in the daily report. There are some good rules about how to frame such a paper. Intelligence managers need to find out from policy officials what kinds of studies would be useful, as well as the scope and timing of the work. This will give managers a handle on who should do the analysis. Usually, this means an individual analyst ends up drafting a study and analysts from other components are asked to review the drafts to make comments, or offer additions or corrections. This is known in the intelligence business as "coordination."

PACKAGING INTELLIGENCE

Once the intelligence system is satisfied with the study, it can then be packaged in a form to suit the consumers. Packaging intelligence is an important step. There have been many cases where an intelligence product has turned out to be less than useful because it was too long, too complicated, or classified at a level that prevented it from being used by the very consumers who needed it. In one particular case, my office produced a secret study that contained a fold-out chart in a pocket at the back of the publication, that was designed to allow readers to read a lot of the study's data, much like the maps that one would find in issues of the *National Geographic* magazine. When I canvassed our readers to find out what they did with the study, I asked as well about how useful the chart was. Most respondents said that they were reluctant to unfold the chart for fear that they might not get it back in its holder and thus be penalized for a security violation. In that case, poor packaging had rendered one part of the study quite useless.

Many intelligence consumers, because they are policy officials appointed by the party in power to make the administration's policies, have little patience with intelligence that tells them what they don't want to hear. They do not want education, they want support. They want intelligence to help them with their agenda and they want the material to be actionable. They do not want to be told that the world is different than they think, or that the policies they have chosen may not work. This was part of the problem in the buildup to the Iraq war. In that sense, DHS leaders will be no different than policy officials in the more traditional national security-oriented agencies.

Another way for the DHS to produce in-depth studies is to contract them out to consulting firms, a practice common throughout government. Many firms have cleared analysts who may have the kind of expertise in some obscure specialty that is not available on an agency's staff. These consulting firms tend to attract former intelligence officers who understand the system, so producing useful intelligence is an art they have already mastered. Even the CIA does this from time to time, when they need a specialist.

MILITARY ANALYSIS

Things are a bit different in military intelligence, where the intelligence function is traditionally part of any military staff. Military intelligence is designed for a variety of demands, including support for war fighting, for planning, and for weapons procurement. While some military intelligence functions are integrated into the U.S. Intelligence Community and supported by the National Foreign Intelligence Program (NFIP), a great deal of them are not. They are part of the Pentagon's tactical intelligence system specifically designed to support military operations, are generally run by the intelligence components of the armed services, and do not fall under the aegis of the DCI or the IC.

Nonetheless, at the national level, defense intelligence analysis is produced and delivered in much the same way as the intelligence analysis produced by the CIA or the State Department. The Defense Intelligence Agency (DIA), founded in 1961, was created to bring intelligence analysis previously grounded in the services to national military decision makers. Neither the CIA nor the State Department could fulfill that function and neither was intended to do so. In 2002, the DIA issued a history of its first years, which explains in great detail the thinking behind its creation.[12] The DIA also uses consultants for intelligence production, turning to firms whose staffs are heavily populated with former military personnel.

While the future of the DIA began to be questioned in 2003, the need for military intelligence was not. Clearly, military intelligence has to be woven into contingency plans, weapons procurement policies, strategy, as well as war fighting, so it can't disappear. The unit that does the military intelligence production, however, could be changed. In fact, the entire issue of structural reform in intelligence is once again being raised and will be explored later.

General Odom has suggested that since the CIA does not make major contributions to any of the military intelligence tasks, it ought to be disbanded. He is again quite wrong. The CIA's intelligence analysis is widely read within the DIA and finds its way into the DIA's products, even if no formal coordination takes place. The experience of the Iraq war in 2003 shows that the CIA can make a significant contribution to war fighting intelligence as well. There might have been a time when this was not the case, but recent developments in intelligence sharing between military intelligence and the CIA clearly have overcome many of the obstacles to cooperation. This includes special operations, a subject that will be examined later.

THE ESTIMATE

The final significant category of product in intelligence has been known for many years as "the Estimate." It is the most controversial and difficult of all the products that an intelligence agency produces. It is seen by intelligence managers as one of the most important inputs to the policy process, although policy makers rarely give the Estimate high marks. In theory, intelligence estimates are supposed to forecast the future, but this is really impossible. Mankind has long sought ways to predict the future with little success, trying everything from examining the entrails of chickens or goats to seeking to find truth in tea leaves or tarot cards; none have proven to be accurate. The CIA has, of course, tried such things as well, but in the end has been forced to rely on human judgment, if not to predict the future, at least to try to forecast the most likely course of events in a world filled with uncertainty and surprise.

The construction of the Intelligence Estimate as a formal IC product dates back to DCI Walter Bedell Smith who took over the CIA in the aftermath of the failure of U.S. intelligence to forecast the North Korean attack on South Korea in 1950. Smith created the Office of National Estimates and Board of senior "Wise Men" to oversee the creation of the estimates. Some of the early estimates have become public and they form an interesting window into the art of intelligence forecasting. Many of the early estimates focused on whether or not the Soviets were going to attack the United States or its NATO allies. Over time, these publications became far more wide-ranging and eventually began to cover forecasts of developments in most parts of the Third World as well as in the USSR and China, our traditional adversaries. It was just such an estimate that fostered the controversy over Iraq's weapons program before the 2003 war.

DRAFTING THE ESTIMATE

Usually an individual analyst at the CIA (but sometimes in other agencies) was selected to write the initial draft of an estimate with inputs from around the rest of the IC; then, comments, suggestions, or criticism would come in from around the IC as the draft was coordinated; finally, representatives from the IC agencies would meet to finalize the estimate, demanding changes in accordance with instructions from their senior managers. Sometimes protracted negotiating sessions lasted well into the night as the representatives argued over words and phrases. If agreement could not be reached, the dissenting agency was asked to write a footnote explaining the dissent and who had made it.

Once the agreed text was finalized, the estimate would be sent to the Board of National Estimates and the lead analysts would be summoned to defend the Estimate in front of the board. It felt to many much like defending a thesis in front of a doctoral committee at a university. The

Wise Old Men would question and probe, more changes would be negotiated, and finally the Estimate would be sent off to key policy consumers. We believed, however naively, that each consumer was waiting eagerly for the estimate to arrive so that sensible policy could be made from it. In reality, many of these ponderously prepared publications would be opened by subordinates, and many went unread except at relatively low levels.

THE NATIONAL INTELLIGENCE COUNCIL

When Bill Colby became DCI in 1975, he revamped the estimates process and created a National Intelligence Council to replace the Board of Estimates. Under the new system, which still exists, the National Intelligence Officers (NIOs) who made up the council would select the analysts to prepare the estimates and oversee the finished products. Then they would go to the National Foreign Intelligence Board (NFIB), made up of the directors of the IC agencies, for a final review before being sent to the White House.

Senior managers at the CIA always thought that the estimates were the premier products of the IC. Policy officials, however, admitted in surveys and feedback loops that the estimates were usually too long and complicated to read in their entirety, but that they might skim the executive summaries in the front. At working levels, however, the estimates received greater scrutiny, although it seemed clear from the surveys and other studies that the estimates were not driving policy. The best one could say was that the estimates were educating policy officials. Clearly, established policy agendas, lobbying, and other factors went into the decision process. Nonetheless, those of us at the CIA who wrote such estimates always operated on the theory that policy makers were eagerly awaiting our judgments so that they could decide what to do.

It's hard to judge the validity of the estimates process. Many estimates were close to predicting the outcome of future events, but often failed to anticipate all the variables, so it would be difficult to say that an estimate was completely correct in its forecast. One study done years ago suggested that estimates were right about as often as they were wrong, but getting it right was not always the desired outcome. Instead, a discussion of the most likely scenarios that might develop and ideas about how to tell which scenario was unfolding was as valuable as trying to predict the future. Again, because failed estimates were more likely to become public than successful ones, it would be difficult to create a scorecard.

DIALOGUE WITH USERS

Sometimes, a dialogue with policy users about the direction estimates were taking could have been useful, but there was reluctance among intelligence managers to permit or encourage such a dialogue, since the IC representatives had not yet reached an accepted conclusion. Managers feared, perhaps quite rightly, that providing an informal draft of the estimates to users might confuse and distract them, if the final version differed considerably from the draft. Still, some kind of interactive method might have been valuable compared to the rather bureaucratic system that prevailed throughout the cold war.

If nothing else, the estimates process did force analysts to come to grips with their beliefs and their evidence in regard to the future and made them articulate and defend their ideas among their intelligence colleagues. While there are still world situations that require the kind of thoughtful look ahead the estimates are supposed to provide, estimates as an intelligence art form seem to be less and less useful as time goes on.

One of the main drawbacks of the estimates is that it is hard to produce in fast moving situations. During the cold war, analysts found themselves producing Special National Intelligence Estimates (SNIE—pronounced *snee*) with a shorter focus than the six months to a year scope of the more formal NIE. These could be done in a matter of days from draft to NFIB approval, but these required a certain level of surge capacity in the system, which did not always exist. Even if an analyst could be broken out to write a SNIE, there was still the coordination and approval process to bless the SNIE before delivery.

What harried policy officials really wanted, they sometimes said, was to have an expert come to their offices and provide answers to questions, or have a dialogue on a hot issue. Intelligence managers were not always comfortable with this because they preferred to give policy officials an agreed agency position on an issue, rather than the views of one particular analyst. Most analysts would probably admit that they were already cognizant of the varying positions of colleagues in other agencies and would have no trouble explaining to policy officials the range of views held within the IC. Having done this sort of thing from time to time, I would have to say that a dialogue with a policy official can sometimes be much more useful than a printed or electronically delivered paper. Policy makers who won't spend more than a few minutes reading an NIE might well spend an hour discussing the issue, so the analyst can provide a great deal of intelligence in such a dialogue.

MILITARY ESTIMATES

The NIEs produced by the National Intelligence Council (NIC) traditionally look at political and economic developments abroad. General Odom complained in his book on fixing intelligence that this was not helpful to military planners, so there was no utility in CIA analysis. In fact, the NIC—which most people believe is mostly a CIA entity even though it is supposed to represent the entire IC—was not set up to support the Pentagon directly but rather to provide their judgments to the White House and National Security Council. The NIC did produce estimates on strategic military issues, but not for the purposes of war planning or weapons procurement. That job was properly left to the DIA and its Defense Intelligence Officers (DIOs).

The DIA's inputs to war and contingency planning, as well as weapons procurement, are more threat analyses than traditional estimates. They have to be longer range because the weapons design and development process can stretch out over as long as ten years; thus, military intelligence has to anticipate what the world will look like so military hardware and strategy can be prepared accordingly. This kind of intelligence analysis is not usually coordinated outside the DIA, although analysts from all the agencies discuss these kinds of topics from time to time.

ESTIMATES FOR HOMELAND SECURITY

It's hard to see how the traditional style of intelligence estimates would be useful for homeland security. The kinds of threat analysis the DHS will have to do will likely fit a shorter time frame, so DHS analysts may never be called on to write the kinds of formal, coordinated estimates that were a hallmark of the cold war. In fact, they may have to produce analysis that looks more like what is written in the private sector than the typical intelligence products in government. The private sector is working on developing methodologies for threat assessments that could become the kind of product the DHS would find most useful.

In government, especially in the CIA, it has long been a rule that analysts do not give policy advice to decision makers. The idea is to maintain a neutral stance untainted by political pressure or ideological bias and there are good reasons for this. Intelligence officers do not want to become part of any debate about policy. If they were seen as biased toward a particular policy position, their analysis might be dismissed as favoring one side against another. While they do want their analysis to be actionable—usable by policy officials—they do not want to be part of the action.

In the private sector, however, an entirely different approach is common, encouraged, and usually expected. Whether the intelligence in the private sector is written by intelligence specialists inside the company or by consultant firms to whom an intelligence task is outsourced, the product should contain not only an explanation and exploration of a problem, but also some idea about what to do about it. For example, in risk analysis, a study might be done to determine if a particular country is a good place to make an investment. The resulting product will contain not only information about such things as the country's infrastructure, its governmental stability, and its economic conditions, but also the security situation and dangers a company might face. The study will give company decision makers a recommendation about the feasibility of an investment, and whether the time is right to do business. Sometimes such studies conclude that the country is too dangerous or unstable to support a sensible investment.

Similarly, in competitive or marketplace intelligence, analysts not only seek to answer questions for a firm about its competitors, but also make recommendations for action. Leonard Fuld, a competitive intelligence expert, relates a number of "war stories" in his books on the subject that illustrate this point nicely.[13] In one case, Fuld not only found out why a firm was losing market share to its competition, but also how the firm might solve the problem. He recommended that the firm defeat its competition by buying the opponent and adopting its manufacturing techniques. This style of analysis, which requires that the analyst not only understand an adversary but learn what to do about a problem might have real application in homeland security.

In many respects, DHS intelligence will operate much like private sector intelligence in collecting, analyzing, and distributing information both within the organization and to users at the federal, state, and local levels, as well as in the private sector. Private firms usually build intelligence units into the company when they have continuing need for intelligence for strategic planning, for investment decisions—especially overseas—and for threat analysis. Sometimes, firms choose to rely on outside consultant firms for specialized intelligence collection and analysis, either to avoid the cost of a built-in unit, or because the consultant firm might provide more useful analysis, untainted by inside politics or bureaucracy. The DHS could have an intelligence unit internally and outsource some of its intelligence needs, just like its corporate counterparts.

GIVING USEFUL ADVICE

Intelligence analysis from the DHS will be most useful if, like its counterparts in the private sector, it provides not only an evaluation of intelligence inputs, but also some suggestions about what to do, especially in the area of threat analysis. When DHS Secretary Tom Ridge raised the national threat level from Yellow to Orange early in 2003 and then again at the start of the war against Iraq, he was only able to say that intelligence had suggested an increased threat of terrorism, but he was unable to say that any specific targets or plots had been uncovered. Because of fears that terrorists might use biological or chemical weapons, the first alert caused a run on duct tape and plastic sheeting, although Ridge then went on national TV to suggest that what he really wanted was for Americans to prepare an emergency supply kit for future use. Many state and local governments said that they were already at about as high a state of alert as they could manage, so the lack of specificity in the warning was of no help to them.

The DHS needs to develop an intelligence "art form" that not only provides more specifics about threats, but includes some advice about what to do. This is especially important in the intelligence the DHS will provide to state and local governments. All states and most major cities have already established some kind of homeland security system and have facilities to match in some way the 24/7 watch center at the DHS. They will not have, however, the kinds of high-level clearances that are common among the watch centers at the federal level. Thus, the DHS has to make sure that the intelligence it produces is not so highly classified that it cannot be distributed to state and local officials, or to the private sector. This is not as hard as it sounds.

All during the cold war, the CIA provided intelligence to its partner intelligence services in foreign countries at the secret level. Having prepared some of these myself, I can attest that they can carry a great deal of useful intelligence, without getting into sensitive areas that might require more restricted distribution. The DHS can prepare the same kind of product, but just as in private sector intelligence, they can add in, where appropriate, the kinds of advice that state and local governments might find helpful. The DHS intelligence officials can draw on the resources of its many agencies to obtain the operational information, just in the same way that many private firms draw upon internal company resources for intelligence information.

Intelligence analysis is a critical component of any intelligence system. The DHS will not lack for advice as it moves to establish the analytic intelligence component it needs to support its internal needs as well as those of federal, state, and local governments who are all trying to keep us safe. In examining the DHS budget for FY2004, which began in October 2003, the DHS planned for rather modest and very specific intelligence activity, mostly focused on threats to America's infrastructure.[14] The department planned to upgrade its command center, improve its ability to produce threat assessments, a critical element in planning, and develop a system for guiding intelligence collection. Over time, however, homeland security intelligence has to have a broader mandate if it is going to be useful to its broad range of intelligence consumers.

Cops and Spies

One of the issues that created headlines in the aftermath of 9/11 was the clear disconnect between the FBI and the CIA. One reporter described it as one of the longest running feuds in government, and while it may have been surprising to the public, to law enforcement and intelligence veterans it was nothing new. This conflict involves a lot more than just the typical Washington battle over turf. Whether or not it contributed to the alleged intelligence failure on 9/11, it raises some serious issues for homeland security.

Except for a brief period during the U.S. Civil War, the nation has never had an internal security service like the British MI-5. In fact, we are the only major industrialized nation in the world that does not have such a service. There are a great many reasons for this. Lafayette Baker's draconian Secret Service, set up during the early days of the Civil War, arrested people without warrant and jailed them without trial.[1] This led to the notion that any such service had to be open, subject to strict legal constraints, and well controlled.[2]

J. Edgar Hoover, the founder and leader of the FBI, understood very well that his agency, as a kind of federal police and investigative service, had to be above reproach. FBI Special Agents had the power of arrest and were armed. The Bureau, as many call it, was far more open than the internal security services of most nations, which was clearly what the public wanted. It was certainly not a secret police. In fact, Hoover understood the value of giving the FBI a squeaky clean image. To that end, he supported radio shows and movies that made the FBI look good and when TV came along, Hoover backed a fictional series on the FBI.

Hoover trained his senior agents in public relations and did everything he could to make the public see his special agents as "the good guys." While most Western internal security services hid behind secrecy and anonymity, Hoover opened the FBI to the public, hosting tourists in the downtown FBI headquarters and having his agents give weapons demonstrations, while passing out bullet-marked paper targets to fascinated visitors. Tourists could peer through windows into the forensic labs and see artifacts from famous criminal cases the FBI had solved.

Meanwhile, the FBI was using undercover operations, including wiretaps and "sting" operations along with other surreptitious methods, to snare the bad guys. During Hoover's reign, the FBI appeared to do no wrong and the public seemed to trust the agency to obey the law while doing everything it could to defend it. There were problems, but mistakes were hidden, agents who got in trouble were either forced out or exiled to remote locations, and the FBI's image remained untarnished.[3]

THE FBI AND INTELLIGENCE

In the days before World War II, Hoover tasked his agents with stopping possible Axis espionage or sabotage operations, even though the political mood in the United States at that time was one favoring isolation from the growing threat of war in Europe. In fact, Hoover wanted the FBI to become the lead intelligence agency for the U.S. government, but President Franklin Roosevelt had other ideas. When FDR created the Office of Strategic Services (OSS), the best Hoover could do was to obtain an agreement that the OSS would stay out of any operations in Latin America, where pro-Nazi sentiment was growing in Argentina and Chile.

When FDR asked General Donovan in 1944 to make recommendations for a postwar intelligence service, Hoover had no trouble finding out what the general had in mind. Hoover was determined to kill the proposal, which would have established a civilian-controlled central intelligence service, and he allegedly leaked the plan to a journalist with the suggestion that the proposed service would be a "secret police" along the lines of the Nazi Gestapo. When the stories hit the press, Donovan's ideas were quickly set aside. After FDR's death, President Harry Truman, probably impressed by Hoover and the media, not only fired Donovan and broke up the OSS, but accepted the idea that the war was over and intelligence could revert to military control.

Still, it was only a few months later, in January 1946, that Truman established the position of Director of Central Intelligence (DCI), created the National Intelligence Authority, and the Central Intelligence Group. Truman referred to Admiral Sidney Souers, the first DCI, as his "chief snoop" and Hoover was once again left out of the intelligence loop. In 1947, Lieutenant General Hoyt Vandenberg, the second DCI, wisely stipulated that the new Central Intelligence Agency would not engage in "police, subpoena, or law enforcement or internal security functions."[4] Those rules still apply. Hoover's suggestion that the CIA might become a secret police was thus made moot; the CIA would concentrate on foreign intelligence. Since there was no other agency to take on internal security matters, it fell to the FBI to fulfill that role.

NO POLICE POWER

Interestingly, the CIA and the Congress made such a strict interpretation of the rules against CIA police activity that, for many years, the CIA had to use police officers from the General Services Administration to guard its facilities. It was only in the 1980s that the CIA finally was able to hire its own guard force, but their police authority was restricted only to the CIA main compound and its other buildings. When Pakistani terrorist Mir Aimal Kansi attacked CIA officers waiting to drive into the CIA headquarters in 1993, the CIA security force could do nothing more than summon the Fairfax County police, although they subsequently stationed a guard at the road entrance to the headquarters.

As the cold war developed, a neat division of labor was established between the FBI and the CIA. The Bureau would handle counterespionage and carry out internal security investigations within the United States, while the CIA would pursue intelligence about potential spies and other threats to the United States from abroad. Information was supposed to be shared between the agencies, but in the early days, there was not much real cooperation. The FBI did send reports from wiretaps and other investigations from time to time, but Hoover mandated that the CIA was to communicate with the FBI through one—and only one—designated agent. I can remember when I was a Latin American analyst in the 1960s, meeting with FBI agents in regard to issues in my field of interest, the agents were not allowed into the main headquarters area but were confined to the visitors area on the first floor.

In the 1950s, James J. Angleton, the chief of CIA counterintelligence, and Hoover apparently made an agreement that the CIA would handle internal spy cases, if they arose, and the Bureau would stay away. This story surfaced years later in the wake of a spate of spy cases, including that of Edward Lee Howard, a former CIA officer who defected to the Soviets in the 1980s. When it became apparent that the CIA had failed to advise the FBI on a timely basis about firing Howard, the Congress wanted to know why and the Angleton-Hoover agreement was revealed, but since both parties were dead, the agreement could not be confirmed.[5]

OFFICIAL TIES

Of course, official ties between the FBI director and the DCI were maintained at the National Foreign Intelligence Board level, but a story appeared suggesting that Hoover had become so angry at the CIA that he refused to speak with DCI Richard Helms. I know this is false because at one time during the Nixon administration, while I was at the Justice Department to give a briefing, Helms and Hoover emerged together from the attorney general's office, deep in conversation, but Helms paused long enough to introduce me to the legendary FBI director. For the average CIA officer in those days, however, there was no more connection to the FBI than there was to the Bureau of Labor Statistics.

Ill will between the CIA and the FBI surfaced again during the Watergate scandal in 1972 when it became known that a former CIA officer hired by the Committee to Reelect the President (CREEP) and his associates— including a former FBI agent—had broken into Democratic Party Headquarters at the Watergate complex in Washington and had been caught. The Nixon administration then sought to have the new FBI Director L. Patrick Gray assist in a cover-up by asking DCI Helms to claim that the break-in was part of an ongoing CIA operation. When Helms refused, he was fired and sent off to be ambassador to Iran. Most CIA officers probably understood that this was all part of Washington political machinations and had little to do with the real work of the two agencies.

While both the FBI and the CIA were concerned about such problems as espionage and terrorism, the two came at these issues from different directions. The CIA wanted to recruit penetrations and informants and learn as much as it could about ongoing operations. The FBI wanted to make arrests and win convictions. The joke at the time was that "the CIA wanted to string along the bad guys, while the FBI wanted to string them up." For the CIA, making arrests meant the end of intelligence gathering; for the FBI, the arrests and convictions were the endgame. The clash between the two cultures was therefore inevitable.

WORKING TOGETHER

After Angleton's departure from the CIA, there was one area where the CIA and the FBI were able to cooperate and join forces; targeting the Soviet intelligence apparatus both at home and abroad. Much of this cooperation was kept under wraps, but was revealed in the book by the CIA senior insider Milt Bearden and *New York Times* reporter James Risen.[6] Although there is no way to tell which writer made the specific contributions to the text, this is the most authoritative description of the anti-Soviet operations to appear in recent memory.

According to the authors, the FBI and CIA not only worked together to combat Soviet efforts to penetrate the U.S. government—especially in regard to getting inside U.S. intelligence—but also cooperated in training new CIA case officers and FBI agents to work against the "Main Enemy." As various espionage cases surfaced, the press and several authors made it appear that the two agencies were not communicating or cooperating, but Bearden and Risen explain in detail how this was far from the truth. While they did work together against Soviet spying, their cooperation in regard to terrorism did not receive much attention at first.

When terrorist cases began to rise in the 1980s, DCI Bill Casey decided to establish a Counterterrorism Task Force which eventually became the Counterterrorist Center (CTC). The idea was to bring representatives from all the agencies concerned with terrorism together in one place to share information and develop countering strategies. Both the CIA and FBI would be represented and would be forced to work together. Later, a similar center for counterintelligence would be established as well. In theory, this was a fine idea and seemed to work well. The centers were clearing houses for intelligence, but we now know that this only worked when the agencies shared all that they knew. Clearly, as we know from 9/11, some information never reached the centers, as each agency seemed to guard jealously a few of its most sensitive secrets.

FROM THE FBI TO THE CIA

Another important element in improving contacts between the FBI and CIA was the appointment of Judge William Webster to be DCI in 1987, after the untimely death of DCI Casey. Webster had served nine years as director of the FBI before accepting the DCI assignment and he came to the CIA with little experience in foreign affairs. Although some CIA officers were critical of Webster and slammed him as an "incompetent," those of us who worked closely with him saw quite a different picture. He was a quick study and his public speeches after the Iran-Contra affair, in which several CIA officers were implicated, did much to calm public perceptions about the U.S. intelligence system.

Webster had brought with him several senior FBI agents, including Bill Baker, who took charge of the Public Affairs Office. Baker sought to improve contacts between the CIA and the FBI, despite reluctance to cooperate on the part of some in both agencies. Still, a series of spy cases revealed that cooperation could only go so far. In 1985, the CIA fired Edward Lee Howard, a trainee still in his probationary period with the agency, after a routine polygraph exam revealed that he had been involved in drugs and a minor criminal operation. Howard had been preparing for an assignment to Moscow, but when he was let go, the CIA failed to alert the FBI—apparently based on the old Hoover-Angleton agreement that the CIA would police its own spy cases. After Howard defected to the USSR, the Congress asked a lot of hard questions about the failure of the CIA to inform the FBI about the case until it was too late to stop him.[7]

THE AMES CASE

The Howard case was small potatoes compared to some other spy cases that surfaced during this period. No one knew it then, but about the same time in 1985, Aldrich Ames, the CIA counterintelligence specialist and Russian speaker, had begun spying for the Soviet KGB. The Ames case generated five books and several articles. Most of the literature focused on how the CIA failed to catch Ames while the FBI was able to stop him. This misses several important aspects of the case.[8]

Although it took nine years before Ames was actually arrested, a dedicated team of CIA counterintelligence officers were on the case practically from its beginnings. Naturally, when the agency began to lose its agent network inside the KGB and GRU, senior CIA officials wanted to pursue the case internally because no one was sure, at first, that a "mole" was loose in the CIA. Eventually, CIA and FBI cooperation led to the identification of Ames as a Soviet penetration of the agency, and then a criminal case was built against Ames and his wife. Most of the literature depicted Ames as a bumbling drunk, but he was a lot more devious and clever than that. Agency officers knew he was up to something, but it was hard to prove.

Milt Bearden wrote that Ames, who in his early days suffered from bad teeth because of his heavy smoking and wore nondescript clothes to work, suddenly turned up at CIA headquarters wearing fancy suits and smiling with capped teeth.[9] His spiffy Jaguar was certainly not the only high-priced set of wheels at the agency, but was unusual for someone of his grade. He acknowledged to his friends that he had paid cash for his Arlington house, but told everyone that his wife's wealthy family made it all possible. It was all a scam.

KGB ERRORS

Although Ames was the KGB's first serious penetration of the CIA, the Russian service really mishandled the case. The KGB gave Ames too much money and his free spending led in part to his downfall. The Soviets held meetings with Ames in the open, relying on his agency assignment of recruiting Soviets to protect his contacts with them. The Russians quickly executed the KGB and GRU officers betrayed by Ames, instead of turning them into double agents. The executions sent an unmistakable signal that something had gone sour in the CIA's agent network.

Since the revelations of the Ames case, we now know that FBI Special Agent Robert Hanssen had also been a spy for the Soviets and had helped betray the U.S. penetrations of Soviet intelligence. Hanssen's behavior was even more bizarre than that of Ames, but again careful counterintelligence cooperation between the CIA and FBI led to his arrest and imprisonment.[10] Now, Bearden and Risen have teamed up to claim that there might well have been another Russian mole in the American intelligence system and that this person was instrumental in betraying the American agents.[11] The authors offer no evidence to support this supposition and we are not likely to know, of course, until the Russians tell us, which is highly unlikely.

The spy cases have caused the Congress to force the CIA to bring in FBI counterintelligence specialists to run their counterintelligence operations. This was supposed to compel the CIA to tell the FBI up front when it detected suspicions of espionage within the intelligence system. The old Angleton-Hoover agreement was dead. The CIA would still develop counterintelligence data abroad, but at home, countering espionage was to be the jurisdiction of the FBI, even within the secret agencies.

OTHER ISSUES

Counterintelligence isn't the only problem pressing the CIA and FBI to work more closely together. Countering terrorism is the first priority, but the two agencies have to work together against other targets including the narcotics trade, industrial espionage, global organized crime, and weapons proliferation, as well as against espionage by foreign intelligence services. So far, the record of cooperation is mixed. Today, FBI agents serve in the Terrorist Threat Integration Center along with intelligence officers from the CIA and the other intelligence agencies, but that does not tell us much about how well they cooperate. Before 9/11, FBI agents were assigned to the CIA Counterterrorist Center, but clearly some intelligence was not shared.

CIA officers are supposed to be assigned to the FBI Counterterrorist units around the country, but not much has been said about what they might contribute. In 2002, the FBI had planned to establish 56 of these centers, but by 2003, the number of planned Joint Terrorism Task Forces (JTTFs) had risen to 84; although it was not clear that all of them were operational. At the same time, the number of FBI legal attaches overseas continues to grow, much to the dismay of CIA officers who used to have liaison with host intelligence and security services to themselves. As of April 2003, there were 46 U.S. embassies around the world with FBI legal attaches on permanent assignment, according to the head of the FBI's

Office of International Operations.[12] At the same time, a number of CIA analysts have been assigned to FBI headquarters, presumably to assist the bureau in creating an intelligence analysis capability. The problem of cooperation and coordination between the CIA and FBI, however, seems to remain a troublesome issue and is based on cultural, procedural, and operational problems that have led some observers to refer to this as the "cops and spies" dilemma.

SHOULD SPIES BE COPS?

The spies and cops formulation was first laid out by Stewart D. Baker, a lawyer and general counsel for the National Security Agency (NSA) from 1992 to 1994, writing in the journal *Foreign Policy*.[13] Baker used the term "spies" to mean intelligence officers in general, although CIA officers would never refer to themselves that way. Likewise, Baker thought of any kind of law enforcement officials as "cops," although that is not the way that FBI agents think of themselves. They are investigators, not policemen, although they do have the power to arrest and carry weapons. Since Mr. Baker's article appeared, others have begun to use the same terminology, even if it is technically incorrect. It is a handy way, however, to think about the differences between intelligence and law enforcement.

Michael Turner, a former CIA analyst and now a professor of international relations, has described some of the cultural differences between the cops and spies.[14] CIA officers, especially those who work in the Clandestine Service, have always been reluctant to share information, even within the CIA. Turner says this "cloak-and-dagger" mentality is pervasive and stems from a fear that somehow the identity of recruited agents—the real spies—or other sources will be compromised if reports from agents are turned into intelligence analysis. If Clandestine Service officers are reluctant to share intelligence with their counterparts in the CIA's analysis directorate, it's no wonder that they are even more reluctant to share with outsiders like the FBI.

The FBI also wants to protect sources, but for different reasons. The FBI wants eventually to make court cases, and divulging information might compromise evidence that could be used to obtain a conviction. According to Benjamin and Simon, rules of evidence prevented FBI agents from sharing information with intelligence if that information was to be taken before a grand jury.[15] The Patriot Act has relaxed that restriction, but old habits die hard, especially in large bureaucracies. The old problems persist: intelligence officers want to exploit sources and law enforcement personnel want to make arrests and obtain convictions. The two goals are incompatible.

DIFFERENCES IN END GOALS

The operational and methodological differences between intelligence and law enforcement in general are strong largely because of differences in the end goals of the two communities. Much of what the FBI wants in criminal cases is evidence, gathered and protected according to specific rules, but available to the defense in disclosure. The CIA does not want evidence, which is case specific, but rather intelligence that can identify problems and warn of threats. Under these circumstances, there should be no question about why the two agencies operate with different rules and according to different methods, or why there is a divide between intelligence and law enforcement at many levels.

Although many law enforcement agencies from the FBI to state and local police have intelligence units, the kind of information they seek is different from that sought by intelligence agencies such as the CIA, DIA, or NSA. When the CIA recruits sources, it wants to establish a controlled, secret, and continuing relationship so that it can obtain information not available through other methods.

The CIA wants an agent who has good access to the information, is reliable, and who can maintain a clandestine relationship over time. In such a relationship, the CIA will eventually be able to determine if the agent has such qualities, but sometimes the information may be less than perfect, subject to the agent's biases and contacts, and may conflict with other source data. Above all, the agency has to protect the identity of the agent; revelation could mean arrest, torture, or death. Thus the CIA often keeps its activities secret to protect sources as well as the methods of gathering intelligence.

The FBI typically works in an entirely different fashion toward a different goal. Its sources have to be protected too, but they are usually targeted toward solving a crime. Eventually, the identity of the sources may have to be revealed in court, although there are some cases where a penetration of a group may last over time. The methods used to obtain the information may also come under the scrutiny of a court. In fact, the FBI might have to demonstrate in court that the information was obtained according to legal rules. FBI agents have to be prepared to appear at trial and testify for the prosecution. This would be completely unacceptable to intelligence officers working undercover, because once their cover was blown, they could no longer operate as intelligence collectors.

INVESTIGATIVE OR EXCULPATORY

Stewart Baker divides law enforcement information into two categories, investigative and exculpatory. The former is essentially intelligence, pointing at situations that may be of interest from a law enforcement perspective, identifying the "bad guys," describing their activities, pinpointing their locations and targets, and, if possible, providing information about their vulnerabilities. As Baker points out, this kind of intelligence is of little use to criminal investigators and prosecutors. He notes that "Intelligence that cannot ultimately be introduced in court as evidence borders on the worthless" as far as law enforcement is concerned.[16]

What law enforcement really wants is exculpatory information that can be used to obtain a conviction in court. Because this information must eventually be revealed to the defense in a trial, protection of sources and methods becomes impossible. Further, Baker writes, prosecutors cannot be depended on to protect sensitive intelligence since their motivation is to convict criminals, and defense attorneys will certainly try to defend their clients by demanding information they know the government will be reluctant to reveal.

In the Iran-Contra affair, for example, the government refused to prosecute a CIA station chief in Latin America because the CIA feared that critical information would be revealed at trial. In several of the espionage cases, the U.S. government seemed eager to reach a plea bargain with the intelligence officers caught spying, so that defense efforts to subpoena classified information about the cases—information the defense knew the government would be reluctant to reveal—did not arise. Further, it seemed at the time that the government feared that a court case might create a constitutional challenge to the Foreign Intelligence Surveillance Act (FISA), which had not yet been tested in the courts. In the wake of 9/11, the FISA has been upheld by the Foreign Intelligence Court of Review, suggesting that even if a challenge were to reach the Supreme Court, it might well be declared constitutional in today's conservative atmosphere.

NEW RULES

While intelligence cannot play by law enforcement rules, the reverse may no longer be true. The firewall that the government thought had been created by the FISA to separate intelligence and law enforcement has been declared null and void by the FISA review court. This means that law enforcement, specifically the FBI, may task the intelligence agencies to collect data that might be used in court, and that the kind of surveillance permitted under the FISA could be used by the prosecution in a court case. As demonstrated so clearly in the Ames case, prosecuting an espionage case required that after a counterintelligence investigation had identified an American spying for a foreign power, the more rigorous rules of a criminal investigation had to be followed actually to bring the case to court. For example, after an investigation had pinpointed Ames as a Russian spy, a new warrant under the Omnibus Crime Bill was obtained by a team of criminal investigators, thus preserving the firewall between intelligence and law enforcement.[17]

THE NICHOLSON CASE

The Nicholson case is another good example of how the transition from counterintelligence to criminal investigation worked. Harold J. Nicholson was a fast-track rising star in the CIA's Clandestine Service, but his career seemed to have become derailed when he was assigned to a training slot after serving as chief of station in two posts abroad. Nicholson, apparently frustrated by the changes in his career prospects, and buffeted by a failed marriage and money troubles, decided to volunteer to be a spy for the Russians. Nicholson began his spying activities right at the end of the Ames case in the 1990s. He may have learned about what had happened to Ames and perhaps had decided that he could do better, but, in fact, he turned out to be surprisingly incompetent at espionage.

Nicholson turned up on the counterintelligence radar when he had difficulty with a polygraph exam. Unlike the Ames case, however, the CIA's Office of Security quickly took note and pursued the case. Nicholson made it easy for the FBI agents trying to catch him. He was observed photographing secret files with a document camera he had brazenly requisitioned from the CIA's Office of Technical Services. Although Nicholson had checked his office for possible video surveillance before he started copying, he missed the probe entirely. Later, when he went to Singapore to hand over papers to the Russians, his efforts to throw off surveillance failed and he was easily seen meeting with his Russian handlers. He was arrested in 1996, and in a plea bargain, agreed to cooperate in a damage assessment. In this case, the CIA–FBI cooperation was praised by the press and Congress.

FAWAZ YOUNIS

Another example of how intelligence and law enforcement could cooperate is detailed in the case of Fawaz Younis, one of a group of Lebanese terrorists who had hijacked a Jordanian airliner in 1985 and then arranged to have TV cameras present when they blew up the empty plane.[18] Younis was also implicated in the hijacking of TWA Flight 847, in which an American serviceman was murdered and his body thrown out on the tarmac. The Justice Department was eager to bring Younis back to the United States for trial. Under U.S. law, in a case involving a foreign national living abroad but indicted in a U.S. court, the United States can invoke "extra-territoriality" and request that the FBI bring the accused back for trial, as long as this does not violate the sovereignty of a foreign nation. Thus, Younis had to be lured into international waters or airspace so that the FBI could make the arrest. The job of luring Younis out of Lebanon fell to the CIA.

Again the two agencies wanted to maintain the firewall between them, so that there was a smooth transition from the intelligence operation to law enforcement. According to former CIA official Duane "Dewey" Clarridge, the CIA recruited a buddy of Younis to lure him onto a boat with the promise of liquor, sex, and gambling. The boat, in international waters, was in fact part of an FBI sting operation, and even had female FBI agents dressed in bikinis as part of the operation. Once Younis was identified by the CIA, it was up to the FBI to make the arrest after the terrorist had boarded the boat; CIA officers were not supposed to be present when the arrest was made. Younis was then spirited back to the United States, tried, and convicted.

AUM SHINRIKYO

Cooperation between the FBI and the CIA against terrorism can be seen in a case that occurred before 9/11, but is instructive in that it shows how law enforcement authorities can task intelligence for data without compromising either legal restrictions or intelligence sources and methods. In March 1995, Aum Shinrikyo, a Japanese-based religious cult and erstwhile terrorist organization, sought to bring attention to its cause by injecting deadly sarin gas into the Tokyo subway system.[19] Twelve people were killed and thousands injured. CIA officers in Tokyo learned that Aum Shinrikyo had a branch in New York City, not far from the Times Square subway station. Of course, the FBI wanted to move quickly to make sure that the group was not planning a similar attack in New York so it tasked the CIA to gather what information it could about Aum Shinrikyo in Japan while the Bureau obtained a FISA warrant to put the New York branch under surveillance. It turned out that the New York group had no plans to attack the subway, and a crisis was quickly averted.

In order to manage the hand-off from counterintelligence gathering to criminal investigation, the Clinton administration established a committee within the Justice Department to determine when the shift would be made from intelligence to law enforcement, but it seemed to be more a temporary arrangement than a permanent fix. No results had been announced when President Clinton left office. Attorney General John Ashcroft had not tackled the problem before 9/11 and now it seems that legal decisions in regard to the FISA and the passage of the Patriot Act have made the issue moot.

AMENDING THE FOREIGN INTELLIGENCE SURVEILLANCE ACT

Since 9/11, the need to maintain the various separations and firewalls between intelligence and law enforcement seem no longer to be necessary or desirable. In fact, the Patriot Act served to amend the FISA to be sure that FBI agents in the field would no longer have to provide substantial evidence of terrorist or espionage activity to obtain a FISA warrant for surveillance, but merely demonstrate that there was reason to suspect such activity—a far lower standard. These changes in the law were driven by what seemed to be a failure before 9/11 both by FBI field agents and their supervisors at headquarters to understand the standards for obtaining a FISA surveillance warrant.[20]

In addition, the judgment of the FISA Court of Review suggested that the Congress, in passing the FISA, never intended that there should be a firewall between intelligence and law enforcement; although this had been the policy since it was implemented. Now, issues related to the FISA and relations between intelligence and law enforcement will be managed by the Justice Department's Office of Intelligence Policy and Review (OIPR).[21] When these decisions were handed down, it was too soon to judge whether or not changes in the rules would lead to changes in the FBI and its relationship with intelligence.

In a lead article on the FBI in *U.S. News and World Report* in May 2003, the reporter points out that the FBI has never been focused on preventing crime and many questioned whether or not the bureau could shift into a new mode.[22] Clearly, part of the failure to pick up the planned terrorist attack on the United States was caused by a mind-set among FBI supervisors that they could not investigate Middle Eastern men taking flight training because the trainees were in the United States legally and had committed no crime. FBI Director Mueller insisted that field agents still seek guidance from headquarters, limiting their freedom of action when they see a situation that ought to be pursued. The CIA follows the same kind of rules, requiring its case officers to report back to headquarters before they take an action and following through with an after-action report. This is supposed to protect the case officer from second-guessing by superiors and ought to work the same way for FBI field agents.

Many FBI agents who have been around the Bureau for a while wonder what will happen to the cases they have been running against bank robbers, white-collar crimes, espionage, and narcotics.[23] These kinds of cases are far more common than terrorism and do affect the internal security of the United States. While Director Mueller has sent out word that terrorism has top priority, federal prosecutors and the Congress will surely press the FBI not to drop its work against these other targets.

The same holds true for the CIA and the other intelligence agencies. Developments abroad cannot be ignored, from North Korean missile activity and nuclear weapons to African revolutions and South American politics. The White House will not excuse the Intelligence Community if the president and his key officials are surprised by a situation that requires action, even if it is not related to terrorism.

INCREASED COOPERATION

Clearly, cooperation between the FBI and the CIA has increased in fighting al Qaeda and other terrorists. The two agencies were able to snatch Mir Aimal Kansi in Pakistan and bring him to the United States for trial. Kansi was the lone gunman who, in 1993, shot CIA officers waiting to enter the headquarters compound. Although he took refuge in Afghanistan, he was lured out of hiding in 1997 in a clever operation. Similarly, several key al Qaeda leaders were captured by cooperative efforts overseas. Although capturing these officials cut them off from further information about what the organization was doing, the utility of learning a great deal from interrogation was worth the effort. It's not clear that any of them would have been willing to become agents for the United States. Arresting them fulfilled President Bush's mandate to bring them to justice.

THE WRONG MAN

Despite this growing cooperation in the field, there are troubling cases that show that tension between the FBI and CIA is inevitable. In the first case, a CIA officer who had been working in counterintelligence against the former KGB and its successor agency, the Russian SVR, was targeted by the FBI as a mole and the Bureau began a relentless operation to find evidence against him. The CIA officer, Brian Kelley, had been working the case against U.S. State Department officer Felix Bloch, who seemed to be a Soviet agent within the U.S. diplomatic corps.[24] The FBI apparently thought Kelley was cooperating with Bloch and put Kelley under tight surveillance.

Eventually Kelley was forced to take administrative leave from the CIA while the FBI built its case against him. When Robert Hanssen was arrested in February 2002, the FBI finally realized that Kelley was not a spy, but it was too late. Kelley's 20-year career in the CIA was in tatters and was further damaged when David Wise, the hustling writer who has published several books on spy cases, identified Kelley in his book on the Hanssen case. Kelley, who had served undercover throughout his career, was characterized by Wise as the "Wrong Man."[25] DCI George Tenet had tried to have Wise's publisher delete Kelley's name from the book on the Hanssen case to protect what was left of Kelley's career. When Wise found out, he wrote a self-serving piece in the *New York Times* claiming that the CIA had tried to censor his book. The evidence the FBI had obtained from a Russian informant made the case against Hanssen, and not Kelley.

THE BAER CASE

Bob Baer, the former CIA case officer, accused the CIA of a witch hunt in the aftermath of the Ames case, which suggests that the case against

Kelley was all part of an effort to respond to congressional pressure to be sure there were no more Soviet moles in the CIA. Baer does not mention the Kelley case, but he does describe in detail the poisoned atmosphere at the CIA when hundreds of officers were forced to undergo polygraph exams. Baer believes that the FBI agent in charge of CIA counterintelligence after the Ames case was determined to "get" the CIA. Baer says that the move was part of an effort by then-FBI Director Louis Freeh to dismantle the CIA, aided and abetted by CIA leaders who refused to stand up for their people.[26]

It's no wonder that Baer was bitter. His second encounter with the FBI came after returning from the operation in Iraq in 1994–1995 to try to foment a coup against Saddam Hussein. The effort went nowhere, probably thwarted by the ability of Saddam's formidable intelligence and security services at that time to infiltrate any such efforts. When Baer got back to headquarters, he was told that he was under investigation by the FBI for plotting to assassinate Saddam, which at the time was banned by Presidential Executive Order 12333.

Baer was particularly incensed that the FBI was investigating him under criminal statutes and not the Executive Order. His supervisor told Baer that he could have an attorney if he wished but that his career would be over if he brought one in. The CIA, of course, had its own staff of lawyers to protect the organization. Baer blamed President Clinton's former National Security Adviser Anthony Lake for the effort against him, but there was no independent evidence of this. In the end, Baer was not indicted and the charges went away. Of course, the George W. Bush administration would have been quite happy if the CIA had been able to assassinate Saddam and gave specific orders in 2002 to make him a target. When Saddam was captured in 2003 he was then protected as a prisoner of war.

IMPLICATIONS FOR HOMELAND SECURITY

Baer's denunciation of the FBI, as well as his own CIA masters, reflects some of the long-standing tensions between the two agencies—the cooperative effort against terrorism notwithstanding. What, then, are the implications of the cops and spies problems for homeland security? Although both the CIA and FBI counterterrorist centers are co-located with the Terrorist Threat Integration Center (TTIC) at some unnamed location in northern Virginia, this tells us very little about how well these units will communicate with each other. So far, the Department of Homeland Security has said that it will depend on these units to provide much of its intelligence input.

The overall management of the centers and the force that will make them cooperate lies with the DCI and the FBI director, but these two leaders do not have the same boss. The DCI reports directly to the president, while the FBI director works for the attorney general. The DCI nominally coordinates the government's intelligence activities, but in reality, has little control over any of the agencies except the CIA. This leaves the issue in the hands of the president himself, but modern presidents have been happy to divorce themselves from direct control of intelligence activities.

Since the Intelligence Oversight Committees in the House and Senate were established in 1976, the Congress has become increasingly involved in oversight of intelligence, but aside from control of the budget and the efforts to manage the system through the intelligence authorization legislation, there is not much the Congress can do to make the system function effectively. There is no single office, outside of the White House, to deal with the spies and cops problem. It depends on cooperation between a variety of entities and the ability of the various chiefs in Washington to make the system work.

Students of political science find it difficult to accept the notion that personalities and not governmental structure are the determinants in regard to the efficiency of government. Nonetheless, some overhaul of the system ought to be considered to make sure that intelligence and law enforcement work together in the interests of national security in general and homeland security in particular. The challenge of intelligence reform to meet these needs have often been discussed but no action has resulted. It is certainly a subject worth further exploration.

Should We Have an MI-5?

One of the issues that emerged from the terrorist attack on the United States was the potential need for a domestic intelligence service to mirror the work of the U.S. Intelligence Community overseas. While Director Robert Mueller worked feverishly in 2003 to build such a capability into the FBI, some former intelligence leaders as well as members of Congress suggested that we needed an organization comparable to the famous British MI-5, the designation for its Internal Security Service. One of the most persistent supporters of creating a new agency was Lieutenant General William Odom, the former director of the NSA and a veteran of army intelligence, but he was not alone.

After the results of the Congressional investigation into the alleged intelligence failure before 9/11 was released, Senator John Edwards introduced legislation to establish a homeland security service along the lines of the British system.[1] It also appeared that the study commission under Tom Kean would make a similar recommendation. Despite these recommendations, the issue was quite troubling to many who were already criticizing the George W. Bush administration for its heavy-handed tactics in dealing with suspected terrorists and immigration violators.

The United States has never had an internal security service, except for the brief period during the Civil War when Lafayette Baker sought to root out Confederate sympathizers in the North. His draconian tactics offended many, so when the new Secret Service was created after the war, its focus was limited to protecting against counterfeiting and other financial crimes. At the time, and stretching into the twentieth century, Americans thought they were immune to the kinds of problems plaguing the European states, including particularly subversion and insurrection against the existing regimes, as well as the usual issues of terrorism, espionage, and organized crime. Even the attempt by the Confederacy to leave the federal union was not an insurrection, since the South did not want to overthrow the government in Washington, but only sought to secede from it.

In subsequent years, as the Europeans girded for war, we did not have to worry about threats to the stability of the federal government and we are still safe from such threats. Perhaps this lack of a serious threat to overthrow the government from within has been a critical factor in avoiding the creation of an internal security service. We never thought we needed it until faced with terrorism here at home.

MI-5

The British created the MI-5 in 1909, but its first leader, Vernon Kell, admitted that he really did not comprehend the full extent of his mandate when he was appointed.[2] In typical British fashion, the establishment of the service and the appointment of its leaders was not debated in Parliament or made public. In fact, it was not until the mid-1980s that the service and its counterpart the MI-6, the Secret Intelligence Service (the British equivalent of the CIA) was given a legislative basis. A parliamentary committee was established for oversight and the name of the leader of the MI-5 was revealed. The British were either pleasantly surprised or genuinely shocked to learn that the head of the MI-5 was Stella Rimington, a career Security Service officer and its first female chief.

The MI-5 operates within Great Britain to gather and analyze intelligence information much like its counterpart the MI-6 does abroad. The MI-5 has no police power, no arrest authority, or any of the other trappings of a law enforcement agency. When action is needed, the MI-5 has to turn to the special branch of Scotland Yard or police services to make actual arrests. Other European internal security services such as the French DST operate in a similar fashion. Today, Germany has a comparable internal security service, the BFV, the Federal Office for the Protection of the Constitution, and internal security services can be found in most industrialized countries.

FEARS OF A SECRET POLICE

What seems to frighten Americans most is not that we might have a version of the MI-5, but that an internal security service might become the kind of secret police and investigative service common in dictatorships.

There are plenty of examples, but perhaps none worse than the Nazi Secret State Police (Gestapo) of the World War II era or the NKVD of Stalin's Soviet Union. Dictatorships need an internal security service to stay in power, so they give it a great deal of support and appoint leaders they trust. The most recent example was the *Mukhabarat* of Saddam Hussein, an intelligence and security service headed by one of Saddam's tribal chiefs from his hometown of Tikrit. After Saddam was driven from power, the excesses of his security service became known in rather gruesome detail. It resembled in many respects those of such security services as the infamous *Stasi,* the Ministry of State Security of the former East Germany.

Other such draconian services of the modern era include the dreaded *SAVAK* of the late Shah of Iran, and the *Securitate* of Romania under its former dictator Nicolae Ceausescu. What all these dictatorial security services had in common is that they had police power and they appeared to be uncontrolled. Their intent was to create fear among the populace through brutal tactics. They were known for torture, they used prisons maintained in horrible conditions, and they did not operate under any kinds of legal constraints.

Because they had such complete power, the dictators very often appointed only close relatives or trusted friends to lead the security services, purging them from time to time of anyone who might threaten to get out of line. After all, we know of several cases where the head of the security service tried to overthrow the regime he was supposed to protect. That is how former security chief Manuel Noriega allegedly came to power in Panama and how Najibullah was able to overthrow his predecessor in Afghanistan. Is it any wonder, then, that people in the United States question the wisdom of having an internal security service?

THE CANADIAN EXPERIENCE

Actually, the United States is facing a problem that our northern neighbor Canada has already solved, although there are still some questions about the solution. During the period between the two world wars and then again after World War II ended, Canada's federal police organization, the Royal Canadian Mounted Police (RCMP) thought the major danger facing Canada was Communist subversion. It was much the same kind of attitude fostered by J. Edgar Hoover and the FBI in the United States, but the Bureau was dealing with other federal crimes on a scale unknown in Canada. The Mounties had tried to foster the same kind of image as the FBI, loyal and clean servants of the people. The RCMP supported radio shows and movies that depicted the Mounties in their scarlet tunics and campaign hats as heroes. The major difference between the FBI and the RCMP, then as now, is that the Bureau is strictly a civilian organization while the RCMP is a quasi-military uniformed force; otherwise their roles are similar.

After World War II, the RCMP successfully penetrated the Communist Party of Canada.[3] When Igor Gouzenko, a code clerk at the Soviet Embassy in Ottawa, defected in 1945 and revealed that a Canadian scientist was leaking nuclear secrets to the Soviet Union, the Mounties gained even more support from Parliament for their anti-Communist operations. The RCMP developed a crack surveillance team, known as the "Watchers," comparable to the "Gs" of the FBI, to try to root out other Soviet spies and Communist sympathizers.

While the RCMP was competent at striking back at Soviet espionage, it was less successful against domestic subversion and terrorism in Quebec. After a series of kidnappings and murders by the Front for the Liberation of Quebec (FLQ) in the 1970s, the RCMP was called to task for failing to anticipate what had happened. A special commission's investigation showed that the RCMP was poorly equipped to deal with a crisis in Quebec. Few officers and troops of the RCMP spoke French and even fewer were rooted in Quebec Province. In one case, the RCMP managed to gather a great deal of data about the FLQ but could not readily translate the material.[4]

THE CREATION OF THE CANADIAN SECURITY INTELLIGENCE SERVICE

After an investigation by a government commission, the RCMP established a security intelligence unit that was supposed to be staffed by new civilians untainted by RCMP traditions. Unfortunately, the new unit did not perform as well as had been expected and in 1984, Prime Minister Pierre Trudeau was able to convince the Canadian Parliament to establish the Canadian Security Intelligence Service (CSIS).[5]

The CSIS might well be the model for a U.S. internal security service if the United States wanted to have one. It is an intelligence rather than an investigative service and is part of the Office of the Solicitor General of Canada. It's leaders generally have been political appointees without significant intelligence experience, but unlike its British counterpart the MI-5, the CSIS has been publicly recognized from its first days. It has both collection and analysis units just like the CIA, but with a domestic focus. It has no police power, but must rely on the RCMP or provincial authorities when action is needed. It has, until recently, had no role to play abroad, although there have been discussions within the Canadian government about creating a foreign intelligence service. In the fall of 2003, Ward Elcock, the director of the CSIS, hinted that the CSIS was indeed starting to play a role in foreign intelligence collection, although he would not reveal the details. Until now, Canada has been one of the few major powers in the world without such a service. Traditionally, Canada has received its foreign intelligence from the United States and Great Britain.

To assure Canadians that the CSIS would be a force for good and that there would be no abuse, the Security Intelligence Review Committee (SIRC) was established as an oversight mechanism. The committee, made up of former members of the government, was to make sure that there were no violations of human and civil rights. The SIRC was to review the situation after five years to determine if the system was working, and issue a public report on its findings. Since that time, the value of the SIRC as an oversight mechanism has been brought into question along with an effort by some members of Parliament to create an oversight committee in the legislature, similar to the British oversight system.

REVAMPING THE FBI

The dilemma of trying to create an internal security and intelligence unit within the FBI thus mirrors the same challenge as the one the RCMP faced in the 1970s. The RCMP was not ultimately successful, but that is not to say that the FBI can't do better. In many respects, the new FBI that Director Mueller is creating could look a lot like the CIA in terms of institutional structure, although the mission is quite different. The present investigative force will, in addition to its law enforcement duties, have the job of gathering domestic intelligence through its field offices around the United States, just as the CIA's directorate of operations does now. Other domestic collectors will come from DHS units including agents from the Border, Immigration, and Customs units, the Secret Service, and the Coast Guard.

State and local governments, particularly the police, will contribute to the intelligence collection matrix based on tips, informants, and observation. For example, a recent article in a local New Jersey newspaper described quite well how such a system might work.[6] One detective in Mercer County was selected to be the county counterterrorism coordinator. As such, he was responsible for contacts with the FBI's JTTF and the state office of counterterrorism, New Jersey's ATTF. This system was replicated in each county. The coordinators not only pass intelligence to the FBI, but also serve as the focal point for intelligence passed by the FBI to the coordinators. Admittedly, this means drawing down resources that might otherwise be devoted to fighting more normal kinds of crimes. Reports of suspicious activities that might have been linked to terrorism usually turn out to be narcotics-related activity, or other kinds of crime, so there are benefits to the operation in any event.

The FBI's analysis unit parallels that of the CIA Directorate of Intelligence, but focuses primarily on the domestic situations uncovered by the operational units. Other data feeds into the FBI's analytic division from American foreign and military intelligence. The analytic division is not made up of FBI special agents but is staffed by trained civilian analysts. The CIA already has in place an analytic training facility called the Sherman Kent Center which might have been used to train FBI analysts, but the Bureau has decided to create its own analysis training center— although it might benefit from existing courses at the CIA or DIA on the critical aspects of intelligence collection and analysis. The FBI is moving aggressively to hire and train the new people it will need to make the scheme work. Ironically, as Mueller moved aggressively to remake the FBI, some members of Congress criticized the bureau for failing to keep up with its more traditional targets of drugs and white-collar crime.[7]

COUNTERINTELLIGENCE METHODOLOGY

The methodology of counterintelligence (CI) is well known and has been practiced around the world for many years, but it has expanded as the targets have grown. There are both offensive and defensive measures. At first, CI meant countering espionage and subversion, but it has grown in most countries to include countering terrorism, organized crime, and where there are concerns, countering the flow of illegal narcotics. The basic principles of CI are the same no matter what the targets, but security and internal intelligence services find that certain techniques work better than others. The legal constraints vary from country to country as well, so it is difficult to generalize about restrictions or controls on CI. In general, democracies have such constraints but dictatorships do not.

Countering espionage traditionally means recruiting an agent or asset inside the target intelligence service to find out whether or not it has successfully penetrated one's government, especially if it has an asset inside the intelligence or counterintelligence service. This was the method used to identify and arrest FBI Agent Robert Hanssen; an agent penetration of the KGB helped identify him.[8] After the Ames, Nicholson, and other spy cases, it became clear that we had done to the Soviets the same things they had done to us, and for the same purpose.

Of course, recruiting an agent inside an adversary intelligence service is not so easily done and that may be the reason that there are relatively few such cases over the years of the cold war, and even fewer in the post–cold war period. They usually surface only when the spy is arrested and his or her identity is made public. Such cases make headlines when they become known, but the reality is that agent penetrations of intelligence services don't happen all that often. Sometimes, penetrations are revealed by defectors, who turn over the names of agents as a way of establishing their credibility to the service to which they want to defect.

A Soviet KGB defector, Vitali Yurchenko, gave his interrogators enough information in 1985 to identify both Ronald Pelton of the NSA and Edward Lee Howard of CIA, both of whom were spies for the Soviets.

Apparently, at about the same time, a Chinese defector fingered Larry Wu-tai Chin, the CIA translator dispatched by Chinese intelligence to get inside the U.S. system. Americans are usually horrified, however briefly, when it turns out that Americans have betrayed their country in this way, although we fully expect that others will betray their countries on our behalf.

SURVEILLANCE

Another good technique for determining the targets and operations of a hostile intelligence service is through surveillance, both physical and electronic. Most good counterintelligence services have trained surveillance teams, such as the FBI's "Gs" or the RCMP's "Watchers" who are adept at following targets on the street without being detected, in spite of the fact that most intelligence operatives engaged in espionage are trained equally well to detect and avoid surveillance. Sometimes, operatives on the way to meet an agent will spend hours "laundering themselves," by taking devious routes so that they cannot easily be followed.[9]

Over the years, most intelligence services have acquired some knowledge of the key operatives in hostile intelligence services and they know that surveillance of these key people may eventually lead to an identification of their agent networks. Combined with physical surveillance, electronic surveillance is another good way to help pinpoint an adversary. Before the advent of modern communication systems, this meant phone taps and bugs, but now has expanded to include surveillance of a variety of portable devices and computers. The 1978 Foreign Intelligence Surveillance Act (FISA) was originally designed to ease restrictions on surveillance of foreign agents in the United States; overseas such restrictions do not apply. The CIA can carry out surveillance abroad without having to worry about breaking U.S. laws, although the operations are carefully supervised by CIA managers.

COUNTERING TERRORISM

Countering espionage is not part of homeland security but clearly it ought to be, as I have argued previously. The target of greatest importance over the past few years however, has been terrorism; no one opposes the idea that it ought to be given full attention. Unfortunately, the techniques that are most effective in stopping espionage do not work very well against terrorists. It is extremely rare to be able to penetrate a terrorist cell because most terrorists operate in small groups where the members of the cell are well known to each other. Recruiting one of these fanatics, as most terrorists seem to be, is unlikely. We do know that terrorists, even though they should know better, can be vulnerable to surveillance, especially electronic surveillance of their communications. The United States has managed to get its hands on several key al Qaeda leaders using this method.

Similar methods have been used successfully over the years by the FBI and the Secret Service against organized crime, counterfeiting, and in cooperation with the Drug Enforcement Administration, against narcotics producers, shippers, and dealers. Although not given high priority, at least some of these counterintelligence issues will be targeted by elements of the DHS. Interestingly—in what appeared to be a bureaucratic maneuver—the responsibility for financial crimes, formerly a key target for the Secret Service, was shifted to the FBI. Naturally, the Secret Service complained but will probably cooperate with the FBI after the turf battle is over.[10]

THE LACKAWANNA SIX

Just as in the conflict between law enforcement and intelligence described previously, there can be a conflict between law enforcement and politics in regard to surveillance. This might well have been the case in regard to a group of suspected terrorists in the Buffalo, New York area that some in government thought was a sleeper cell just waiting for the right signal from Osama bin Laden to carry out a terrorist operation. In the high state of alert after 9/11, the CIA and the FBI could not agree about the nature of this group, but the White House was not prepared to give law enforcement officials much leeway because it could not take the chance that the group might carry out a terrorist operation while the FBI was still developing evidence against the alleged cell.[11] It turned out that the group, now known as the Lackawanna six, were not really terrorists at all.

All six of the men were born in the United States of Yemeni parents and were practicing Muslims. They were recruited early in 2001 by an al Qaeda operative to go to Afghanistan to take part in the jihad, although they apparently had no idea that a real plot against the United States was in the works. All six quickly became disillusioned with the situation and returned to the United States: after 9/11, they realized that they might fall under suspicion, so they developed a cover story about going to Pakistan for religious training and kept their heads down. Meanwhile, the Buffalo office of the FBI received an anonymous tip about the six, suggesting that they were part of a terrorist sleeper cell. The FBI quickly put them under surveillance, but found no evidence that they were plotting an operation. The CIA, on the other hand, thought they were dangerous and should be stopped.

In the post–9/11 atmosphere, the pressure to prevent another terrorist strike was very high. Early reports suggested that the FBI was moving against them too quickly and might miss their connections to other groups. Finally, the six were arrested and charged with training for terrorism, a crime that might put them in jail for ten years. The fact that one of the six offered to help the FBI with its investigation seemed to carry no weight. The government claimed that it had stopped a terrorist operation, but the reality is quite different. After the six were arrested, both a deputy attorney general and Governor George Pataki of New York played the case as the disruption of a very real terrorist cell. The *New York Times* reporters who investigated the case, however, pointed out that the involvement of the six in terrorism was ambiguous at best, and so the arrests were hardly a victory in the war on terrorism.[12]

INFORMANTS

Another good source of counterintelligence information comes from informants. These are not recruited agents or assets, but may from time to time be able to provide information they pick up and are willing to turn over, usually for some small sums of money. Police sometimes call such people "snitches," but the reliability and availability of their information varies. A hallmark of many dictatorships and draconian security services, the pervasive use of informants to report on neighbors, co-workers, and even family, is the kind of activity that really frightens people about any kind of internal security service. In a democracy, the use of informants needs to be very carefully controlled.

Sometimes, people will notice strange or unusual activity in their neighborhood and will call the police to tip them off. The danger is that they will identify innocent activity and waste police time for no good reason. For example, on the anniversary of 9/11, a woman in a restaurant in Georgia thought she overheard men of distinctly Middle Eastern appearance discussing a plan to bomb a target, so she called police. The men were eventually stopped in Florida after a rather extensive manhunt and the shutdown of 20 miles of an interstate highway, but they turned out to be medical interns, not terrorists. No bombs or weapons were found.[13]

In June 2003, more horror stories began to appear about terrorist tips that turned out to be false and resulted in serious harm to innocent people who had been fingered by tipsters.[14] Shortly after the terrorist attacks on 9/11, eight men of Middle Eastern descent were rounded up in Evansville, Indiana, shackled and jailed for a week based on a tip to the FBI. Although the men were never charged and were released, four of them had their names entered into a terrorist database so that they could not fly on commercial aircraft or even get jobs. Eventually, the FBI took action to have their names expunged from the list. In some cases, tipsters denounced people just to get them in trouble and in one incident, a woman was sentenced to one year in jail for giving false information against her ex-husband, who turned out to be innocent but was then charged with immigration violations because he had missed school while in jail. While informants can be useful, they can also create a good deal of mischief, as many cases illustrate.

INTERROGATION

A useful tool in counterintelligence is the interrogation of defectors, prisoners—including those taken in wartime—and individuals rounded up as illegal aliens. The image of the cruel interrogator sitting behind a bright lamp as the subject cowers before him is mostly the stuff of fiction. The reality can be a lot worse. Americans taken prisoner in wartime or even travelers who run afoul of the law in many foreign countries find out that harsh, brutal interrogation, complete with torture, is not uncommon. Although many countries have signed the Geneva Convention regulating the treatment of prisoners of war, the rules are often broken or bent to satisfy the need for intelligence. Unfortunately, revelations about American treatment of Iraqi prisoners at what was once Saddam Hussein's infamous prison at Abu Ghraib demonstrates that U.S. soldiers or private contractors will behave in much the same way without careful screening, training, and supervision.

During the Korean War, some American prisoners of the Chinese or North Koreans appeared to have been "brainwashed," especially the few who chose to stay behind in the Communist North or China after the war. Studies undertaken at the time revealed that the Communists have used a combination of sleep deprivation, food withdrawal, and similar psychological methods to break the prisoner's will to resist. The American experience in the Vietnam War was even worse as severe torture was inflicted on many Americans, many of whom were able to survive and tell their stories after the conflict.

Despite this gruesome history, the United States has, until recently, avoided such tactics in interrogations because torture and physical duress are not the best ways to obtain useful and accurate intelligence. A good intelligence interrogation requires establishing a controlled situation in which the interrogator dominates the subject but at the same time creates an atmosphere in which the subject actually looks forward to the interrogation and becomes eager to cooperate. This can be accomplished by giving the subject special food or cigarettes during the interrogation, or creating a more pleasant atmosphere than the subject experiences in a cell. The interrogator must be sure to keep the questions and answers on track to make sure that the answers are consistent. There are other techniques, including the "good-guy, bad-guy" approach often seen on TV crime shows, and the use of already available intelligence—or another subject—to play off against the person being interrogated.

USE OF TORTURE

In my opinion and experience, the use of physical duress and torture is not likely to provide truthful information as the subject tries desperately to stop the pain by spewing out whatever information he or she thinks will satisfy the interrogator. Nonetheless, the use of some psychological treatment can prove useful and is not considered torture. This includes disrupting the subject's circadian rhythms by keeping lights on and spacing food at odd intervals, or solitary confinement. These steps are designed to weaken the subject's will to resist without causing any real damage.[15]

During the cold war, successful interrogations of defectors and prisoners did indeed produce useful intelligence, much of it at a rather low level. During my Air Force assignment in Korea in 1958, for example, defectors from North Korea were able to provide useful information about North Korean equipment and training methods. We only had to be careful to keep the defectors out of the hands of our South Korean colleagues, who seemed to prefer harsher interrogations that sometimes rendered the subjects incapable of speech.

Milt Bearden and Jim Risen cite the infamous case of Soviet KGB officer Yuri Nosenko, who defected to the United States in 1964 and was held as a virtual prisoner in CIA facilities for three years because James Angleton, then head of counterintelligence at the CIA, was convinced that Nosenko was a "provocation," sent to the United States to feed the CIA false information.[16] Angleton had been deceived by an earlier defector, Anatoly Golytsin, who said that all defectors who came after him would be double agents. Although Nosenko provided good intelligence during interrogation, he was not believed until it was too late. Angleton then went on a hunt for Soviet moles within the CIA, which only ended when he was fired by DCI Bill Colby. Even after he left the CIA, Angleton would call in to the CIA Operations Center occasionally to report sightings of foreign agents and demand that action be taken to round them up.

INTERROGATION AND AL QAEDA

Surprisingly, interrogation has been a useful tool in collecting counterintelligence information about al Qaeda, despite the fact that these people are supposed to be fanatics unwilling to cooperate in any way with the infidel West. According to press reports, several of the key al Qaeda leaders captured in Afghanistan or Pakistan, including Ramzi bin Al-Shib, and Abu Zubaydah have been willing to talk to interrogators. Although it is impossible to tell from these reports the circumstances of these interrogations or the nature of the intelligence revealed, government spokesmen have indicated that the subjects have been cooperative.

This became apparent in June 2003 when Attorney General John Ashcroft announced that the interrogation of Khalid Shaikh Mohammed, another of the key al Qaeda leaders captured in Pakistan after 9/11, had led to the arrest of Iyman Faris, a naturalized U.S. citizen born in Kashmir, who had been actively seeking terrorist targets in New York, including the Brooklyn Bridge.[17] Faris, a truck driver from Columbus, Ohio, had been recruited before the 9/11 attacks, but only became active in terrorist plotting in 2002.

According to press reports, Faris was not acting alone. Based on the discovery of the plot, security was tightened around the bridge and other possible targets leading Faris to determine that the planned attack could not succeed. He reportedly then sent a message to al Qaeda that "the weather was too hot," meaning that the plot was unworkable. Faris received a 20-year jail sentence after a plea bargain to avoid a trial and a potentially stiffer penalty.

While key al Qaeda leaders have provided useful intelligence after their capture, this is less certain in regard to the Taliban fighters captured during the Afghan campaign and taken to a prisoner of war camp set up on the Guantanamo Bay Naval base operated by the United States in Cuba. Guantanamo is a relic of the pre-Castro period, and actually was established after the Spanish-American War. Fidel Castro has never tried to force the United States out of this bastion, probably because he would have a hard time doing it. The advantage of using Guantanamo is that it is a technically foreign territory and the prisoners held there are not subject to the protection of the U.S. Constitution or U.S. laws.

It is not likely that we will learn the details of whatever was acquired during interrogation of these prisoners, although the FBI says that it has gathered useful intelligence. Once released, the prisoners are likely to denigrate the United States for their treatment and exaggerate the situation in which they found themselves, but as fighters for the Taliban, they won't receive much sympathy in the United States. Nonetheless, civil libertarians, concerned that many of the prisoners are being punished without trial, have been seeking some way to have them released. In 2003, the International Red Cross determined that the prisoners were suffering from mental diseases brought on by the uncertainty of their situation, but the Bush administration was not, at the time, prepared to permit their release.

ENEMY COMBATANTS

Perhaps even more troubling is the use of presidential power to declare a person an "enemy combatant," which enables the government to detain the person without benefit of due process. Two U.S. persons were given this status after 9/11, including Jose Padilla, a U.S. citizen, who had converted to Islam while in prison and Yasir Hamdi, a U.S. citizen captured in

Afghanistan. Padilla was alleged to be trying to build a dirty bomb, although the evidence revealed in the press was not convincing. Hamdi was supposed to be a Taliban fighter. Both were jailed in military prisons without benefit of counsel and in theory could be held indefinitely. In June 2003, a third person, Ali al-Marri, was declared an enemy combatant and taken from a federal jail, where he was being held on terrorism charges, to an unidentified military prison. Al-Marri, a citizen of Qatar living in Peoria, Illinois, was supposedly an al Qaeda fighter.[18]

The situation of those detained in the United States for immigration violations has produced another set of problems. After 9/11, the attorney general ordered that all male noncitizens of Middle Eastern descent over the age of 16 had to register with immigration officials, be photographed and fingerprinted, and prove that they were in the country legally.[19] Of the approximately 82,000 who registered, about 13,000 proved to have some irregularity in their status and were either deported or faced with deportation proceedings. Many had roots in their communities, were married to American citizens, and believed that they were here legally. Before 9/11, these kinds of visa discrepancies would have been considered administrative issues, but the crackdown turned them into criminal proceedings and led to the detention of a great many otherwise-innocent people.

NO APOLOGIES

In June 2003, Glen A. Fine, the inspector general of the Justice Department, issued a report on the situation noting that of the 762 men arrested after 9/11, few had ties to terrorism, but they had been held in "harsh conditions" without access to lawyers, and some had suffered physical and verbal abuse.[20] After the report was issued, the Justice Department said that it would tighten up the rules on arresting and detaining terror suspects, but the attorney general himself said in public testimony that he made no apologies for what had happened.

In December 2003, the Syracuse University Transactional Records Access Clearinghouse (TRAC) released a report confirming that only a handful of people have received long sentences for involvement in terrorism.[21] In the two years since 9/11, about 6,400 people were somehow suspected of terrorism, but only about one-third of that number were actually charged, and 879 were actually convicted. The median prison sentence in these cases was only 14 days, suggesting that most of the cases did not really involve terrorism at all. Only five people were sentenced to lengthy prison terms. For its part, the government argued that the short sentences meant that terrorists had been stopped well before they had actually carried out their planned operations, while civil libertarians thought the numbers meant that in most cases, prosecutors really had no evidence to support the charges.

On June 18, 2003, President Bush issued a new policy on racial profiling, restricting its use in regular criminal cases, but permitting officials to detain people of a particular "ethnicity" if it appeared that person of a similar background had been engaged in terrorist activity.[22] This policy confirmed the procedures for registering men of Middle Eastern background or any other ethnic group that the government believed was a potential threat. Of course civil libertarians in the United States tried to oppose these racial and ethnic crackdowns, but with little success.

THE USA PATRIOT ACT

The Congress has given the government several tools to fight terrorism and its supporters through the USA Patriot Act, passed rapidly after 9/11 and signed into law by President George W. Bush in October 2001. The Patriot Act gave the government, especially the FBI and the intelligence agencies, increased authority to put suspected terrorists under surveillance, reinforced money-laundering laws, and created a new series of federal crimes related to terrorism so that they could be dealt with at the federal rather than the state level.[23]

The Patriot Act cut some of the barriers between intelligence and law enforcement by amending and strengthening the Foreign Intelligence Surveillance Act (FISA), and permitted increased surveillance of suspected terrorists or foreign agents. Some of the provisions of the Patriot Act have a "sunset clause" which will end the increased governmental powers at the end of 2005. Efforts by the Bush administration to extend and strengthen the Patriot Act in 2003 failed to achieve much support in the Congress, although that could change if there were another terrorist spectacular as on 9/11.

DEFENSIVE MEASURES

The various active or positive counterintelligence operations are usually just one side of the coin. Defensive measures are also important in combating terrorism, espionage, and global crime. In the intelligence world, as in the rest of government and the private sector, defensive measures are considered to be a security rather than a counterintelligence issue, but they are critical, nonetheless.

The first priority of intelligence in countering espionage is to make sure that the intelligence workforce is dependable, loyal, and not vulnerable to recruitment by hostile intelligence services. This means that each and every employee, from the directors to the cleaning forces, have to be carefully and individually scrutinized, their backgrounds checked, their psychological makeup examined, and their credentials verified. It is a time-consuming and expensive process, but we know it works. In the entire history of U.S.

intelligence, the number of traitors has been relatively low compared to many other countries and experience shows that the U.S. Intelligence Community maintains one of the most stable workforces anywhere.

For the intelligence workers, however, it means that in order to gain employment, they must give up certain rights of freedom and privacy that are well protected in the private sector and even in other parts of government. The intelligence workers agree to undergo periodic polygraph interviews, make their personal and financial histories available, maintain the secrecy of their work even after they leave the service, and subject themselves to possible dismissal by senior management without cause. In reality, the system is far less draconian than it sounds and thousands of young people over the past few years have tried desperately to get into it, although only a relative handful have been hired.

DIVERSITY OF THE WORKFORCE

One serious issue has been the diversity of the workforce. In the period after 9/11, the CIA as well as the other agencies, pushed to attract candidates with Middle Eastern and Asian backgrounds, but it was not clear that potential recruits could pass the rigorous background screening, especially if they still had close relatives living abroad in countries not closely allied with the U.S. During the cold war, despite the need to attract new hires with Eastern European and Soviet ethnic roots, security officials feared that having close relatives behind the Iron Curtain could make a potential recruit vulnerable to blackmail or pressure from hostile intelligence services.

Similar biases affected candidates for many years who were homosexual, although in the 1980s, the leaders of both the CIA and NSA determined that sexual orientation should not be a barrier to hiring, because open admission of homosexuality would prevent the threat of blackmail. Other kinds of biases affected minority candidates, especially from the black community, which found few role models in the upper ranks of the agency. Although the intelligence agencies do not release many statistics about the work force, it looks as if some of these problems are slowly being overcome.

Once on board, intelligence professionals, clerical staff, and support personnel all have to be trained in proper security procedures, which are fairly well standardized throughout the IC. A key factor in security is "security awareness," looking out for problems that might arise, even if it means making a derogatory report about a fellow employee. In the case of Aldrich Ames, for example, several of his co-workers reported that they were concerned about his behavior, although they couldn't be sure what he was up to. If security officials had been more scrupulous in following through, Ames might have been stopped earlier in his career as a Russian spy.

PHYSICAL SECURITY

Physical security is important in intelligence work, but no more so than in the private sector. The U.S. Intelligence Community protects its facilities in much the same way as any high-tech firm would. In fact, in my experience (admittedly anecdotal), some high-tech firms I have visited seem to have more rigorous barrier entry systems and surveillance controls than in government. This is not so much a problem for the CIA or NSA which are located in areas where the general public does not have much contact with them and where they do not entertain visitors other than those on official business. For years at CIA, we arranged visits by college-age school groups, but only under carefully controlled situations. Since 9/11, security has been tightened and such visits have been restricted.

The FBI, because it allows tourists to visit, although in carefully controlled tours, has to be more careful about visitors, as do some of the other government agencies that regularly interact with the public. Over the past decades, security has gradually tightened in all government facilities, including the Capitol Building, because of random acts of violence as well as the general threat of terrorism.

While security in U.S. facilities can be controlled, the situation is a lot more problematic overseas. U.S. embassies, which house most of the intelligence activities of the United States outside the country, have traditionally been designed to be open and accessible, even though security studies have shown them to be vulnerable to penetration and to terrorism. That was brought home to the CIA in 1983 when the U.S. Embassy in Beirut, Lebanon was bombed and almost the entire CIA station was lost.[24] After the al Qaeda bombings of the U.S. embassies in Kenya and Tanzania in 1998, the Department of State, which had been lukewarm about beefing up security at embassies abroad, finally realized that diplomacy had to give way to protection. New U.S. embassies, such as the rebuilt one in Kenya or the new one in Ottawa, Canada reflect the heightened awareness of the need for security.

TRACKING PRIVATE CITIZENS

One of the most controversial aspects of the government's security measures concerns efforts to collect and analyze data about private individuals to determine if they might be involved in terrorism in some way. A storm of controversy erupted in 2002 when it became known that the Defense Advanced Research Projects Agency (DARPA), a Pentagon internal think-tank and new projects development office, was trying to develop a system for collecting data on private citizens. The project was headed by retired Rear-Admiral John Poindexter, who had been a key figure in the Iran-Contra Affair during the Reagan administration. Poindexter had been indicted in that particular scandal, but was pardoned by President George H. W. Bush. His role in the new project only fueled the controversy.

The new project, called at first the "Terrorist Information Awareness" system involved a feasibility study to try to learn if there was sufficient data in already existing databases to track persons who might be involved in terrorism. When the project's existence became public, there was a great outcry about what appeared to be a potential invasion of individual privacy. Several U.S. senators, including some conservatives, immediately introduced legislation to try to derail the project. In order to keep the project going, the Pentagon changed the name of the effort to the "Total Information Awareness" system and said that nothing would be implemented until the Congress had a chance to review it. In the end, the project was killed and Admiral Poindexter resigned.

Meanwhile, other personal data collection systems were quietly being put into place to do much the same sort of thing. According to press reports, the FBI is putting together a "Terrorism and Intelligence Data Information Sharing Data Mart" to link data from state and local police systems into a system that can be mined for possible patterns of terrorism.[25] Another FBI database is tracking violent gangs with a potential for terrorism, as well as extremists of various stripes. A police intelligence network called RISSNET has been established to track anyone suspected of a crime, whether or not the individual had been convicted. The list reportedly includes a wide range of people, from peace demonstrators to motorcycle gangs and even the gun lobby.

THE "DO NOT FLY" LIST

The Transportation Security Administration (TSA), in addition to running the security systems at U.S. airports, has developed a database to track all passengers flying in and out of the United States and has created a "do not fly" list to keep potential terrorists from using commercial aircraft for any reason. This has had some unfortunate consequences. Variations in the way names are spelled, especially in transliteration from Arabic or other Middle Eastern languages, has forced some people to undergo enhanced security screenings at airports just because their names resemble those on the "do not fly" list. Efforts to correct the system seem to be fruitless, although the TSA did announce in June 2003 that persons listed in error could have their names removed if they submitted three certified forms of identification directly to the TSA.[26] Other names that appear in the databases may be there in error, and many people may be in these databases without their knowledge and with no way to correct the problem.

One potential solution to this would be to establish a national identity system, similar to those used in many European countries, in which each person resident in the United States would have a standardized photo ID card which would have behind it a complete dossier on the person that could be checked if needed. The individual would have the opportunity to review the file periodically to make sure that there were no errors in it. In that sense, the system would resemble the credit check system already in place in the United States. Anyone who wants to see his or her credit file can apply to review it, at no charge, and make necessary corrections to it. It may come as a surprise to those who have not yet done this to find out just how much personal information is contained in these credit files. They show what could be done if the government decided to become more intrusive in this regard.

PUBLIC REACTION

It seems clear from the public's reaction to suggestions about a national identity card or Total Information Awareness that the American people are not willing to trade privacy for security. Although they might have been willing to make such a trade-off immediately after 9/11, as soon as things calmed down a bit and reality set in, the more normal reaction to increased government intrusion into private lives returned. This suggests that any effort to create an internal security system, however sensible it might look on paper, will not be accepted by Americans who value their privacy and individual freedoms more than they seem to fear terrorism or other threats. In many European countries—and around the globe—the traditions are quite different. The right to privacy has never existed at the same level as in the United States, so internal security systems, national ID cards, internal passports, and other controls have long been accepted. But not here.

While creating a new internal security service may make sense to intelligence veterans such as General Odom—especially if there were a total overhaul of the American intelligence system, as he recommends—the political reality in the United States is that the creation of an internal security service is not likely to gain popular support. Odom does not deal with such sensitive issues as protection of privacy and civil rights nor does he suggest how such a system might be controlled and regulated. The course taken by the FBI to create a carefully monitored internal intelligence system within the Bureau, still in the infant stages in 2003, is probably the best chance we have of enhancing national security while protecting American freedoms.

8

Special Operations

Throughout American history, presidents have used secret intelligence resources to support U.S. foreign and security policy abroad. These resources have been designed to use secret agents and operations to carry out policy in such a way that the direct hand of the United States was hidden and that the president could deny knowledge of the operation. These operations are not for collecting and analyzing intelligence. In the United States, this kind of activity has come to be called covert action; some who oppose such action call it "dirty tricks."

U.S. covert action operations are primarily run by secret agents who are recruited to carry out particular tasks rather than to serve as spies. They may be recruiting and training guerrilla fighters, carrying out political or economic operations, they may be involved in deception operations to fool an enemy, or they could be circulating disinformation—usually false information wrapped around a nugget of truth—to discredit an adversary or enhance our own image. Guerrillas in turn could be carrying out sabotage operations or partisan warfare. The aim of the covert action operator is to hide the hand of the United States in the operations. The CIA has learned over time, however, that any covert action is probably doomed to failure unless it is part of some larger scheme of foreign policy. Covert action operations, by themselves, are rarely successful.

Special operations work in much the same way, except that the United States uses its own troops to carry out unconventional warfare, usually in conjunction with some irregular force we are trying to support. Special ops are often designed to supplement ongoing regular military operations, although they can certainly be carried out by themselves. American military forces could arm and train partisans while fighting side-by-side with them. Usually, the role of the United States in such special ops cannot be hidden, even though the American forces try to look as much like their foreign compatriots as they can. For example, in the war against the Taliban in Afghanistan in 2001, the Green Berets wore local dress and grew beards to resemble their counterparts in the U.S.-backed Northern Alliance, although they fooled no one with these disguises.[1] This procedure did allow them, however, to blend in to reduce attention to their presence. Such operations have been used throughout U.S. history, although they only became institutionalized in the U.S. military after World War II as Special Forces, the Green Berets, and in unique service units such as the Army's Delta Force, the Navy Seals, and the Air Commandos. The United States has considerable experience with covert action and special operations, and we know that these kinds of operations can work to protect the nation against its foreign enemies. Whether or not covert action and special operations can work for homeland security has yet to be determined, but it appears that the two could be useful, at least overseas.

In working toward homeland security, there are several policy goals for the federal government as well as for first responders at the state and local levels, including the private sector. These include *detection* to root out threats, *prosecution* to bring offenders to justice, and *prevention* to set up defensive barriers. Taking a page from the Israeli government's security policies in fighting against terrorists harbored among Israel's Arab neighbors, policy options might also include *preemption* to take out terrorists or other threats before they can strike, and *retaliation* to strike back at the enemy to make any attack very costly. If the United States adopts policies of preemption and retaliation, then the use of covert action and special military operations would seem to be well suited for such tasks.

EARLY USE OF SPECIAL OPS

In the wars against the Taliban in Afghanistan and Saddam Hussein in Iraq, special ops received a good deal of attention from the media, as if it had just been invented. In fact, Americans have been using such unconventional tactics since the earliest days of the republic. The planners of the revolution against British rule in Colonial America established a secret committee to gather arms and ammunition in case there was a confrontation with the British regulars who occupied Boston after the French and Indian Wars. During the Revolutionary War, irregular military units harassed the British, who complained that the Americans fought like Indians, rather than in the European fashion the British expected.

Robin Moore, writing about the U.S. Green Berets in Afghanistan, mentions Rogers' Rangers, a Revolutionary War precursor of today's special operations forces.[2] As it turns out, Rogers' Rangers were Americans who fought for the British in the French and Indian War. Rogers, a Tory in the Revolutionary War, later tried to reconstitute the Rangers to fight with the British against the Revolution, but with little success. Other irregular groups, such as Knowlton's Rangers, did fight on the American side.[3]

George Washington understood that his only hope of winning against the British required using secret means to deceive, confuse, and harass them, while at the same time secretly seeking foreign assistance against the King's forces. Washington used covert action to convince the British that his forces were too weak to fight, or sometimes that they were too strong to ignore. In one of the more famous cases in December 1776, Washington sent a secret agent, a supposedly Tory butcher named John Honeyman, across the Delaware to report to Hessian soldiers near Trenton that Washington's rag-tag army could not possibly attack them. The Hessians took time off to celebrate Christmas and Washington's forces fell on them, defeating them at Trenton and Princeton, giving the colonials their first significant victories in battle, and laying the groundwork for the French to come in on the American side.

After the Revolution, the newly created nation sought to expand its power and territory, partly through the use of secret agents dispatched right from the White House to bribe, cajole, or organize settlers in foreign-held territory on behalf of the United States. Thomas Jefferson thought various Indian tribes might be bought off in this way and James Madison sent agents to foment uprisings in the Spanish-held Floridas so that Americans could come to the aid of the insurgents and gain the territory. Unfortunately, irregulars under former Georgia Governor George Matthews got into trouble around St. Augustine and the U.S. government had to plead with the Spanish for their release.[4]

SPY COMPANIES

In the Mexican War in 1846, General Winfield Scott, "Old Fuss and Feathers" as he was known to the troops, landed his forces at Veracruz and established what he called "spy companies" of Mexicans, many of whom were willing to cooperate with the "Yanquis" after they had been liberated from jail by the invading Americans. This was a combination of intelligence and guerrilla warfare, as the spy companies not only served as scouts, but also as foragers and saboteurs.[5]

During the U.S. Civil War, both sides had forces set up either for intelligence or for special operations. The most famous unit was probably that of

Confederate John S. Mosby, whose raiders struck into Federal forces throughout the war. President Lincoln, meanwhile, used covert action to prevent the European states from recognizing the Confederacy as a legitimate nation. Lincoln's agents sabotaged ships and arms destined for the South, and spread propaganda and disinformation against the rebels.[6]

No U.S. president was more involved with both covert action and special operations than Theodore Roosevelt, who secretly encouraged Panamanian revolutionaries in their effort to throw off Colombian rule and gain independence for the Isthmian state. Of course, Roosevelt had won fame during the Spanish American War as the leader of the Rough Riders, volunteer cavalry in the battles to free Cuba. His support for the Panamanian revolution won the United States the right to occupy the Canal Zone and build the Panama Canal, a sore point with Panama for nearly a century.[7]

ROOTS IN WORLD WAR II

The systems we have today for covert action and special operations all have their roots in World War II. There were many examples during the war—far too many to relate here—but the Office of Strategic Services (OSS), William "Wild Bill" Donovan's intelligence organization, began a tradition of secret operations that carried over into the CIA. Future CIA Directors Bill Colby and Bill Casey were both OSS covert action hands. Colby was part of a Jedburgh guerrilla team that parachuted into Nazi-occupied Norway, while Casey ran operations to support the French resistance before the invasion of Normandy. Their stories are well known, but there is another OSS operative whose activities have recently become public and whose story illustrates quite well how special operations really work.

Robert Kehoe was a young army sergeant assigned to the OSS in 1944 and who parachuted under Nazi machine-gun fire into occupied France to support partisans of the French resistance and prepare for Allied troops to move into western France after the Normandy landings.[8] Kehoe and the French partisans evaded Nazi search parties, set up communications nets, and carried out sabotage missions, all with the Nazis hot on their heels. His tale has appeared in the CIA unclassified journal *Studies in Intelligence* and makes clear how dangerous and difficult these operations can be. Kehoe was one of our instructors when I undertook my early training in the CIA and seemed to be a rather academic and bookish person. None of us realized at the time the incredible daring he had shown during his OSS days; he never mentioned any of this to us at the time.

While General Douglas MacArthur and Admiral Chester Nimitz, who ran the war in the Pacific against Japan, wanted nothing to do with the OSS, the outfit was nonetheless engaged in the China-Burma-India theater of operations under General "Vinegar" Joe Stillwell. The OSS units were sent in to support guerrilla operations against Japanese army forces in the region. These operations spread throughout the area and involved interaction with nationalist and communists elements in China, and in Vietnam, then part of French Indochina.[9]

THE COLD WAR HEATS UP

After World War II, when the CIA was created, it became the action agency for covert action as the cold war began to heat up. In 1948, the new agency was asked to keep the Italian Communist Party from winning an open and free election. Using tactics that would have been well known to big city politicans in America, the CIA campaigned secretly for the Christian Democrats. The Soviets tried to aid the Communists, but without success. This early victory in the cold war was the beginning of CIA's covert action mandate and led to clandestine operations throughout the period, albeit with mixed results.[10]

After General MacArthur's daring landing at Inchon, South Korea in 1950, special operations and covert action were used to support the UN Command in relieving U.S. and South Korean military units that had been driven into a defensive perimeter at the South Korean port city of Pusan. In 1958, I was assigned to an Air Force intelligence collection unit located outside Seoul and learned later that the unit had at one time been run by the mysterious "Mr. Nichols." His operations had included sending agents into North Korea by boat from Inchon and allegedly kidnapping North Koreans to bring south for interrogation. By 1958, all these operations had ended, but the fleet of boats used for the operations remained at Inchon— although most were in need of repair.

Military-style covert action figured into several operations in Europe during the early post–World War II period. The CIA supported Greek partisans who were working to prevent a Communist takeover. In my early days in the agency, I met several officers who had taken part in air drops to the partisans, kicking supplies out of old World War II aircraft to the guerrilla fighters. Later, as a member of the Association of Former Intelligence Officers, I learned of other CIA operations, including one in which a French-speaking officer had been parachuted into Dien Bien Phu in Indochina, to assist the French forces in their failing operation to hold on to their colonial empire in the region.

The notion of using unconventional tactics against our main enemy in the cold war, the Soviet Union, dates back to a 1955 National Security Council directive (these were called, in typical Washington bureaucratese, "non-skids") that directed the CIA to use political action, propaganda, subversion, support for underground and guerrilla movements, and deception against world communism, which meant in those days, the USSR, the Peoples Republic of China (PRC), and their allies.[11] At the time, the U.S.

military were beginning to create an unconventional force, although the emphasis in the military sector continued to rely on the use of "massive retaliation," strategic bombers and later strategic missiles, to deter any attack on the United States.[12]

SPECIAL FORCES

In 1952, the U.S. Army established the Tenth Special Forces group, and the Navy set up the Sea-Air-Land teams (Seals), while the Air Force created a small Air Commando force.[13] Tom Clancy, in one of his nonfiction works, has written a short history of these forces, pointing out that they were so small, at first, with such small budgets, that even Pentagon leaders did not fuss about the possibility that these forces might tred on the turf of conventional units. Set up originally to work with so-called "stay behind" guerrillas in the event of a Soviet invasion of Western Europe, the Special Forces were eventually targeted against Communist insurgents in the spreading "wars of liberation" as former imperial powers gave up or abandoned their colonial holdings. The most famous of these wars took place in the former French Indochina, at first in Vietnam and Laos, and later in Cambodia. The battles in Vietnam and Laos showed that CIA covert action units and the military Special Forces could work together against a common enemy, although at the time it was seen more as competition than cooperation.

PLAUSIBLE DENIAL

Meanwhile, the CIA was working to carry out the White House mandate to battle World Communism through the use of covert action. Much has been written about these activities, a great deal of it critical of the CIA, as if it had chosen to run these operations without the direction or approval of the president. In fact, the operations were designed to keep the president's hands clean, making it appear that the U.S. government was not sponsoring the operations at all, thus giving the president "plausible deniability" so he could say that he was not aware of the secret activities. In reality, of course, the CIA's involvement in the operations was hard to hide, but the deniability factor seems to have worked. The few historians who write about intelligence have seen these operations as the work of a secret government within the CIA, which somehow raised money for them and ran them without approval from either the White House or the Congress.[14]

As later investigations showed, the CIA was receiving directions for these operations from secret White House committees, operated usually below the president's level but including his close advisers, with the support of key members of Congress, some of whom asked not to be given details of the planned activities. There was no secret government, but the politicians were not unhappy that the CIA had to take the heat, especially when one of the operations went sour.[15]

More and more details of these operations have been revealed over the years, based in part on an agreement by several DCIs to declassify the documents and make the material available to the public. In 2003, for example, documents relating to the overthrow of the elected government of Guatemala under Jacobo Arbenz Guzman in 1954 began to appear on the public record. While the CIA is proud of having released the formerly classified information, at this rate contemporary historians will have a tough time learning about more recent events. Nonetheless, most of the information is sufficiently well known for us to draw some lessons from the cold war covert action experience.

LESSONS LEARNED

Just as in the case of espionage operations, most covert action is directed by intelligence agency case officers, but they rarely do the actual work. This falls to trusted agents; their task is to find the resources and manage the operations so that the hand of the United States is not visible. These agents, sometimes called "agents of influence" to distinguish them from the agents who steal information, are recruited and handled in much the same way as their "spy"counterparts, but their goals are different. These action agents are the ones who pass money, arms, or other assistance to groups the CIA is trying to support, while avoiding the attention of the opposition or local security services that might get in the way of their operations.

All through the cold war, secret operations maintained the mandate stated in the original presidential directive, but the specifics were always coordinated with the White House committee and reported to the key members of Congress, who would make sure the money was there when it was needed. The results of these operations were a mixed bag; while some of them may have made sense to policy makers at the time, to the modern observer they seem short-sighted, perhaps even foolish and counterproductive. For example, the overthrow of Arbenz in Guatemala, driven by the mistaken belief that he was a Communist with ties to Moscow, rather than a reformer who had popular appeal, led to decades of civil war in a country that has yet to recover fully from the violence and economic ruin of this period.

The rise of the theocracy that still rules Iran, and which has become a citadel of anti-American activity in the area, could be traced back to the CIA operations in 1953 that led to the ouster of leftist Prime Minister Mohammed Mossadegh. The CIA helped return Shah Reza Pahlavi to his throne, but the vacillating Shah tried to be both a benign and popular dictator, and succeeded at being neither benign nor popular. His ouster by

Islamic radicals in 1978 and the rise of the theocracy under Ayatollah Khomeini might not have been possible if true democracy had been allowed to flourish in Iran. At the time, however, Mossadegh's plans to nationalize American and British oil interests in Iran, coupled with fear of Soviet encroachment into the northern part of the country, drove U.S. policy without heed to its long-term consequences.

A CONSISTENT ERROR

Another consistent error in covert action operations is the belief that an operation that works in one place will work equally well elsewhere. Policy planners tried unsuccessfully to bring down Sukarno in Indonesia and Fidel Castro in Cuba using the methods that had worked for them in Iran and Guatemala. The full story of the failure in Indonesia has never been released, although we know enough to conclude that policy officials pushed for Sukarno's ouster in 1958 in the face of objections from the CIA, but the result was a disaster after covert operators bowed to White House pressure. Since Indonesian General Suharto was able to drive Sukarno from power later, achieving independently what the United States wanted, the case has not received the same attention as the more notable covert action failure in Cuba.

The attempt to oust Castro began during the Eisenhower administration, based on the notion that given the opportunity, the people of Cuba would rise up to drive out the new Communist dictator. Intelligence analysis during this period drew the opposite conclusion: that the Cubans who were left on the island after many middle- and upper-class people were either driven into exile or killed, supported Castro's revolution. Nonetheless, the plan to land a militia of Cuban exiles developed a life of its own, spurred by the CIA's Director of Plans (Operations) Richard Bissell, who was deeply committed to the plan. Bissell defended the plan, refusing to recognize its flaws and problems, even though some of the supposedly secret action had begun to leak out. President Kennedy, who inherited the plan as well as DCI Allen Dulles and Bissell, let it proceed, trusting that the intelligence professionals at the CIA actually knew what they were doing.

Of course, the invasion at the Bay of Pigs was a total disaster. The poorly trained and equipped exiles hit the beach and were quickly wrapped up by Castro's forces. The air cover provided by the CIA had little effect, and no one rose up within Cuba to aid the invaders. There were far-reaching consequences. Dulles and Bissell were forced to resign and the CIA's credibility took a severe blow, even though the intelligence analysts had correctly forecast what would happen. In the face of this challenge, Castro sought increased aid from the Soviet Union, leading eventually to the Cuban Missile Crisis. Some critics of the Kennedy administration still argued years later that the president should have used regular United

States military forces to back the invasion, but this might have led to a wider conflict for which the United States was, at the time, ill prepared.[16]

COMPETING FOR HEARTS AND MINDS

In the years after this defeat, the CIA continued its covert action campaign, as the agency sought to compete with the Soviets for the hearts and minds of the uncommitted nations in the Third World. Although the United States and the Soviets never actually confronted each other directly, except perhaps over Cuba, American and Soviet surrogates did fight on a variety of fronts in Southeast Asia, in Africa, and in Latin America. Most of this activity was hardly covert and did little to hide the hands of the intelligence services on both sides.

In the United States, press revelations about these activities, as well as efforts to infiltrate or stop the antiwar movement during the Vietnam period, led to growing concerns that, as Senator Frank Church charged, the CIA was a "rogue elephant," running amok, planning and carrying out secret operations without oversight or control. There were allegations of attempted assassinations, drug experiments, infiltration of peace and student groups, and secret funding of extremist groups. The final allegation, that the CIA had tried to overthrow the democratically elected government of Salvador Allende in Chile in 1973, led Church and counterparts in the House of Representatives under Congressman Otis Pike to hold hearings to find out the truth. These hearings mark a watershed in both the management and control of secret operations in the United States.

CONGRESSIONAL OVERSIGHT

When congressional investigators learned that the CIA's secret operations were all directed by the White House—whether controlled by Republicans or Democrats—and supported by key members of Congress, they were probably shocked. It was not what they had been led to believe over the years. Even the overthrow of Allende could not be laid at the feet of the CIA, although President Nixon had pushed the DCI Richard Helms to bring down Allende's leftist regime. The CIA had indeed sought to encourage Allende's ouster, but General Augusto Pinochet, Allende's army chief, told agency operatives that he neither needed their advice nor their weapons. Although Allende probably committed suicide in the Casa Moneda, the CIA is still blamed by some historians for his death as well as the coup against him.[17]

Still, the results of the Church and Pike Committee investigations led both Houses of Congress to establish Intelligence Oversight Committees. This move made a great deal of sense, but it ended the tradition laid down by the Founding Fathers that intelligence, especially secret operations, was an executive function and that congressional involvement would jeopardize secrecy. Legislation was passed that required the president, through the DCI, to inform the Intelligence Oversight Committees of planned secret operations on a timely basis. Although the committees could not veto the operations, they could cut funding or intervene with the president if they disagreed with the plans.

In addition, President Gerald Ford issued the first Presidential Executive Order defining the roles of the various agencies in the Intelligence Community, ratifying the role of the DCI as chief intelligence officer, and prohibiting assassinations and drug experimentation. Presidents Carter and Reagan issued similar versions of this order, serving as a reminder to the Congress that intelligence and secret operations remained an Executive Branch function, efforts by the committees to micromanage the intelligence process notwithstanding. Controversy over intelligence operations and management has continued unabated ever since the oversight system was established in 1976.

HOSTAGES IN IRAN

In 1979, after the fall of the Shah of Iran and the rise of the theocracy, the CIA warned President Carter and the State Department that if the United States were to provide asylum to the terminally ill Reza Pahlavi, radical elements in Iran might well invade the U.S. Embassy in Tehran. The warning went unheeded. When the Shah entered the United States for treatment after spending brief exiles in Egypt and Panama, radical young zealots invaded the U.S. Embassy and took the staff hostage. Unfortunately, the secret files, including those of the CIA station, which would normally have been destroyed after the warning, were kept in the safes until the radicals were at the gates. There was too little time to burn the files, so they were shredded. Later, the Iranian revolutionaries, using a great deal of patience, were able to reconstruct some of the secret material.

Meanwhile, several embassy officers were able to take refuge in the Canadian Embassy nearby and the CIA mounted a rescue operation which was successful but not known to the public until many years later when the CIA chief of the operation, Antonio Mendez, was able to recount the adventure in a book.[18] Mendez, undercover as a Canadian film producer, actually flew into Iran, despite the danger of discovery, and was able to exfiltrate the officers, disguising them as part of his film crew.

Although some of the hostages at the U.S. Embassy were released soon after the takeover, most were held prisoner. Rumors surfaced years later that Ayatollah Khomeini, Iran's spiritual and political leader, wanted to free the hostages but was afraid to give the order for fear that the Iranian guards might not obey him and make him look weak.

A FAILED RESCUE ATTEMPT

As the hostage crisis dragged on, the Carter administration decided to mount an operation to rescue the hostages, using a combination of U.S. Army Delta Force commandos, a new unit of the Special Forces, and CIA operatives. It was poorly planned, not well rehearsed, underequipped with the wrong aircraft and crews, and turned into a major disaster for the Carter White House. Although CIA agents on the ground in Tehran had confirmed the location of the hostages and arranged to get them to the soccer field that was to be the rescue site, the military taskforce never reached the city.

By the time the helicopters reached Desert One, the landing and refueling site outside Tehran, several of the helicopters had been forced to drop out due to a sand storm and mechanical difficulties. Colonel Charlie Beckwith, the Delta Force commander, determined that he had too few copters to continue the mission and decided to abort. In the process, a helicopter crashed into the refueling aircraft on the ground, several soldiers were killed, and President Carter had to report on television to the American people that the mission had failed. It was a blow from which his administration never recovered. The hostages were dispersed after the failed rescue attempt to prevent another try and were held prisoner until President Reagan took his oath of office as Carter's successor nearly a year later.

In writing about this mission, General William Odom blames the failed rescue on poor intelligence from the CIA, but clearly the mission should have been better planned and rehearsed with a greater number of properly prepared helicopters to take account of the possibility of weather or mechanical failures. Apparently the Carter administration tried to manage the operation quietly for fear that it would leak to the press and would be stopped before it even got started. President Carter might have been better off politically if that had happened.

General Odom reports that in the wake of the failure, the U.S. Army developed its own clandestine operational capability, called the Intelligence Support Activity (ISA), to make sure it had the capacity to support future special operations without having to rely on the CIA.[19] In addition, an army general was assigned to the CIA's Directorate of Operations to make sure that CIA covert action in support of military special operations was properly planned and coordinated. Odom is scathing in his criticism of the CIA's lack of interest in supporting the military in this regard, but my personal experience is quite different. I knew several of the officers involved in handling liaisons with the military, and they were both eager and competent in making sure there was good cooperation. This was made evident in the Balkans and in Afghanistan after 9/11.

DRIVING THE SOVIETS FROM AFGHANISTAN

The last vestige of traditional cold war covert action may have been demonstrated earlier in Afghanistan as the Reagan administration sought to drive the Soviets, still the "main enemy," from their occupation of that country. The Soviets had invaded Afghanistan in 1979 to prop up a failing Communist regime which had seized power after a military coup had ousted King Zahir Shah some years before. Soviet political leaders, concerned about developments in the Soviet Republics on their southern border, and following the Brezhnev Doctrine to support Marxist-Leninist regimes, saw great value in keeping Afghanistan within its sphere of influence. The Soviets treated Afghanistan as a buffer state in the same way that it maintained control over its Eastern European empire in the West. The Reagan administration was determined to bring all of it down.

In order to weaken the Soviet hold on Afghanistan, which was then ruled by Achmed Najibullah (Najib), the former chief of Afghan intelligence (KHAD), the CIA enlisted the aid of Pakistan's intelligence and security service, the Interservices Intelligence Directorate (ISI).[20] The aim of the CIA/ISI operation was to try to unite the various tribal factions and warlords opposed to the Soviet presence into a coalition. The combined groups would then be supplied with Soviet-style arms and ammunition, passed through the CIA and ISI to the fighters, called the *mujahideen*, or sometimes just the *muj*.

The operation had really begun at the end of the Carter administration, but Milt Bearden, the CIA officer who ran the operation, pointed out that the effort bore little fruit until Reagan's second term.[21] The factions were not eager to work together and the Soviet weapons the CIA gave them did not work well enough against the professional troops the Soviets were using in Afghanistan. The tide changed when the United States decided to provide Stinger shoulder-fired surface-to-air missiles to the *muj* to drive the Soviets from command of the airspace over Afghanistan. Some senior CIA officers objected to this policy because they feared—quite accurately as it turned out—that the missiles might be sold to the wrong people or fall into the hands of terrorists. Nonetheless, the Reagan White House pushed the Stinger operation, which was even more successful than planners had hoped.

SOVIET PULL-OUT

As the Soviets began to lose aircraft and the ability to support their troops in the field, President Gorbachev decided that it was time to cut his losses and withdraw from Afghanistan. The CIA predicted that Najib would soon be driven from power after the Soviet pull-out, but that did not occur. The *mujahideen* began to turn on each other in a struggle to see which group might take over the country, which led to the rise of the Taliban, mostly young radical Muslims, steeped in a brand of Islam even more fanatic and restrictive than the Wahabism of Saudi Arabia. Eventually, Najib was forced to flee and the Taliban gained control of most of the country. They instituted an even more rigid theocracy than that of Iran and, as we now know, provided a base for Osama bin Laden to establish al Qaeda as a serious terrorist force.

After driving the Soviets out of Afghanistan, U.S. special operations forces began to prepare for contingencies that might require their special skills. This was evident in Panama in 1989 when President George H. W. Bush decided that Panamanian dictator Manuel Noriega had to be pushed out because of his growing ties to Cuba, to drug lords, and his harassment of American citizens in the country. Special operations forces were used extensively to fight the Panamanian Defense Force (PDF) and grab Noriega after he had taken refuge in the home of the Papal Nuncio in Panama City.

SPECIAL OPS IN IRAQ

In the first Gulf War against Iraq, the Special Forces were not used initially because General Norman Schwarzkopf preferred conventional military operations, but the Special Forces did eventually gain acceptance in the battles to drive Saddam Hussein's forces out of Kuwait. Schwarzkopf complained that he had received little support from intelligence during the campaign. At the time, the CIA's Special Operations Group, after a period of intelligence budget cuts, had shrunk to the point that there was little it could have done had it been asked. The use of Predator drones and a strengthened CIA special ops capability, had they been available during that time period, might have been able to do what Schwarzkopf wanted in terms of scouting out the battlefield.

In the aftermath of the Gulf War, with Saddam still in power in Baghdad, the CIA did carry out a plan to try to have opposition elements overthrow the dictator but with little success. The plan was given only half-hearted support by the Clinton administration, and when John Deutch became DCI, efforts to work with the opposition forces, some of whom were considered "dirty," led to the collapse of the operation. Bob Baer, the former CIA officer who spearheaded the operation—and who was later investigated by the FBI for his efforts—has described this fiasco nicely.[22]

REBUILDING CAPABILITY

According to *Jane's Defence Weekly*, which follows such developments rather closely, the rebuilding of the CIA's Special Operations Group really began in 1997 when George Tenet took over as DCI.[23] After 9/11, when the George W. Bush administration decided to take out the Taliban in

Afghanistan, the CIA was ready to put its Special Operations warriors on the ground. It appears that many of them were military Special Forces veterans who had left the service but who were recruited effectively by the CIA to use their skills to fight the new enemy, interrogate captured Taliban and al Qaeda forces, and direct the warlords and their troops. Aided by ready support from CIA headquarters, including air drops of supplies and cash, the Special Activities operatives quickly moved in. This came to national attention when Johnny M. Spann, a former Green Beret, was killed in an attempt to interrogate Taliban prisoners in Afghanistan. The CIA revealed his name to the press because he had given his life for the country and his sacrifice could be recognized without compromising ongoing operations.

Meanwhile, the military's Joint Special Operations Command (JSOC) was also moving into Afghanistan. Unlike the CIA, which depends on native forces to carry out its goals, the JSOC troops fight their own battles. Secretary of Defense Rumsfeld apparently saw military special operations, featuring small, highly mobile units as the wave of the future for the United States. Toward that end, in 2003, he appointed a former JSOC commander, who had already retired, to come back on active duty to serve as Chief of Staff of the Army and made clear that he wanted the military to become more flexible in the future.

Rumsfeld also supported growth in military intelligence capability, including increases in the Defense Humint Service.[24] While the defense intelligence and special operations forces probably outnumber their counterparts in CIA, the CIA can operate more surreptitiously than the military, and can move in and out of places more quietly. Thus, the CIA could track al Qaeda forces in Pakistan as civilians without raising the kind of political fuss that might accompany the use of armed military forces.

THE SECOND IRAQ WAR

In the second war against Iraq in 2003, the JSOC and the CIA showed that they could work effectively together against a common enemy. The CIA special activities operatives could identify and target Saddam Hussein and his henchmen so that the special ops forces could go after them. According to some reports, a military Task Force 20 was set up to find Saddam and his sons, but by mid-2003, they had had no success finding the former ruler. They were able to track down many of his key aides, however, so that both military and CIA interrogators could glean intelligence from the captives. Then in July 2003, an informant reportedly identified Saddam's sons Uday and Qusay in Mosul in northern Iraq. When the two refused to surrender, a firefight ensued and the two were killed by troops from the U.S. Army 101st Airborne Division. While it might have been better, from an intelligence perspective, to capture the two alive, fears that they might somehow escape led to the assault on the house they occupied.

FINDING SADDAM

In the fall of 2003, the new U.S. military commander in the Middle East, General John Abizaid, reportedly disbanded both Task Force 20 as well as Task Force 5, which had been fighting in Afghanistan, and replaced them with a new force called Task Force 121.[25] The idea was to streamline the operations and put them under one operational commander. The new unit would continue to hunt for Osama bin Laden and his followers, but much of the emphasis was on capturing Saddam Hussein, who seemingly had gone underground in Iraq, but continued to issue messages from time to time exhorting Iraqis to continue their guerrilla campaign against the Coalition Forces.

Finally, in December 2003, Saddam was captured through a combination of good intelligence and a careful and well-planned military operation. It appeared from press reports that military intelligence personnel actually tracked down Saddam by creating a matrix of known Iraqis who were tied to the former dictator.[26] This matrix, known as the "Mongo Link," led to those who might know where Saddam was hiding, and eventually to the underground "spider-hole" where the bearded and scruffy Saddam was found.

The creation of the Mongo Link is a good illustration of how intelligence really works at the tactical level. Intelligence personnel from the Army's 4th Infantry Division were able to piece together bits of information from informants, patrols, and intercepts to show how Saddam's support network was keeping him from capture. Eventually, the intelligence led to the capture of a key aide to Saddam, who gave up Saddam's hiding place after what was described as a grueling interrogation.

The successes of the Afghanistan and Iraq campaigns suggest that a combination of military Special Forces and CIA Special Activities operatives could be useful if the United States decided to carry out preemptive or retaliatory strikes against terrorists overseas. Although the proscriptions against assassination, as contained in President Reagan's Executive Order 12333, remain in effect, the president can override this order if he chooses to do so. Both Presidents Clinton and Bush made clear that killing Osama bin Laden, Taliban leader Mullah Omar, or Saddam Hussein would be acceptable, although bringing them to trial might be preferable. The same might hold true for any terrorist who can be identified as planning to attack the United States.

PROBLEMS WITH ASSASSINATION

The downside of an assassination policy, as the Israelis found out when they tried to kill all the Black September terrorists who had taken Israeli athletes hostage at the 1970 Olympics in Munich, is that a false identification could lead to the murder of someone who was completely innocent. In that case, the Israelis killed an innocent Arab waiter in Lillehammer, Norway, a crime that the Norwegian government could not forgive. This means that if the White House wants to use intelligence and military special operations for preemption or retaliation against terrorism, it better have a plan put together and not rely on spur-of-the-moment decisions.

The shortsighted nature of covert action during the cold war makes clear that a planning and decision-making system ought to be established to deal with these issues on a continuing basis. This could mirror the committee system that was used during the cold war to plan covert action operations. Such a committee ought to include senior officials from the National Security Council staff, the State Department, the Department of Defense, and the CIA, as well as analysts and operations experts. The committee ought to consider both short-range goals and the long-term effects of any covert action or special military operation directed against terrorists, members of global crime groups, narcotics kingpins, or anyone else who threatens our security.

SPECIAL OPS IN THE UNITED STATES

The question yet to be resolved is how preemption and retaliation might be used within the United States. Since the end of World War II, we have generally been comfortable with taking defensive measures at home but have not been prepared to have covert action against our enemies take place within the United States. Overseas, our attitude has been quite different. Even though most kinds of covert action and special operations are either illegal or will violate the sovereignty of the nation in which the action takes place, this has not deterred the White House from approving such operations, nor has the Congress sought to stop them in most cases.

Given the restrictions on the use of secret intelligence resources within the United States, any effort to preempt terrorists domestically will have to be handled either by the FBI or by state and local law enforcement. The USA Patriot Act and the FISA may make this easier. According to some reports, the FBI claims to have preempted a number of planned terrorist acts after 9/11, but has not made public any details, so as to protect its sources and methods. Law enforcement officials will be seeking ways to gather enough intelligence to identify terrorist operations in the planning stages. A conspiracy to carry out terrorism is sufficient legal reason to bring terrorists to justice.

A NEED FOR HONESTY

The system of controls now in place, in which the executive branch has to report plans for covert action to the Intelligence Oversight Committees, or special military operations to the Armed Services Committees of the Congress, ought to give the American people some confidence that their representatives in Washington are giving such activities close scrutiny. This requires, however, a certain degree of honesty on both sides. When President George W. Bush and his aides made a case for war against Iraq, at first the assumption was that the president had access to secret intelligence that he could not share with the public or even the Congress because of its sensitivity. President Bush argued that Iraq's possession of weapons of mass destruction (WMD), its attempts to build nuclear weapons, and its ties to al Qaeda, made it necessary to invade Iraq and take down Saddam Hussein before he could attack the United States.

In the aftermath of the war, it became clear that the White House had manipulated intelligence to convince the American people that an invasion of Iraq was necessary, even though the Bush administration could not even convince the UN Security Council to support the attack. When no WMD were found, no ties to al Qaeda were discovered, and the nuclear development issue turned out to be based on forgeries, an outcry arose. Many thought both the Congress and the American people had been duped, although it was hard to argue that the overthrow of Saddam's regime was a bad thing.

The lessons learned here are clear. If the White House wants to carry out covert action and special operations, it is going to have to justify this to the peoples' representatives. Dishonesty in this process will cost any administration dearly and lead to skepticism about its policies, no matter what the justification.

Understanding the Department of Homeland Security

It is always difficult to write about bureaucracies because they are subject to frequent change. In the federal government, this is particularly true because administrations only have a mandate for four years, and the political appointees who head the various agencies and fill key policy positions usually stay only about two years before they burn out, or are lured by more lucrative jobs in the private sector. It is amazing that so many people are eager to fill the Schedule C political appointments, which typically pay the same salary as senior military officers receive, and require back-breaking six- or seven-day work weeks, 12 to 15 hours a day. Yet, there are enough of these folks waiting in the wings in any administration that the assignments rarely go begging. In that regard, the new Department of Homeland Security seems to be having some trouble.

The DHS had only been officially in business for six months when the press began an assessment of its performance as part of a look back at the events of 9/11. The DHS did not receive very good grades in these assessments, even though Secretary Tom Ridge was trying to manage an overhaul of government that was even more complicated than the last major departmental creation, that of the Department of Defense in 1947. One could make the argument that the first Secretary of Defense, James Forrestal, had a much easier task in an atmosphere of peace in the postwar world. Secretary Ridge is trying to make the DHS work in the midst of a war on terrorism that some say might last as long as the cold war—about fifty years.

BUREAUCRATIC ADVANTAGES

In 1947, Forrestal had some real bureaucratic advantages over Ridge and the DHS. The first secretary of defense had a building, the Pentagon, that could hold all his key policy makers and defense chiefs. The War Department became the Department of the Army with only a name change while the secretary of war position was downgraded from cabinet level to one lower rung on the bureaucratic ladder. The navy did not have to do anything, although its secretary, too, would report to the secretary of defense instead of the president. The new U.S. Air Force moved up in the bureaucracy, becoming an independent service instead of just a part of the army, and its secretary became the equal of the two older services. All in all, this major reorganization worked well, despite the usual grumbling and turf battles, and President Truman could preside over a rather peaceful three-year transition to the new system before it received its first test in the Korean War.

Of course, the strain of the work led Secretary Forrestal to develop a severe mental breakdown in 1949, forcing President Truman to ask for his resignation. Forrestal then committed suicide, jumping out a window of the hospital where he had gone for treatment.[1] Secretary Ridge, however, does not seem to be the sort to succumb to such problems, as far as anyone can tell.

A MODEL FOR GOVERNMENT

Creating the DoD also gave the government the ability to plan for all the military services together instead of having two separate offices competing for military funds. Today, joint planning in the DoD is a model for the government. Only in the DoD is long-range planning a reality, and with increased emphasis on jointness, the DoD shows how turf battles can be minimized and cooperation fostered. The most significant obstacle facing defense planners and managers is the stubbornness of the system in resisting change. President George W. Bush became a strong supporter of Defense Secretary Rumsfeld's efforts to modernize the U.S. military, but the administration had to fight off entrenched bureaucrats, and members of Congress who objected to any changes that might affect their constituents. Meanwhile, senior military officers, who had spent most of their careers fighting the cold war, had a hard time adjusting to new thinking. Still, the 2003 war in Iraq showed that the military was adapting successfully to Rumsfeld's new ideas.

A MORE DIFFICULT PROBLEM

Creating the DHS was a much more difficult problem for everyone involved. In fact, it was only with some reluctance that President Bush agreed to establish the department. He faced a situation where the Congress was intent on having the new organization and the president, in the aftermath of 9/11, could hardly veto the legislation.[2] According to statistical studies, DHS is the third largest government component; the Pentagon ranks number one, followed by the Department of Veterans Affairs.

The task of merging 22 agencies and about 160,000 people into the new department was handicapped by the lack of buildings to house them, few communications and computer systems to support them, no clearances for many of the workers, and—except for the Secretary himself—little effective leadership. According to press reports, more than fifteen people turned down the chance to become the DHS chief of the unit that was to contain the department's intelligence staff and other key positions were equally hard to fill. Finally, retired military officers were found for some of the positions, because they would be easier to recruit than politicians.

According to Rand Beers, a former White House staffer, officials in the White House somewhere below the president's level tried to prevent Secretary Ridge from recruiting the best people for the top spots in the DHS. They were equally uncooperative in planning and budgeting for the new department.[3] Certainly, they permitted Ridge to take some hits from the press, but the secretary always seemed upbeat in responding to criticism. DoD officials, accused of failing to support Ridge by not attending his meetings, denied the charge, pointing out that Paul McHale, the assistant secretary of defense for homeland defense, was ready to send military officers to work at the DHS. Other sources have told me that a number of military officers were "borrowed" from the Pentagon to assist in putting the DHS Watch Center together until it could find a regular civilian cadre.

SCATTERED PERSONNEL

Most of the agencies brought in to the DHS were fully functioning parts of other departments and had facilities already assigned to them. Many DHS employees were not in Washington at all, but were scattered around the United States, especially along border regions.[4] According to a Syracuse University study, only 8.6 percent of DHS employees were assigned within the Washington metropolitan area.

The problem for DHS management was that they had to coordinate the work of the 22 agencies they inherited while these disparate groups were still housed in their former departments, without the kind of communication systems that would enable them to respond easily to new tasking from new bosses. In two cases, that of the Coast Guard and the Secret Service, their directors insisted that they should report directly to the secretary of the DHS rather than to an undersecretary as originally planned. The two services took the original plan as a demotion, so they fought and won their battle for independence. Each now reports directly to the secretary.

UNFAIR CRITICISM

The press is, in my view, criticizing the DHS unfairly. Ridge and the few senior officials who have stuck with him have an unenviable task. Some of the senior leadership is already bailing out of the DHS, and more are likely to depart as Bush's first term winds down. This happens throughout government, but is more acute at the DHS where the loss of leadership is more keenly felt as the system is only starting to work. Mr. Ridge's deputy quit to go back to the Pentagon, his chief of staff alienated many with his "brusque and secretive" behavior, and Ridge himself was slammed for his lack of attention to detail.[5] Apparently, the leadership ranks at the DHS were kept lean in accordance with Republican aversion to big government, but this did not stop the Bush administration from creating its own homeland security policy bureaucracy within the White House.

The leadership of the various agencies is hampered as well by endless requests from members of Congress and their staffs for testimony or data. This represents the usual effort by Congress to micromanage the executive branch, or gain political advantage, mingled with honest requests for information. Because the Congress has not yet consolidated oversight of homeland security into one committee for each House, DHS management has to be accountable to a host of masters. Reporting to Congress can easily suck up most of the management resources of the DHS if it is permitted to continue.

DIFFERING SYSTEMS

The DHS bureaucracy is complicated by the fact that while some agencies were taken in wholesale, such as the Coast Guard and the Secret Service, others were mixed together. The mergers were made more difficult by differing personnel management systems, varied pay and benefits packages, and a variety of training backgrounds. For example, 3,500 customs agents and 2,050 immigration agents came together from their two entirely different agencies, with different rules and procedures, even different uniforms. They not only had to be crosstrained, but had to learn new rules created by more stringent security policies. Then in August 2003, before crosstraining even got underway, Secretary Ridge announced that the Air Marshal Service, which was part of the Transportation Security Administration of the DHS, would be melded with the customs and immigration unit, and all three would be trained so that they could perform any of the functions of their units. It made sense but caused headaches too.

By the summer of 2003, the former customs agents and immigration officers were starting to move into the 25 field offices that had been used before by one or the other of the services.[6] One former customs officer complained that the immigration officers were not really "agents" and did not have any criminal investigative experience. The immigration officers thought they were more experienced than the agents in the former customs service. Now these two forces are going to have to learn to be stand-by air marshals as well as work together. As a sign of progress, a senior DHS official testified in a Congressional hearing that at least the various services are now wearing one uniform, all with DHS patches.

DHS STRUCTURE

At the risk of describing a bureaucracy that is constantly changing, it is important to understand the variety of functions within the DHS and how the offices are structured. The DHS was organized at its inception in March 2003 into five main directorates. These included Border and Transportation Security (BTS), Emergency Preparedness and Response, Science and Technology, Information Analysis and Infrastructure Protection (IAIP), and Management. Of these five, three of them were the federal equivalent of first responders. BTS, IAIP, and Emergency Preparedness, which used to be the Federal Emergency Management Agency (FEMA), were the units that would respond to a terrorist attack, or to other threats to homeland security.

The unit that has received most of the attention since DHS was "stood up"—current Washington bureau-speak for "inaugurated"—is BTS. It is the largest of the DHS directorates, containing 80 percent of DHS employees.[7] The Transportation Security Administration (TSA) was moved in wholesale from the Department of Transportation. These are the people who search shoes and check carry-on luggage at the airports. They have not been wasting their time. In one month alone, over 640,000 potential weapons, including concealed knives, hidden guns, and other such material was seized by TSA inspectors. They even found a loaded gun concealed in a child's teddy bear.[8]

CONSISTENCY IN SCREENING

Most critics seem to agree that the TSA has brought an annoying consistency to air travel security, as far as passengers are concerned, but has fallen short in other areas. The TSA was able to put in place a checked baggage screening system by the end of 2002, as it had been ordered to do by the Congress, but this meant that some major airports had to put the truck-sized baggage screening machines right out in the passenger check-in areas of the airport. The TSA had not yet developed a system for screening package shipments in September 2003 when a man managed to hide himself inside a container and had himself shipped by air from New York to Dallas. He ended up paying more for his air freight transportation than he might have spent for a regular ticket, but this caused a storm of controversy among members of Congress who are pressing the TSA somehow to develop a zero-defect security system.

The TSA planned to spend $20 million in 2004 to develop cargo shipment screening technologies, according to an agency spokesperson.[9] There are other areas where security at airports needs work, including checks on ramp agents, baggage handlers, and security procedures. After a man managed to spend the night in a parked aircraft at one airport, more procedures had to be changed to prevent such incidents. The TSA cannot possibly manage a system that is totally foolproof, and the situation was made worse when politicians zeroed in on the TSA as a way to attack the Bush administration.

PROTECTING THE BORDERS

Other main units in BTS include the Bureau of Customs and Border Protection (CBP), largely the former Customs Service, and the Bureau of Immigration and Customs Enforcement (ICE), the former Immigration Service. These are the people who are being crosstrained, along with the Air Marshal Service that was part of the TSA. Secretary Ridge believes that combining these services will enable BTS to have surge capacity in the event of trouble, since agents from all the units will be trained to handle immigration, customs, and air marshal duties. The Bureau of Citizenship and Immigration Services, which was the last element of the former Immigration Service to become operational within the DHS, finally got underway in 2004, but it seemed to be understaffed. There were many complaints about lengthy processing times for visa renewals and other matters not directly related to security concerns.[10]

Border and Transportation Security has also acquired personnel from the Department of Health and Human Services, the Animal and Plant Inspection service from the Department of Agriculture, and the Federal Protective Service, which was part of the General Services Administration. Federal Protective Officers are security police who guard federal buildings.

DISASTER MANAGEMENT

The Federal Emergency Management Agency, or FEMA—as many still refer to the Emergency Preparedness office—has always been a first responder in times of natural disasters or manmade crises. It came over to the DHS pretty much intact and in the fall of 2003 was prepared for the hurricane season as it has always done since its inception. The Coast Guard continued all its regular functions, including coastal search and rescue, while increasing its border and harbor protection duties. The Secret Service remained on the front line for the protection of key individuals in government, patrol of diplomatic facilities in the United States, and protection against counterfeiting.

Another addition to the Bureau of Emergency Preparedness and Response is the Office of Domestic Preparedness (ODP), which moved from the Department of Justice to the DHS. The ODP is responsible for training first responders in dealing with chemical, biological, and radiological weapons. It provides training at a former army base in Alabama, but because of limited resources, it is clearly unable to handle more than a small percentage of the vast number of prospective trainees at the state and local levels each year. The hope seems to be that each successful trainee will return to his or her local service and train co-workers in approved techniques and equipment usage. The ODP is also a conduit for funds for training and equipment, and technical assistance to first responders.

INFRASTRUCTURE AND INTELLIGENCE

Information Analysis and Infrastructure Protection (IAIP) is supposed to be the directorate that contains the intelligence function of the DHS and indeed, 641 of the department's employees are listed as intelligence officers, but there is no functioning intelligence unit in the DHS outside of the watch center at DHS headquarters. Some intelligence officers were assigned to the infrastructure unit, which was transferred to the DHS from the FBI; the cyber-security unit—which was supposed to have nearly eight hundred people, but in reality had only 92—came to the DHS with only 22 professionals. All the rest decided to stay with the FBI.[11] Other intelligence officers may be found in the Coast Guard, the Secret Service, or assigned to the FBI's joint task forces. Some are reportedly assigned to the Terrorist Threat Integration Center (TTIC); the rest are unaccounted for.

Former Marine General Frank Libuti, who became the undersecretary for IAIP in 2003, was not himself an intelligence veteran and he lost his assistant secretary and intelligence expert, CIA veteran Paul Redmond, soon after IAIP came into being. Redmond received harsh treatment at a Congressional hearing when he admitted that the DHS had not established a functioning intelligence unit. Redmond blamed it on the fact that the DHS had no secure communications or facilities for such a unit. After he was raked over the coals, he submitted his resignation for reasons of health. Libuti then found another retired Marine officer, Bill Parrish, to take Redmond's place. Both Redmond and Parrish were counterintelligence experts, so that may say something about the plans for whatever intelligence unit is eventually created at the DHS. Eventually, the role of assistant secretary was filled by a retired army general, Patrick Hughes, who had previously served as director of the Defense Intelligence Agency.

SOME FUNCTIONS MISSING

Because of the lean staffing at DHS headquarters, some functions that the DHS should have had at the top seemed to be missing. Except for having a press spokesman for the secretary, there seems to be no public affairs unit. We know from long experience in the CIA that if the DHS does not tell its own story, others will tell it in ways that the DHS may not find helpful. That may be the reason why so few people outside the homeland security community are aware of the real progress that has been made in information sharing and other services.

The DHS should have had, as well, a congressional liaison staff to manage requests for information and testimony from the Congress. If this function is not put together, the Congress will bury the DHS in requests and senior managers will spend all their time on Capitol Hill instead of in their offices. A congressional liaison office can also make sure that DHS testimony is consistent and accurate. Otherwise, DHS managers will look foolish and confused if their answers to the endless stream of inquiries are inconsistent.

The planning and budgeting function at the DHS ought to be placed at the director's level. At the beginning, the DHS reportedly had to turn to the private consultants for this function because the department had no one to perform this work. Planning and budgeting is a real problem in the U.S. government because it has never been able to get beyond a one-year budget cycle. That is, budgets have to be submitted each year, even for projects that stretch out over ten years or more. The Congress retains this system, in my opinion, because representatives in the House, where budget issues are dealt with first, might lose control of the budget if it stretched beyond the two years of their terms.

In any event, this means that long-range planning is very difficult. Of course, government budgets are drawn for the fiscal year, with planned expenditures for the next four years; these are not real numbers, but wish lists. For a start-up department such as the DHS, being able to do long-range planning is essential if the various agencies in the new system are ever to be truly integrated. The DHS needs a strategy for the future, but so far it is too new to have had the luxury of planning for systems integration. One area where work sorely needs to be done is in the area of intelligence. DHS has to fulfill the expectations of both Congress and the people at large that they will have a functioning system for intelligence analysis.

HOMELAND SECURITY COUNCIL

One aspect of homeland security management that has gotten little attention is the Bush administration's creation of the Homeland Security Council (HSC) and the policy making apparatus that goes with it. The Homeland Security Council is the counterpart of the National Security Council (NSC), but most people don't seem to realize that both of them are just subsets of the president's cabinet and not separate organizations. According to the White House announcement, the HSC was established soon after 9/11 "to coordinate all federal, state, and homeland security activities."[12] This was done well before the creation of the DHS was even considered. While the DHS has taken over some of the coordinating functions originally assigned to the HSC, the council has become the president's chief advisory body on homeland security issues at the White House level.

The NSC includes the president, vice president, secretaries of state and defense, usually the attorney general, and the national security adviser. The Chairman of the Joint Chiefs of Staff and the Director of Central Intelligence are members as well. The president can add anyone else to the list if he wishes. The national security adviser heads the staff at the White House that supports the NSC and does the leg work to provide whatever information the principals need when the time comes for decision making. The NSC's main function is to assist the president in making foreign and national security policy. The HSC replicates this structure on a smaller scale, but its purpose is to make domestic security policy.

The HSC consists of the president, vice-president, the secretaries of DHS and defense, the attorney general, and whomever else the president might appoint. One would expect that HSC meetings would include the DCI, the FBI director, and the NSC adviser. The HSC has a small staff to support it under an executive secretary and the law establishing the HSC specifies that there could be joint meetings of the NSC and HSC.

POLICY COORDINATING COMMITTEES

To do the groundwork for national security policy, the NSC has a number of Policy Coordinating Committees (PCCs) made up of senior policy officials from the various parts of the NSC. This committee system was set up during the Carter administration and has been used in one form or another ever since. The PCCs are supposed to work out policy options and recommendations for the NSC, which then helps the president choose policies to be implemented. A similar system is supposed to support the HSC.

Typically, PCCs are chaired by the appropriate staff member from the HSC and attended by representatives of the other agencies at the assistant secretary level or even lower. These are working-level committees, which means that every input they make in reaching a policy decision or making recommendations on policy options has to be carefully coordinated within their own agencies or departments. It is a process followed throughout government, but when such committees deal with national or homeland security issues, the meetings are usually classified at least at the secret level. This may be one of the reasons why so little about the Homeland Security Council or its work has become public.

There are supposed to be eleven PCCs for homeland security and the first on the list is one for "Detection, Surveillance, and Intelligence."[13] Among the others are committees for law enforcement and investigation, WMD consequence management, transportation security, and domestic threat response. There is a committee for public affairs, but even that one seems to have been kept under wraps.

EXAMINING THE BUDGET

We can tell a great deal about where the DHS is going in the future by examining the budget it has made public.[14] In the U.S. intelligence system, budget details and even the total figure are rarely made public, precisely because a study of the budget would reveal a great deal about the IC's plans and programs. The DHS is under no such restriction, so studying the budget can tell us what kinds of changes to expect in the year to come. Although the budget figures only cover one year, it seems likely that the new initiatives will continue into what budgeteers in Washington call "the out years."

In regard to intelligence matters, the DHS plans to expand and upgrade its watch center into the DHS Command Center or Homeland Security Operations Center (HSOC). In addition, a threat assessment system will be created with a focus on threats to the nation's infrastructure along with a unit to guide intelligence collection and provide strategic warning. These are the kinds of intelligence analysis functions suggested earlier that ought to be part of the Information Analysis and Infrastructure Protection (IAIP) part of the DHS.

Funds in the FY 2004 budget are included for creating a national communications system to respond to emergencies and to share information with state and local governments. What is not clear in the budget is where the intelligence analysts will come from to staff this system. So far, based on the experiences of university students who have applied for positions at the DHS, recruiting is slow and riddled with bureaucratic stumbling blocks. Obtaining security clearances for the new hires will likely slow down the hiring process even further.

THE VISA PROCESS

The DHS plans to expand its control over the immigration and visitor process by eventually taking over the entire visa-granting system now run by the Department of State,[15] which was severely criticized after 9/11 for its lax visa policies that allowed some of the 9/11 hijackers into the country. According to press reports, DHS officials will be granted diplomatic status and will be stationed permanently overseas to run the visa application process. Meanwhile, travelers to the United States have begun to complain about the new rules, which require visas for visitors from many countries, outside of our close allies in Europe. Nonrefundable fees, the limited number of visa-granting posts, and the tedious process of filling out lengthy application forms, along with the requirement for a personal interview, have cut into both business and leisure travel to the United States. Many students have decided not to pursue university studies in the United States because it is easier to go elsewhere. Budget money for FY 2004 seems to be directed toward strengthening controls rather than easing entry.

Significant increases in the DHS budget are allocated toward increased border and port security. The DHS wants to expand and improve the Customs-Trade Partnership Against Terrorism (C-TPAT), a system designed to enlist the assistance of foreign manufacturers and importers to protect against terrorist use of shipments to the United States to hide weapons or explosives. There are increases in funding for the Container Shipment Initiative, which will enable inspectors overseas to examine containers at the point of origin, which is much more effective than trying to inspect them when they enter the United States.

The TSA will get money for an explosive detection system for the nation's airports and is trying to develop new technologies for cargo inspections as well. A great deal of uninspected cargo is carried on commercial airliners, in addition to the cargo that is shipped by companies such as FedEx. Interestingly, FedEx has instituted a new plan to have its own brand of private air marshals to protect itself and its air fleet against terrorism. UPS reportedly rejected developing an expanded security force and will rely on existing systems for protection.

Money is included in the DHS budget for upgrading the Coast Guard, including purchase of new ships and aircraft, and for improvements in the Secret Service. A significant increase in funding will go to FEMA, including money for disaster relief and the more normal emergency services FEMA has provided in the past. There is an initiative to develop sensors and defenses against biological, radiological, and chemical terrorism as well. There are funds in the DHS budget for developing new protective technologies, and for training.

A LONG WAY TO GO

The DHS has a long way to go before it becomes an effective part of the U.S. government. We should remember, however, that putting together a conglomerate of the size and complexity of the DHS requires patience and cooperation on the part of its members as well as its overseers. Some of the departments of the government, such as the State Department or Treasury, have been in existence since the founding of the nation. To expect Secretary Ridge to have the DHS fully functioning in just a few months is asking for miracles. At least we know he is heading in the right direction. The future of this vast bureaucracy is uncertain at best, but having invested in starting it up, the American people have every right to expect that, no matter who sits in the White House, the DHS will receive support and encouragement as well as money and talent.

Learning about changes in the DHS or related bureaucracies has been made easier by the World Wide Web. Even though the DHS lacks an extensive public affairs function, it has kept its Web site (www.dhs.gov) more or less up to date, so that changes in the system can be reported. In addition, several online journals cover homeland security, reporting on changes in leadership and activities. Change is inevitable in the homeland security system in 2004 as elections draw near. The functions will continue, no matter how the system changes. An effective homeland security system is America's best chance of defending itself against its new enemies.

First Responders

In the aftermath of 9/11, a great deal of attention focused on the creation of the Department of Homeland Security (DHS) and efforts by the federal government to provide for the defense against terrorism and other threats. The fact is, however, that DHS was not the only organization working on security within the United States. That work was and is primarily being done by state and local governments and the private sector. Yet DHS does provide some very useful and helpful functions at the federal level, both to deal with threats to homeland security and to provide support to the first responders at state and local levels.

First responders—or "emergency response providers" as they are called in the Homeland Security legislation—include "federal, state, and local emergency public safety, law enforcement, emergency response, emergency medical" and support personnel. First responders also include private sector security and volunteer organizations who would be the first people to deal with the aftermath of a terrorist attack or some other disaster that inflicted harm on the homeland.[1] There are hundreds of thousands of such people within the United States at the state and local levels, not counting the DHS itself.

Although response to threats and attacks on the homeland generally fall below the federal level, the DHS has its own first responders. The Coast Guard protects harbors and waterways, as well as keeping an eye on ships entering and leaving key ports. For example, there is still a great deal of concern in Boston, ever since 9/11, about liquid natural gas tankers coming into the city's harbor. A terrorist attack on a fully loaded tanker could cause a great deal of devastation in Boston.[2] In this case, the Coast Guard began a patrol to guard the weekly tanker delivery making sure no other ships came close enough to create a hazard. Other key ports and harbors are receiving similar treatment. Of course, the Coast Guard continues its search and rescue missions while beefing up its role as a homeland first responder.

The Secret Service, as part of the DHS, continues its protective services for key U.S. government officials, visiting foreign dignitaries, and foreign embassies and consulates around the country. The Secret Service has lost its charter for dealing with illegal financial transactions to the FBI, but it continues to be responsible for fighting against counterfeiting. This is particularly important because terrorists and global crime groups have found copying the U.S. dollar, especially for circulation abroad, is a good way to finance some of their operations. Even though the Treasury Department began circulating newly designed $20 bills in 2003, with color and other safety marks added, counterfeiters, with easy access to high-tech copy machines, circulated realistic copies within weeks.

ON THE FRONT LINE

The directorate of Border and Transportation Security (BTS), the largest component of DHS, is on the front line to make sure that illegal entry into the United States is curtailed and that shipments, especially in containers, are inspected before they enter the country. This is a tall order, but an increasing number of inspectors are being stationed overseas to check the containers before they are loaded onto cargo ships.[3] Using technical sensors, the inspectors can check for radioactive or explosive devices. The directorate's Bureau of Immigration and Customs Enforcement takes the lead on these issues for BTS, but the directorate is also responsible for inspecting plant and animal imports, and federal law enforcement training, especially for the guard force that protects federal buildings.

Perhaps the most visible of all the federal-level first responders in BTS is the Transportation Security Administration (TSA). Unfortunately, the TSA has been hurt by cutbacks in personnel and funding, and is hobbled by a tendency to run everything from Washington. The TSA has security checkers at 429 airports around the country, manning some 750 checkpoints, but all the procedures are handled by TSA headquarters, even though the system's needs vary around the country.[4] Craig P. Coy, the CEO at the Massachusetts Port Authority, which runs Boston's Logan Airport, noted in November 2003, that local TSA supervisors have no power even to change security lanes when there are back-ups. He argues, quite persuasively, that the TSA ought to give its airport units more flexibility. Although the TSA has confiscated millions of potential weapons since it took over airport security, there is no evidence that even one terrorist attack has been thwarted. Logan airport managers are more sensitive than most, since it was from Logan that two of the hijacked aircraft took off on 9/11.

The TSA, as a federal first responder, deals with breaches of airport security. When the TSA first took over airport security from a host of private security companies, harried travelers ran through security checkpoints to avoid missing flights, or to retrieve items left behind. TSA's response was to shut down the airline terminal concerned, and in some cases, entire airport terminals were evacuated and all passengers had to be rescreened. The chaos and financial loss to airlines and passengers was significant. No terrorists were involved. The TSA has now developed procedures to minimize this kind of mindless response, but terminal evacuations could still take place.

Equally visible as a federal first responder, but only when there is a disaster, is the Emergency Preparedness and Response Directorate, which incorporates the Federal Emergency Management Agency (FEMA). It played a key role in responding to the 9/11 attacks and is continuing this responsibility under the DHS. It will continue to funnel disaster relief funds to its counterparts at the state level. FEMA works closely with state counterparts in planning and exercising for disaster relief, which may turn out to be one of the most important aspects of its operations. For example, in August 2003, FEMA and state emergency management teams from around New England took part in a disaster relief exercise at the Naval War College in Newport, Rhode Island. The exercise simulated both a bioterrorist attack and a hurricane; the plan was to play out the exercise over several years.[5] FEMA was on the front line in providing federal aid to the victims of Hurricane Isabel, which roared on shore in September 2003, just as it had done in previous weather-related disasters before FEMA became part of the DHS. During the fires in southern California later that fall, FEMA was very visible in seeking to set up disaster relief for victims of the blazes.

CONDUIT FOR FUNDS

The DHS serves a number of other functions at the federal level that are significant in providing support to state and local governments and first responders. The DHS is the main conduit through which funds are channeled to state and local governments. This means that state and local jurisdictions have to apply for grants from the DHS, which then decides how much money can be spent for which function. Eventually, the DHS plans to set up regional centers for this process because having 50 states and the District of Columbia all applying for funds to DHS headquarters would require a huge bureaucracy to administer. Having regional centers might simplify and speed up the process. While every state and most major cities are crying for money to finance their own efforts at homeland security, the DHS and the White House have come in for considerable criticism because the money did not come in quickly nor in the amounts that were needed.

According to the Task Force Report from the Council on Foreign Relations, commonly known as the Rudman report after its chairman, former Senator Warren Rudman, first responders at the state and local levels are seriously underfunded.[6] Senator Rudman paints a bleak picture and calls for at least triple the amount of money budgeted for the five years beginning in FY 2004. Other reports suggest that no one knows how much homeland security will cost in the out years, that is, after FY 2004. It seems clear, however, that state budgets for homeland security are stretched thin and federal grants will have to increase if DHS goals are to be met.

Of course, DHS will want to set up some sort of monitoring and reporting system to make sure that the money is actually being spent for the purposes for which it was granted. Already, at the end of 2003, there were reports that some of the money was going to state and local projects that were not included in the grant applications. This should not be surprising, but establishing some kind of monster bureaucracy to oversee spending might well eat up money that could otherwise be used for first responders.

ESTABLISHING STANDARDS

In addition to providing federal funding, the DHS will establish safety and security standards and procedures for dealing with hazardous materials, especially biological, chemical, and radioactive weapons, and for standardized communications systems nationwide. Because most states had already adopted their own systems for protective gear, handling of hazardous materials, and other procedures, some rules needed to be drawn to make sure that common standards were met. The states had to move on these issues without waiting for the DHS to get its act together, but in retrospect, some of the equipment purchased may not have been as good as it could have been, and by adopting standardized handling procedures, the DHS can help the states achieve common methods of operations.

When the DHS was established, the Congress intended that one of its key roles would be passing intelligence to first responders at the state and local level, as well as to security officials in the private sector. As noted previously, this is supposed to be the role of the Directorate of Information Analysis and Infrastructure Protection (IAIP), which is responsible for identifying and analyzing threats to the homeland. While the DHS may have the responsibility for these tasks, it's not clear that they have the capability to carry them out. It is an area in which the DHS has come in for a great deal of criticism, especially from the Congress. It's too early to tell if the increases in budget for IAIP will get the job done.

The infrastructure protection part of the mandate was bolstered when the FBI's National Infrastructure Protection Center was moved to the DHS. Because 85 percent of the nation's infrastructure belongs to the private sector, IAIP will really serve to warn of threats and coordinate action, but in its early stages, the warnings have been far too vague to be of much use. The warnings suggested an increased risk of terrorist attack, but did not provide any specific indication of targets or locations. The private sector cannot afford to beef up security without some actionable intelligence, and, so far, the DHS has been unable to provide it.

At a meeting of the nation's governors in Indiana in August 2003, DHS Secretary Ridge announced that intelligence would be shared with the states, and that five officials in each state would be given top-secret security clearances in order to receive the best information.[7] Of course, the DHS expects that the states will help out by providing intelligence developed at the state and local levels to the DHS watch center in Washington. Ridge also asked the governors to identify potential infrastructure targets in each state, so that protective measures could be planned for the most vulnerable targets.

PROTECTING CYBERSPACE

One of the most critical parts of the infrastructure is protection of cyberspace and telecommunications. The vulnerability of our systems became apparent on 9/11 when communications systems collapsed in New York and first responders were unable to contact each other. The DHS has been working on packaging emergency communications gear in such a way that a mobile facility could be moved into a disaster area quickly to replace damaged systems. The DHS is making good progress in that regard, but critics say that telecommunications, especially Web-based systems, remain a serious vulnerability and a tempting target for terrorism.

Despite dire warnings that al Qaeda would attack America's cyber-based infrastructure, or that Saddam Hussein would do so if the United States invaded Iraq, nothing happened. While we have no way of knowing for sure, it appears that this kind of attack does not achieve the goals terrorists seek. No one dies in a cyber-attack, and the destruction is not visible. Terrorists want a spectacular display of violence, death, and destruction to create fear and shock. Taking down computer systems seems to be too subtle for them.

While the Infrastructure Protection unit of the IAIP came over from the FBI, the intelligence part of it was supposed to be created by the DHS. It got off to a slow start; the IAIP does not have its own intelligence collection system, but has to rely on the intelligence community for most of its inputs. It's not clear that intelligence has been forthcoming. The IAIP has suffered as well from a lack of direction and leadership. It has placed DHS officers in the Terrorist Threat Integration Center (TTIC) but it has not solved one of the key intelligence problems: how to pass sensitive intelligence data and the analysis derived from it, as Secretary Ridge has promised to first responders at the working level, most of whom are not cleared for classified intelligence.

I have suggested earlier that there are ways to do this and the DHS is working on the problem, but it seems clear that the IC agencies that deal in top secret materials are not about to let a DHS unit pass the secrets without stringent controls. Even if clearances are granted to key individuals at the state level, this still does not solve the problem of delivering intelligence to first responders. In June 2003, a CIA officer assigned to work with the FBI's infrastructure unit who moved to the DHS when the unit was transferred, told me that networks are being established to make sure that information can be shared rapidly; the system is working, but the most sensitive intelligence is not yet passing to those who probably need it the most.

COMPARTMENTATION

A Congressional investigation into the matter, a byproduct of the 9/11 inquiry, reported that even when outside personnel with proper clearances are integrated into the FBI, CIA, or TTIC, they are still seen as "foreigners" and do not gain access to some of the intelligence they think they need. This is partly the normal turf battle that goes on throughout government, but it also stems from the old cold war admonition that intelligence personnel should have access only to intelligence for which they had a "need to know." This kind of compartmentation, as it was called, stemmed from the notion that enemy spies were everywhere and that by restricting the free flow of intelligence and information sharing, damage and loss could be limited. CIA operatives also feared that the free flow of agent reporting could somehow reveal the identity of the agents, even though the reporting was set up in such a way that no clues to the agent's identity was in the report.

If the intelligence community and the DHS are going to become effective producers of homeland security intelligence, these leftover relics of cold war procedures really ought to change. They did not stop penetrations of the system and did not limit the damage caused by Soviet agents Ames or Hanssen. These kinds of practices die hard, however, and may not disappear for another generation. Meanwhile, the intelligence that should be shared with state and local emergency officials is not getting to them. There is an alternative.

For several years, the private sector has been able to subscribe to a number of private intelligence services. These services operate on a 24/7 basis to gather and analyze information to provide, albeit on an unclassified basis, information and analysis about world events. They can tailor their products to individual subscribers and they usually employ government intelligence veterans both to gather the material and create the analysis. Of course, this intelligence is all based on open sources, but experience shows that the services miss very little in their analysis. Because they are equipped to gather information from a variety of open sources, far more than any one individual could do, these services can come very close in their analysis to the best that might emerge from the intelligence community. The growing number of antiterrorism task forces could subscribe to these services at relatively little cost and avoid the problems of clearances and compartmentation inherent in obtaining intelligence from the DHS. One such service, Stratfor (www.stratfor.com), has an open Web site that provides a preview of the sorts of intelligence it can deliver.

DUPLICATION IN TASK FORCES

One of the problems Washington is going to have to deal with is what seems to be unnecessary duplication in the antiterrorism task forces at the state and local level. After 9/11, in part to fend off criticism that the federal government, and especially the FBI, had dropped the ball in tracking terrorists within the United States, 56 Joint Terrorism Task Forces (JTTFs) were established in key cities. These units were supposed to be staffed by the FBI, and CIA officers were supposed to be assigned to each unit. Now the number of these JTTFs has grown to more than eighty. No information had surfaced indicating whether or not the CIA has actually made such assignments. Meanwhile, each of the states has established Anti-Terrorism Task Forces (ATTF) of their own, some modeled on the New York ATTF, but many set up according to models developed independently by each state.

The goals of these ATTFs are similar. They are to facilitate intelligence and information sharing with state and local authorities, and prepare to respond to a terrorist attack. The JTTFs, meanwhile, will seek to prevent and disrupt terrorist activity through "aggressive investigation and prosecution."[8] It seems to make sense, over time, to combine these various functions in one unit for each state, if the turf and security problems could be worked out. Key cities could have their own sub-ATTFs. Since all of these units operate on a 24/7 basis, they are extremely manpower-intensive and will eventually eat up their personnel resources, unless they are combined.

The state ATTFs are making progress in contingency planning for disasters, whether manmade or natural. They are even planning the evacuation of major cities, although it seems doubtful that the population of any city in the United States could be quickly moved out. As it is, most cities suffer serious traffic gridlock twice each business day during morning and evening rush hours. Moving an entire population during a crisis would only exacerbate the gridlock and might well trap the population and prevent first responders from being able to move to crisis points. Nonetheless, just the fact that the ATTFs are planning and exercising means that the United States is better prepared for disasters than ever in its history. It might be one of the most useful aspects of the creation of the DHS system.

MEDICAL EMERGENCIES

One area where real success has been achieved in information sharing is in the field of medical emergencies. This is particularly important in the fight against biological weapons; some of the diseases spread by such weapons have a delayed incubation period, so the disease might not appear among an infected population until some time after the attack has actually taken place. Chemical, nuclear, and conventional attacks are hard to miss, but a biological weapon is insidious in that it could spread before being noticed. In the fight against such weapons, one of the key organizations is the Center for Disease Control and Prevention (CDC). It is not part of the DHS, but the DHS has been moving quickly to take advantage of the information sharing network put in place to report on infectious or other diseases.[9]

The CDC became involved in fighting terrorism after the anthrax scare that followed 9/11. The agency quickly realized that it needed to upgrade its communications systems, because health officials were not able to communicate with each other or share data on a timely basis. A new technology was developed as a result of the anthrax scare called the National Electronic Disease Surveillance System (NEDSS). It brings together state and local officials in reporting outbreaks of some one hundred diseases, and facilitates responses.[10] The efficacy of the system was illustrated in the rapid response to the outbreak of the severe acute respiratory syndrome (SARS) virus early in 2003, after it was brought into the United States from China. Another reporting system that will assist in fighting a bioterrorist attack as well as an outbreak of a communicable disease, is the Public Health Information Network, which coordinates exchanges of data among public health organizations nationwide.

After a disastrous fire in a Rhode Island nightclub in February 2003, hospital officials throughout New England realized that they were ill-prepared to cope with the overwhelming number of burn victims that flooded area facilities, so they are working together to develop contingency plans for such an emergency in the future. The next step will likely be some sort of exercise to see if the plans will work, followed by an after-action report that might be shared through publication in the *New England Journal of Medicine.*

PRIVATE SECTOR RESPONDERS

In general, private businesses can do little to fight against terrorism, but they can prepare for the impact a terrorist attack might have on them. After 9/11, private firms in New York impacted by the attack realized that they needed to have evacuation plans, relocation sites, emergency communications, and off-site data storage if they were going to be able to function in a post-strike environment. These steps come on top of beefed up security for protection of property, personnel, and operations, which are the standard security functions for any business. The American Society for Industrial Security (ASIS) has been spearheading a drive to push security upgrades in the private sector and many firms are now adding the position of Chief Security Officer (CSO) to the more traditional senior management roles of Chief Operating Officer (COO) and Chief Financial Officer (CFO).

Private firms have to face more than terrorism in security planning. They have to protect against ordinary crimes, such as robbery, vandalism, fraud, and industrial espionage. Although private firms cannot adopt the more stringent security measures available in government, unless the firm is doing business with the national security elements of the federal administration, there are many steps private firms can take to enhance security. The ASIS has established strict standards for the certification of security professionals, including their level of education, experience in the security profession, and a certification examination, which should enhance security planning and management in the private sector.

Private security begins at the front door for many firms. Since 9/11, a great many companies have adopted barrier entry devices to preclude unauthorized entry into working areas. In the past, gaining entry to many firms only required joining a group of people entering the firm in order to sweep past guards. Sometimes, just looking like you knew where you were going would get you in. Now firms may be using more sophisticated devices such as hand print readers, or eyeball recognition systems, to keep outsiders out.

Private firms have limited jurisdiction outside their own premises and their control usually ends at the limits of the property. Security experts push the use of scanning systems to monitor property, although this means having someone either at a TV control desk or a tape system to record the data for review later. Most property can be well protected just by installing good lighting, which will work as well for homeowners seeking better security.

Of course, many firms are trying to be welcoming to their clients or customers, particularly in retail stores, hotels, or restaurants. In the United States, we have not yet gotten to the point where travelers have to be "wanded" when they enter a hotel, but such practices have been adopted in some countries where security against terrorism is a high priority. In the United States, this kind of security has been adopted for many sporting events which draw large crowds, although in most cases, it seems to be sufficiently loose so as to give the impression of security without being too rigorous.

TIGHTER RULES

Personnel security has been enhanced since 9/11 as well. Private firms have never been able to use the extensive and expensive systems the government uses to screen new hires, relying instead on prospective employees providing their own data, called in security literature "self-revelation." With the increase in personal information on the Internet, checking the background of a prospective new hire requires only a few mouse clicks. Anyone who cares to learn how much of his or her personal data is available need only ask for a review of credit data. This report can run to several pages and can usually be obtained just by asking for it from a credit bureau. Private firms cannot use the polygraph to interview a prospective employee the way the government can, but a careful interview can be quite revealing. Many firms have started to do more extensive checks on prospective senior officials after the scandals involving the leaders of several major companies such as Enron and Tyco.

Private firms are beginning to adopt tighter security tactics to prevent vandalism, especially damage to computer and telecommunications systems. Years ago, it was common to give people advanced notice of their possible dismissal so they could look for other work. Now, a pink slip is delivered accompanied by a security guard who walks the fired employee off the premises so that the potentially angry ex-worker can't destroy electronic data before leaving.

Private security workers are not the police, although in some firms they may be dressed like police officers and in certain circumstances may carry weapons. Even off-duty police who are moonlighting as private security guards usually are enjoined from exercising their police powers, unless the circumstances require such action to protect the public at large. The major role of the security force is to summon the police and detain suspects or protect evidence until the arrival of the cops. In most cases, having a visible protective force, especially in retail stores or in the hospitality industry, is the best way to deter crime.

SECURITY PLANNING

Security managers are responsible for developing the contingency plans for emergencies and this is where private security systems sometimes fall apart. Contingency planning has to be based on a solid threat assessment because it would be too expensive to develop protective plans against all possible threats the way the government does it. Threat assessments are an intelligence function, but most American firms do not have an internal intelligence unit, so they have no one to provide such assessments. So far, neither homeland security at the federal level nor the state ATTFs seem to be ready to provide threat assessments to the private sector. The vague and unfocused warnings provided when the threat level has been increased have done nothing to assist private sector security professionals. Private firms cannot afford to increase security based on such vague warnings and many states and local governments have had to curtail resources for heightened alerts. In the private sector, firms have begun to turn to private intelligence companies to give them the assessments they need for planning.

Contingency plans require exercise to be truly effective, but again the private sector has to be careful about trying out protective plans because of the costs involved. Nonetheless, many firms have started to practice evacuation and relocation, and the use of emergency back-up telecommunications and computer systems. We know from government experience, that systems need to be used periodically or they will not work when they are really needed.

The private security workforce outnumbers the police by about three to one in the United States, but so far, the private security force has largely been left out of the first responder networks that are developing around the country.[11] Charles Connolly, a former assistant police commissioner in New York City, and vice president in charge of security at Merrill Lynch, argues that this army of private security professionals should be part of the fight against terrorism, and that a public–private partnership should be built to take advantage of this large and untapped private force. So far, homeland security planners have not moved in this direction, but Connolly is optimistic that it will eventually happen.

THE MILITARY FIRST RESPONDERS

The last element in the network of first responders is that of the U.S. military, which has an overwhelming presence in the country but has only been tapped sporadically for homeland defense. Before 9/11, the military in this country was primarily engaged either in training for combat operations abroad or management, planning, and administration. There were, to be sure, tasks that engaged service personnel, but they were seen as ancillary to the main mission. These tasks included border protection, countering drug trafficking, supporting state and local authorities in dealing with natural disasters, protecting against weapons of mass destruction, infrastructure defense, and counterintelligence operations, including countering terrorism.[12] In fact, as a matter of public policy, the military services do not want to be first responders within the United States, but some action may be unavoidable.[13]

After the terrorist attack, the military was called upon to play an increased role in homeland security. Most of the forces seemed to come from the National Guard, which were called up by the individual state governors. The most visible role was in the air, as fighter units began to fly combat patrols over the United States in skies completely absent of commercial and private aircraft for the first time in modern U.S. history; two hundred fifty aircraft—including 120 fighters—patrolled the nation, aided by NATO early warning flights. These patrols lasted for several months after 9/11, as commercial air transportation resumed.[14] From time to time, even after the major patrols stood down, USAF fighters scrambled when private aircraft strayed into areas closed to them. No terrorists were involved, but no one was taking any chances.

More recently, the Air Force has been practicing ways to shoot down civilian airliners so as to minimize loss of life on the ground. This tactic would presumably be used if an airliner or cargo plane were hijacked and refused to land when ordered to do so. It's frightening to think that such action might be necessary, but bringing down a hijacked aircraft would be better than having it crash into a building or other terrorist target.

The U.S. military is not supposed to be involved in law enforcement operations, according to the Posse Comitatus Act of 1878, but clearly the rules of engagement are changing. The act was passed after alleged abuses by federal troops during the Reconstruction period in the South after the Civil War, but it has been modified several times by Congress. The military has been authorized to suppress insurrections, and assist in dealing with crimes involving nuclear materials or other weapons of mass destruction.[15] The possibility that the Posse Comitatus Act might be violated was raised in 2002 during the sniper attacks on Washington, when law enforcement officials wanted to use an Army plane for surveillance, but the Army's role in combating terrorism justified its use.

NORTHERN COMMAND

In order to manage the use of military forces for homeland security, President Bush ordered the creation of the Northern Command in 2002.[16] Under normal conditions, the Northern Command (NORTHCOM) is a headquarters only, in reality a part of the North American Aerospace Defense Command (NORAD) at Colorado Springs, Colorado. The commander of NORAD is also the commander of NORTHCOM, but there is a small cadre of personnel, about five hundred military and civilians, devoted solely to the homeland defense mission. The command will be fleshed out when it is needed, so the main function of the NORTHCOM cadre is to prepare for that eventuality.

NORTHCOM will be able to provide intelligence analysis to military forces in the United States through its connection to the NORAD Indications and Warning Center, which will plug into the worldwide military intelligence network. Intelligence from the Terrorist Threat Integration Center (TTIC) should also find its way into this network. In addition, military intelligence units within the United States, primarily devoted to counterintelligence, should be collecting and analyzing threats to military security. Overall, the military units that will serve for homeland defense will not have the kinds of problems with intelligence that affect other first responders.

However it is done, first responders need to have good intelligence for planning and to support operations. This is a subject that DHS ought to address sooner rather than later, but as of mid-2004, only first steps had been taken. Failure to share intelligence was one of the main complaints of the inquiries into the 9/11 disaster, so one would think that the DHS would be eager to solve this problem. The lack of movement is disappointing.

11

Restructuring Intelligence

One of the key recommendations of the Congressional investigation into the 9/11 attacks was to revise America's intelligence system to create a new position of director of National Intelligence to oversee the Intelligence Community (IC) in the wake of what was seen as a catastrophic intelligence failure. It was just the latest effort to make sense out of the IC's convoluted and rather inefficient structure. It's an idea worth examining, even though every effort made over the past sixty years to reorganize the IC has gone nowhere. While there is scant evidence that a more orderly and manageable IC structure would have prevented 9/11, the system is expensive, cumbersome, and lacks the authority at the top to make it work effectively. Surely, there must be a way to fix it.

When President Truman created the position of Director of Central Intelligence (DCI) in January 1946, there was no Intelligence Community, no Central Intelligence Agency, and almost none of the other intelligence agencies that make up today's IC. Truman's first DCI had nothing much to manage and did not report directly to the president, but rather to a National Intelligence Authority (NIA) which was made up of the secretaries of state, war, navy, and Truman's personal representative, Admiral William Leahy, his chief of staff. This was a plan backed by the Joint Chiefs of Staff because the NIA was dominated by the services and the plan kept the intelligence units of the Army and Navy intact.[1]

The plan had been put together by Rear Admiral Sidney Souers, who had served as deputy director of the Office of Naval Intelligence in World War II, and who was Leahy's confidant. Souers was then appointed to be the first DCI, and was given a small staff of about eighty people in a unit called the Central Intelligence Group (CIG), whose job was to pull together intelligence analysis from the military, the State Department, and the FBI. Souers got along well with Truman, perhaps because he had been successful as a private businessman before the war, he came from a background similar to Truman's, although he was a college graduate while Truman was not, and he was a navy reservist and not a career officer. Souers and the CIG began to send intelligence summaries to Truman, which he seemed to value more than the information he had been getting from the State Department, creating a tradition that has lasted in various forms to the present.[2]

TRUMAN'S MIND-SET

To illustrate Truman's mind-set about intelligence, in January 1946, the president named Souers his "chief snoop," and gave him a statue with a black cloak and a dagger, the symbols of intelligence in those days. What Truman apparently wanted was someone to be his intelligence adviser because he did not trust J. Edgar Hoover and the FBI or the State Department. The DCI remains the president's chief intelligence officer, but over the years a number of factors have intervened to dilute that role. There was no National Security Council in 1946, nor was there a national security adviser. There was no Congressional oversight of intelligence, and intelligence was a subject not often covered in the press. There was no IC, and there were no other intelligence agencies vying for the president's attention. In that simple world, it was relatively easy for the DCI to be a trusted confidant of the president.

Director Souers only spent a few months in office, then departed the post to return to the private sector. His successor, Lieutenant General Hoyt Vandenberg of the Army Air Forces, a World War II operational commander and nephew of influential Senator Arthur Vandenberg, took over as DCI in June 1946. Vandenberg took the post knowing that he was slated to become chief of staff of the newly independent Air Force that would emerge from pending legislation to create a Department of Defense in 1947. Meanwhile, Vandenberg expanded the CIG from 80 to 1,800 people and began to work to create an even larger and more independent intelligence agency modeled along lines suggested by former OSS commander "Wild Bill" Donovan.[3]

Although FBI chief J. Edgar Hoover tried to scuttle the new plan, just as he had when Donovan had first proposed it to President Roosevelt, Vandenberg took the wind out of Hoover's sails by agreeing to ban the new agency from most domestic operations, and from having any sort of police power. When the CIA was actually created in September 1947, Vandenberg left for the Air Force and Rear Admiral Roscoe Hillenkoeter, former director of the Office of Naval Intelligence, took his place as DCI and also as director of the new CIA. In creating the dual-hatted position, the Congress was only following the Vandenberg plan to give the DCI both access to the president and a rather large force of professionals to gather and analyze the intelligence the president wanted so badly.

AN INDEPENDENT CIA

The scheme placed the CIA outside the normal channels that then existed for the other departments. The CIA would have no political agenda, no departmental policies to defend, nor would it have a cadre of political appointees as senior officials as in the State or Defense Departments. The only stipulation made by the Congress was that the DCI and the Deputy DCI (DDCI) could not both be military officers. At least one would have to be a civilian. In the course of the debates about creating the CIA, little thought was given to separating the post of DCI from the position as director of CIA. The reasoning at the time, repeated often ever since, was that a DCI without an agency behind him would be weak and lack influence. The DCI's power would derive from his command of the Clandestine Service, a unique intelligence collection arm for foreign intelligence, and an equally strong cadre of independent analysts.

Now the DCI had three roles: he was the president's chief intelligence officer, he was the coordinator of governmental intelligence, and he was the manager of the CIA. The first and last tasks were clear, but what exactly was meant by coordinator of governmental intelligence? In 1947, it did not mean much, but over time as the Intelligence Community grew, it became more significant.

THE INTELLIGENCE CONGLOMERATE

After the creation of the National Security Agency in 1954 and the Defense Intelligence Agency in 1961, the notion of a conglomerate intelligence system became a reality. The DCI did not have control of these new agencies, but he did have a mandate to: "coordinate." To bring the new agency leaders together into the collegial system that was developing, the NSC created the U.S. Intelligence Board (USIB), and in later years, this became the National Foreign Intelligence Board (NFIB). The NFIB was chaired by the DCI and its members were the directors of the intelligence agencies.

This system continues and serves the same purposes as always. The NFIB is the final arbiter on substantive intelligence judgments that go forward to the president and is the group that manages the intelligence system. In the aftermath of the controversy over the intelligence judgments made by the IC in 2002 before the Iraq War about Iraqi nuclear capability, DCI George Tenet pointed out that the NFIB had signed off on the estimates that had gone forward to the White House. In other words, the judgments represented the collective wisdom of the 14 (now 15) IC agencies and not just the CIA.

The mandate to "coordinate" had come to mean different things at different levels. At the NFIB level, it only means that the agency directors meet with the DCI to discuss common problems and issues. At the working level among analysts, it means that CIA analysts discuss their judgments and findings with their counterparts in the other agencies that perform analysis. Overseas, it means that the CIA station chief meets with intelligence counterparts on the country team to make sure that each knows what the others are doing to avoid duplication or conflict.

FORCING THE IC TO WORK TOGETHER

Three significant developments forced the growing IC to have to work together. After the Church Committee hearings in 1976, the Congress created Intelligence Oversight Committees in both House and Senate, and they demanded that the DCI submit one consolidated budget for the IC, rather than having to review several different budgets separately. At about the same time, President Ford issued the first presidential executive order spelling out the role of the DCI and his responsibilities in regard to managing the IC. This led DCI George H.W. Bush to turn to the National Intelligence Programs Evaluation Staff (NIPE), which had been established by DCI John McCone in 1963, but which had not previously played a major role in community management.

The third development that forced the IC to work together was the growing use of intelligence gathering satellites that the agencies had to share. There had to be some sort of mechanism for determining how these systems would be targeted so that each IC agency would have its requirements met. In the Carter administration, these various tasks were assigned to an Intelligence Community Staff of more than two hundred professionals, some drawn from the IC agencies, some hired directly as staff cadre. The IC Staff was headquartered downtown in a building near the White House to make clear that it was a collegial effort and not just another part of the CIA. In order to emphasize his role as overall intelligence coordinator, DCI Admiral Stan Turner set up an office in the Old Executive Office Building next to the White House from which he would run IC affairs.

When the Reagan administration took office, it adopted this system and the new DCI Bill Casey decided to have his deputy, Admiral Bobby Ray Inman, manage IC issues, while Casey would run the CIA and serve as the president's chief of intelligence. This system seemed to work very well indeed, since Casey's close relationship to the president was well known, and the other agency leaders recognized that working within the IC system was the best way to have influence on substance as well as on management issues. Nonetheless, this was still a collegial system. The DCI did not have real control over the other agencies, since most of the people and the money belonged to intelligence elements of the Department of Defense. The DCI could not run the DoD elements, but his position in the administration motivated the agency leaders to cooperate. It appeared to work very well.

MANAGING THE IC

Under this system, the DCI had two community groups that were seen as part of his IC role: The IC staff helped manage the system, especially in regard to putting together the combined IC budget, the National Foreign Intelligence Program (NFIP), while the National Intelligence Council, located at CIA headquarters, served to bring together IC analysts from the various agencies to create National Intelligence Estimates and other IC substantive publications. The CIA was just one of the participating agencies. The FBI, although technically a part of the IC through its counterintelligence component, hardly participated at all. This was not surprising, since most of the emphasis within the IC was focused on foreign intelligence.

At the end of President George H. W. Bush's administration, Robert M. Gates became DCI and moved the IC staff to CIA headquarters, renaming it the Community Management Staff. Now both the substantive and management units were housed at the CIA and gave the impression that the system had been co-opted by the CIA. While the move was made ostensibly to save money by giving up the building downtown, it was a mistake, in my view. It alienated the other agency leaders and reduced considerably the collegial nature of the IC. The situation became even worse when the Clinton administration took office.

President Clinton was not particularly interested in intelligence when he took office because his policies were largely focused on domestic issues. He chose as DCI R. James Woolsey, who had little experience with intelligence matters and with running an organization the size of CIA. Woolsey was bright and articulate, but had little access to the White House. When a befuddled flyer crashed his light plane into the White House, some jokesters said that it was really Woolsey trying to get the attention of the president. Some historians claim that Woolsey was forced out because of fallout from the Ames case, while others thought it was was his lack of meaningful interchange with the White House that drove him to resign. President Clinton's next choice proved even less effective than Woolsey.

After Woolsey's departure in 1995, President Clinton asked Deputy Secretary of Defense John Deutch to take the post of DCI, a position the former MIT professor certainly did not want. He had hoped to become secretary of defense himself, but when that did not work out, he accepted the DCI post, although without much enthusiasm. Unlike his predecessor, who at least understood the nature of the intelligence process, Deutch seemed to have a real outsider's view. One of his key errors came in the wake of revelations that a CIA agent, a Guatemalan army officer, had been involved in the death of an American citizen. Deutch decided to purge the CIA roles of any recruited agents who might have been somehow violators of human rights or those with criminal backgrounds. These people, all foreign nationals, despicable though they might have been, were critical in penetrating groups that might be plotting against the United States. Efforts by CIA Clandestine Service officers to prevent this serious loss of sources were turned down.

THE 1996 REFORM STUDIES

Deutch had no better luck than his predecessor in working with the IC, but during his tenure, several serious and well-organized studies into reforming the IC got underway. One study was sponsored jointly by the Congress and the White House, one was undertaken by the House Intelligence Oversight Committee, and one was sponsored by the Council on Foreign Relations. All these studies appeared at about the same time in 1996 and many of their recommendations were similar. All suggested that the system was generally working well, but that it would be a good idea to give the DCI more say in managing the IC, including more input into the budget process. Although the studies received wide circulation, very few of the suggested reforms were actually implemented.

In fact, the 1996 studies were just the latest in a series of IC reform studies that dated back to the first one in 1949, undertaken by General Jimmy Doolittle of World War II fame, and followed by at least twenty others over the years.[4] Unfortunately, none of these studies resulted in significant changes to the IC, despite the prestige of their authors and the wisdom of their recommendations. The 1996 studies were just the latest in the series; their suggestions that more resources be devoted to intelligence improvements were rejected by budget managers in both the White House and the Congress.

DOING MORE WITH LESS

Beginning even before Mr. Clinton took office, and despite the intelligence demands of the Gulf War, the intelligence agencies were suffering from budget cuts, personnel reductions, and instructions to "do more with less." This meant early retirements for experienced intelligence professionals, fewer posts overseas, and cuts in technological research. Many relatively young professionals, especially those with less than ten years in intelligence, saw no future in a long-term career and chose to move to the private sector where the money was better and the hours were shorter. The CIA shut down its recruiting system, and opportunities in the other agencies seemed to dry up as well. This was another blow to the IC as morale fell and there was little motivation for the agencies to cooperate, each guarding what was left of its turf.

GEORGE TENET AS DCI

In 1997, Deutch decided to return to MIT and President Clinton found that no one close to the White House wanted to be DCI, so he turned to DCI Deutch's deputy and former White House staffer George Tenet to be the next DCI. It was a fortuitous choice. Although Tenet had no credentials as an intelligence officer, he had served on the staff of the Senate Intelligence Oversight Committee as well as in the White House as intelligence coordinator, and he seemed to have no political agenda. He had good connections within the IC and, unlike his predecessor, he seemed willing to listen to advice from intelligence professionals. He proved to be an able leader and soon morale at CIA, which had sunk to new lows, began to go back up.

When George W. Bush took office, perhaps on the advice of his father, who had served as DCI before winning the presidency, Tenet was given a mandate to stay on as DCI, thus depoliticizing the position and returning to the standards set by presidents before Jimmy Carter. For his part, Tenet immediately moved to cement his relationship with the new president. He returned to the practice of giving President Bush daily intelligence briefings, something that had not been common in the Clinton White House, especially in the early years. Tenet made a special effort as well to work more closely with the other IC agency heads to restore the collegiality that had been a hallmark of the system in its formative years.

AFTER 9/11

Along with Director Mueller of the FBI, DCI Tenet had to take the brunt of the criticism of U.S. intelligence after 9/11, although many of the problems in interagency coordination and cooperation were not of their making. The Director of the NSA, General Michael Hayden, also took some heat in the investigations that followed the terrorist strike. As is common in such situations, the cry went up that intelligence had failed and the way to fix it was to reorganize the system. No one was more outspoken than Senator Richard Shelby of Alabama, at that time the Republican chairman of the Senate Select Committee on Intelligence, who called for Tenet's resignation. Fortunately, wiser heads prevailed.

Meanwhile, Brent Scowcroft, President George H. W. Bush's national security adviser, had been chairing a commission to look once again at intelligence reform. The study had begun well before 9/11, but gathered some momentum after the terrorist strike. In December 2001, rumors began to circulate that the Scowcroft Commission was going to recommend that the intelligence collection agencies that belonged to the Department of Defense—the NSA, NIMA (now NGA), and the NRO—should be put under the control of the DCI, so that the DCI would command almost all the major collection assets of the government. In 2002, the study was actually made public and the recommendations were confirmed.[5]

"ONE DOG TO KICK"

Secretary of Defense Donald Rumsfeld had let it be known, after the stories circulated about the Scowcroft Report, that he was not about to let the DCI take away the Pentagon's intelligence collection agencies, especially with troops in Afghanistan and the possibility of war with Iraq on the horizon. In fact, Rumsfeld did more than just express his displeasure; he decided to derail the commission's recommendations before any further damage was done. Soon after the commission's report appeared, Rumsfeld announced that he wanted to create a new position in the Pentagon, Undersecretary of Defense for Intelligence, and give that person oversight of all DoD intelligence components, including the collection agencies, the DIA, and the military service intelligence units. The undersecretary would control the military intelligence budgets, both for national and for tactical (war fighting) intelligence. One intelligence veteran at the Pentagon said that the move was made so that Mr. Rumsfeld would have "only one dog to kick" instead of the "kennel of dogs" he had under the old system, an apt description of Rumsfeld's management style.[6]

This clever maneuver must have had the approval of the president, although he made no comment on the matter. Further, it had to have had the approval of the Senate Intelligence Committee, or the man nominated to be the first undersecretary, Stephen Cambone, would never have been confirmed. In taking the undersecretary's position, Mr. Cambone had become, in effect, the director of Military Intelligence, and had control of most of the intelligence assets, in both money and manpower, of the entire government. The only thing he did not have was direct access to the White House, which still remained the purview of the DCI.

The creation of this new post, with its program and budget control of military intelligence, could be a good move for the Pentagon and the IC, although former DCI John Deutch saw it only as a "power-grab."[7] The undersecretary oversees the Joint Military Intelligence Program, which includes the budget for the DIA, NSA, NGA, and NRO, as well as the Tactical Intelligence budgets for service intelligence units. This means that a more coherent and coordinated programs system will develop within the Pentagon and should make it easier to put together the budget for the IC. Mr. Rumsfeld indicated that he intended that there should be good coordination between the undersecretary and the DCI.

CREATING A DIRECTOR OF NATIONAL INTELLIGENCE

Despite what appears to be a sensible development in military intelligence management, Mr. Rumsfeld's maneuver has short-circuited the recommendations of the Congressional Joint Inquiry into 9/11. Whether Mr. Rumsfeld intended to do that remains a matter of conjecture, but it is not that significant because some of the key recommendations of the Joint Inquiry are probably unworkable anyway. The study recommends the creation of a director of National Intelligence (DNI), who would be separate from the director of CIA and who would have budget and program authority over all national intelligence. The aim was to create one leader who could bring the IC into a coherent whole. While this sounds good in theory, it fails to recognize the conglomerate nature of the IC and the variety of consumers the system has to serve.[8] Yet, there may be ways to make the position of DNI effective.

Intelligence is not just about stopping terrorism, although that is the threat "du jour." The system has to be flexible enough to provide intelligence data and judgments to all levels of government, from the president to war fighters on the ground overseas. It has to focus on targets that range from North Korean missile developments to political in-fighting among our friends and allies. It is not just about homeland security but rather about the broader issue of national security, at home and abroad. For a variety of reasons, the system envisioned by the Joint Inquiry, which would give the DNI almost total control of all the IC agencies, would not only destroy the collegial nature of the IC, but create a militant system of management that would damage morale and inhibit risk taking, two of the key factors in any successful intelligence system. There is a better way.

At first glance, the American intelligence system seems hopelessly confusing, unlike most countries where the several agencies report directly to the chief of government, whether a prime minister or a president. In most countries, however, the intelligence systems are far smaller, easier to manage, and have fewer targets in a more confined environment. In the United States, the budget for intelligence, a secret figure but thought to be in the $35–$40 billion range, exceeds the entire governmental budget of some countries.

The IC requires direction and management that is flexible and imaginative. It has not always had that, but it does today and that ought to be built upon, not torn down. Still, there are ways to make the system even better, the alleged 9/11 failure notwithstanding. If the systems suggested by the Joint Inquiry had been in place before 9/11, there is still no guarantee that the attack on the United States would have been detected and stopped.

SEPARATING THE DCI FROM THE CIA

Starting at the top, let's examine the idea of separating the position of DCI from that of director of the CIA. Combining the two positions was a natural outgrowth of Harry Truman's original idea and while it did not mean much at first, it came under scrutiny only after the development of satellites and budget consolidation. Still, the combined position was designed to lead the cold war fight against an easily defined enemy. The system, as it grew, was focused almost exclusively on foreign intelligence. Homeland security was not an issue. Now, we need a way to lead intelligence both at home and abroad, to bring together foreign intelligence elements with those devoted to domestic security. While the Joint Inquiry panel would create an intelligence "czar," a kind of intelligence dictator, what is really needed is an intelligence leader who could bring the various agencies together to cooperate and coordinate their efforts.

To lead intelligence, we need a professional, not a politician. He or she should be given a tenure of ten years to further depoliticize the position, so that the DNI would not have to worry about independence from the political policies of whatever incumbent is in the White House. This notion of tenure already applies to the director of the FBI and has proven its merit. The DNI must have close and instant access to the White House and the National Security Council and should have an office near, but not necessarily within the White House as a further sign of independence.

The DNI needs to have the close support of a DNI Staff, which would include a community management staff to deal with budgets and programs, and the evaluation of IC systems. The DNI staff should include a collection management system that would bring together representatives of the various IC agencies to establish collection targets and priorities both at home and abroad. The National Intelligence Council, broadened to include national intelligence officers (NIOs) for domestic as well as for foreign security issues, should be downtown as well, with a staff of analysts large enough to support the NIOs. The analysts on the NIC would be drawn from around the community, while the NIOs would be nominated by their agencies and selected by the DNI. The DNI could be supported for indications and warning by the White House Situation Room, which is already plugged into the worldwide Indications and Warning network; there would be no need for yet another 24/7 ops center. All of this should be centralized in downtown Washington, close enough to the seat of power to have an impact on the decision process.

The Joint Inquiry recommended that the post of DNI be a cabinet-level position, forgetting the fuss that was created when DCI Bill Casey held cabinet-level status. Casey thought of himself as a policy maker as well as an intelligence officer. His successor, Judge William Webster made a specific point that he was not part of the cabinet and would leave cabinet meetings after he had given an intelligence briefing. Of course, the DNI would have to be confirmed by the Senate, but the DNI does not have to be a member of the cabinet to be effective. The DNI's role is to make intelligence policy, not national policy. He should, however, be a member of the National Security Council, as the DCI is now.

A JOINT INTELLIGENCE COMMITTEE

The Joint Inquiry recommended that the DNI manage and control the IC, but Secretary Rumsfeld's changes in the DoD have precluded that kind of approach. What is really needed is a way for the DNI to coordinate the IC's efforts to make sure that there is good communication and cooperation. To that end, the DNI should chair a Joint Intelligence Committee (JIC), a practice that has found favor in other countries, especially in Great Britain. The existing mechanism of this kind is the National Foreign Intelligence Board, to which each of the 15 intelligence agency heads belong. In the past, it was really the senior intelligence officials of the agency, or in the case of the FBI, the head of counterintelligence who attended the meetings. The proposed JIC would be a lot smaller then the NFIB and take advantage of several recent developments. The DoD member would be the Undersecretary for Intelligence, the FBI Director would represent domestic security, the Undersecretary for Homeland Security Intelligence would be a member, as would the Director of the CIA. The JIC of five would seek to develop the kind of coordination and cooperation to make the IC work. It would be a collegial system to bring together foreign and domestic intelligence at the highest level. It would not supplant the NFIB, which would continue to exist to carry out overall IC management, and make substantive judgments as the NFIB does now, and it, too, would be chaired by the DNI.

The JIC concept has a precedent in the U.S. Joint Chiefs of Staff, which is a similar collegial council, made up of the Chiefs of Staff of the military services, and chaired by a senior officer selected by the president, with the advice and consent of the Senate. The Chairman has no troops, no agency, no budget to speak of, but because he sits on the National Security Council and has access to the president, the Chairman has a measure of power the other generals do not have. The JCS system has worked since World War II, and the JIC ought to be able to work the same way.

Is there real benefit to making a change from DCI to DNI? I argued previously that it was unnecessary, and that a DCI who could bring the other intelligence leaders together could be successful, even without the command authority envisioned by the Congress or other reformists.[9] In the post–9/11 world, however, there needs to be some way to bring foreign and domestic intelligence together, and creating the DNI position, along with the JIC and IC revisions, might help shift our intelligence system away from its lingering cold war mentality to new thinking.

The Joint Inquiry suggests the creation of a new NIO for Terrorism. I was surprised to learn that there wasn't one, since most of the intelligence agencies had a senior official or group focused on terrorism even before 9/11. If such a position were created, this official would be part of the National Intelligence Council supporting the DNI. Creating such a position ought to be simple enough and could be implemented even if none of the other reforms were made.

REVAMPING CIA

Several former CIA officers have been writing about what's wrong with the CIA and how to fix it. Among the most interesting ideas are those proposed by Bruce Berkowitz, a former CIA analyst, who has called for more "agility" in the U.S. intelligence system to cope with targets that change quickly, that are amorphous, and that do not lend themselves to the kinds of intelligence collection and analysis systems that worked reasonably well during the cold war.[10] Berkowitz believes, and I agree, that we need to break down the "stovepipes" that prevent good communication and the sharing of ideas. One good way to do this would be to end the separation of collectors and analysts that has been a hallmark of CIA since its inception.

The separation is now a mental and cultural one, but when I joined the agency, the two sides were kept apart by armed guards. They are still separated physically, although they do come together in the fusion centers, such as the TTIC. The separation is perpetuated by two distinct cultures. Within the Clandestine Service, there are myths that suggest that analysts are incapable of protecting agent sources or even the cover of the operations officers. On the analysts' side there are myths that depict operations officers as somewhat disreputable and manipulative, and that they skew their source materials to protect operations at the cost of accuracy. Of course, neither side is correct.

Actually, operations officers and analysts are more alike than either side thinks, differing sometimes in the nature of their personalities. In terms of education and experience, they are more alike than they are different. Both sides work toward the same goal, to provide truth to power. The principle that each officer would work within a compartmented system, with his or her "need to know" kept limited so as to reduce damage if an adversary spy managed to penetrate the CIA, is a manifestation of the cold war. In the new war on terrorism, analysts and collectors ought to work closely together and have the ability to communicate quickly to "connect the dots." The cultural barriers and managerial controls need to be changed, but this won't happen from the bottom up. It requires that the director of CIA, whether he or she is DCI or not, direct the changes from the top.

FUSION CENTERS

The Joint Inquiry recommendation to create an "all-source terrorism information fusion center" within the Department of Homeland Security seems to ignore completely the Terrorist Threat Integration Center (TTIC) that was created in 2003. The TTIC, headed by a senior CIA officer, performs all the tasks listed by the Joint Inquiry, but it is independent of the DHS. Why create yet another such center? What the DHS really needs is a more broadly based intelligence analysis unit that should focus on more than the threat of terrorism. It ought to deal with all the threats to domestic security, including global crime and espionage. The DHS already has people at the TTIC and there is no need for more duplication.

The TTIC belongs to the DCI. If the post of DNI is created, should the TTIC maintain its independence and report directly to the DNI? This seems to make a great deal of sense, since TTIC is a service of common concern to the entire IC. It should continue to represent all the intelligence agencies, including those from DoD. The Joint Inquiry makes much of the need for "jointness" in intelligence. TTIC is certainly one model for how such "jointness" can be established, but it requires that the intelligence collection agencies be forthcoming with their data in a usable format. The CIA practice of limiting the use of its agent reports, or the NSA close holds on some intercepted material have to be set aside if TTIC is to function effectively. It seems likely that this would be an issue on which the DNI will have to weigh in, from time to time, given the secretive nature of the agencies involved.

REFORMING THE FBI

No agency has taken more hits or received more criticism, both in the Joint Inquiry and in the press, than the FBI. The Bureau has been slammed as well for its poor performance in rooting out Soviet spy Robert Hanssen. The Joint Inquiry has a great deal of advice for how the FBI can improve itself, but the press seems to be ignoring the rather effective and timely efforts by Director Mueller to fix things. The Congressional recommendations push the FBI to improve its analytic capability as well as its computer technology. Conversations with FBI agents and other employees reveal that efforts to accomplish both tasks are well underway.

Within two years, the FBI should have a fully functioning domestic security analysis component co-equal with its agent cadre. The Bureau will have done all the things the joint inquiry recommended. It will probably still be behind in computer technology, a common problem in government, because of the way the government buys computer hardware and software. The FBI, like its IC counterparts, will likely have to turn to the private sector if it wants to develop a state-of-the-art system.

The Joint Inquiry does not say much about integrating the FBI's new capabilities into the overall work of the IC, but here, too, much has been done. The Congress wants the DNI, the secretary of Homeland Security, the attorney general, and the Intelligence Oversight Committees all to monitor the FBI's progress in making reforms. Surely, this is not only overkill, but would prevent the FBI director from moving quickly to complete his reform program if he had to spend most of his time reporting to so many bosses about his progress. If the government creates the position of DNI, then that person ought to be the one to oversee intelligence developments at the FBI. The Bureau's law enforcement functions ought to remain under the supervision of the attorney general.

DEFENDING THE USA PATRIOT ACT

The Joint Inquiry suggests that the Congress and the Justice Department should take another look at both the USA Patriot Act and the Foreign Intelligence Surveillance Act to make sure that they are working against security threats, but by the time the Joint Inquiry was made public, a review in various quarters was already underway, perhaps not in the way the inquiry intended. In August 2003, Attorney General Ashcroft began touring the country to stump for strengthening the Patriot Act or at least extending those parts of the act that will expire in 2005. He did not seem to receive much support. Meanwhile, members of Congress and the public from both the right and the left began to question the act itself.

Conservatives began to express doubts about the Patriot Act because they saw it as giving the government too much leeway to invade the privacy of citizens or put them under surveillance. At the same time, civil liberties groups were pressing for changes for many of the same reasons as the hard-liners.[11] According to press reports, more than 150 communities around the country have passed ordinances objecting to the act or have ordered that its law enforcement personnel refuse to follow some of its provisions. Since Mr. Ashcroft's meetings were closed to the public, they did not provide the kind of venue for demonstrations and protests that might otherwise have been expected.

While there may be some aspects of the USA Patriot Act that require revision, members of Congress who will likely review the legislation in

2005 must remember that security officials need to have some tools to work with if they are to provide domestic security for the American people while at the same time protecting their human and civil rights. It seems likely that some reasonable compromise can be worked out that will overcome the more questionable aspects of the law, which admittedly was drawn in haste and anger.

RECRUITING NEW TALENT

The Joint Inquiry recommends that a greater effort should be made to recruit, train, and retain the skilled personnel who make up the IC work force. This is an area where a great deal of work remains to be done. During the height of the cold war, the CIA had recruiting offices around the country, staffed by intelligence veterans, that sought to find the best and the brightest on college campuses and through advertising in local papers. The FBI had recruiters, on-duty FBI agents, in many of its main offices who tried to find the right people to put into training to become special agents. Other agencies relied on local and national advertising to attract the kinds of people it needed.

Today, intelligence recruiting looks a lot different, but many of the mistakes made earlier are still being repeated. Almost all the agencies rely on the Internet to facilitate recruiting, with single officers scattered around the country to give out information and do initial screening. It is still a passive system in the sense that potential hires are not "recruited," or sought out, but rather the agencies put up ads or provide information hoping that the right people will see them and apply.

The agencies are still looking for the right skill mix, as they always have, with emphasis on language skills, area knowledge, business or professional experience, or street smarts, but this is risky. For example, the CIA, FBI, and NSA are all looking for Arabic speakers, hoping that people with the right education and work experience, as well as an ability to speak Arabic, will somehow find their way onto the Web to apply. Recruiters should, instead, seek out students or others with those skills and convince them to apply.

The intelligence system is not taking advantage of an enormous change at U.S. colleges and universities in regard to intelligence recruiting. During the cold war, CIA and military recruiters were regularly shunned by many schools, or barred from recruiting on campus. The recruiters became the targets for antiwar or antigovernment protests, and in some cases the recruiters were chased off campus during their appearances. Today, most faculty members welcome intelligence agency recruiters, except perhaps for a few academic holdovers from the cold war period, and are eager to see their students enter military service. Intelligence recruiters ought to develop close ties to those professors on campus who might help them find the students who have the potential to enter intelligence service.

The second problem is that the recruiters expect to find already skilled professionals who fit their needs and who can pass the background and security screening to obtain clearances. What they get are people whose language skills may be less than perfect, perhaps a dialect rather than mainstream language, and whose family or work background prevent them from passing the security tests. The potential recruits may have close family abroad or have traveled in areas that might complicate a background check. Added to that are complications such as youthful drug experimentation, or other misbehavior that tends to create complications for potential applicants.

THE POLYGRAPH

Complicating the security and background checks is the use of the polygraph to conduct a security interview, both for potential new hires and periodically to do security reviews of the regular work force. Although the polygraph can be unreliable, security professionals claim that an experienced operator can use the machine to detect attempts at deception. Certainly, the polygraph tends to intimidate people into being more truthful than they might prefer. Absent some more sophisticated device to detect abnormal reactions in an interview, the polygraph remains the security officer's most effective tool.

After the FBI revealed that Soviet spy Robert Hanssen had never been polygraphed, Congressional critics pressed the intelligence agencies for even wider use of the machine. In the Aldrich Ames case, there seems to be a widespread perception that Ames had beaten the polygraph, but that is incorrect. In two different security interviews, the polygraph showed that Ames was trying to hide information, but in each case, the interviewer eventually concluded that Ames was OK. Ames had defeated the operator, not the machine. I argued previously that more funds should be invested in new systems that might be more reliable than the polygraph.[12] If a breakthrough is to come in this field, it will likely emerge from the private sector rather than through government research.

EDUCATION AND TRAINING

While the military has long expected that new hires would require training to become intelligence officers, the civilian IC agencies always seem to hope that new hires, especially analysts, could just sit down and do the job with minimal orientation. At a conference to discuss intelligence training, I once heard a manager of analysts say that his office was too busy to send his new hires to training; he apologized when he realized how ridiculous that sounded. The CIA has developed an analyst training program, housed in the Sherman Kent Center, to give new hires the skills they need to be successful.

Military intelligence professionals, whether on active duty or as civilians, have the opportunity, beyond their basic training, to attend the Joint Military Intelligence College, which is both a training and education facility.

When I began work as an analyst many years ago, I received no training at all. I had come from seven years experience as an Air Force intelligence officer, however, and had had rather intense training throughout my military service, so I was able to sit down and do the work. Later, as a analyst supervisor, I found that one of my major tasks was to train new analysts, whose only intelligence education had concerned security issues and orientation to CIA.

The Joint Inquiry, in pressing for the development of "jointness" correctly points out that joint training is a good way to break down the "stovepipes" that hinder interagency cooperation. Since basic intelligence skills are common to all the agencies, the DNI ought to seek to create a Joint Intelligence Training Center where newcomers to the field could not only study together, but develop bonds that might be sustained throughout a career. This works for the military and it could work for the entire IC. The only group that might be excluded are those headed for sensitive positions undercover, where their identities have to be protected even from their intelligence co-workers.

The Joint Inquiry recommended that the IC expand its recruitment and hiring of minorities and "first-generation Americans" to create a "more ethnically diverse" workforce. That has always been the goal of the IC agencies, but they have had mixed success. The problem is not so much hiring as it is retention. First-generation Americans from European or Asian backgrounds may do well and can look around and see senior officers from similar backgrounds as role models. Blacks and Hispanics may see fewer such role models and decide that they could do better in the private sector. Although there is hardly a position in intelligence that men can do better than women, women remain a minority in the professional work force. The increasing number of women in university graduate and professional programs may eventually change the ratio of men to women in intelligence.

The Bush administration dealt something of a blow to employee retention in 2003 when it announced that for the second year in a row, federal civilian workers would not receive the pay raise they had been promised, while military personnel would get a bit of a raise. This seemed particularly harsh because political appointees would be eligible for substantial bonuses.[13] Efforts to realign or change the pay of intelligence professionals to be more competitive with the private sector have not made much progress although the issue has long been studied. The DCI now has the authority to make such changes, at least at CIA, but the workers themselves are often reluctant to risk experimentation with a system that might somehow reduce or limit their take-home pay.

ENCOURAGING "JOINTNESS"

The Joint Inquiry, in suggesting that "jointness" be encouraged and implemented among the IC agencies, is overlooking the realities of personnel management in the IC. After the Gulf War in 1991, the U.S. military leadership determined that more "jointness" was needed to overcome interservice rivalry and failure to cooperate. A tour of duty with another service or in a joint command became a prerequisite to promotion, and the military services were ordered to improve interservice communications and logistics. Subsequent military operations in Bosnia, Kosovo, and later in Iraq, demonstrated that "jointness" had largely been achieved. It is not yet true in intelligence.

The intelligence services have always suffered from a mentality that says that a rotational tour of duty with another service or agency is not as important as service at home. This was particularly true in CIA when I served there, and continues to be an issue to this day. Although the military has largely overcome fears of "jointness" and interservice assignments, that may not be true for the civilian components. DIA has reportedly made an interagency rotational tour a prerequisite to promotion, but it is not clear that the other DoD-controlled intelligence agencies have the same attitude. There continues to be serious rivalry between the CIA and the FBI, and neither agency seems to value the services its officers perform for the other.

Even more problematic is the notion of requiring officers, especially analysts, to serve a tour in a policymaking component. While the idea is a good one and should give those who take such an assignment a good feel for intelligence consumers and their needs, the assignment sometimes backfires because the analyst, having tasted the heady world of policymaking, does not want to return to his or her former agency, preferring instead to stay "downtown." There are several cases I know of where the officers who did return from out-of-agency assignments were not given credit for their good performance, but were told that they had to go back to a lesser job and prove themselves all over again. This kind of personnel management has to be overcome if "jointness" is ever to be achieved.

ALTERNATIVE IDEAS

There are more radical ideas about intelligence reform that go well beyond merely creating a DNI or encouraging "jointness." They are interesting approaches to making sense out of the current IC system, but they are far too radical to earn the support of the White House and the Congress, the two bodies that must make them work. One idea, espoused by Mel Goodman, a former senior CIA analyst, would break up the CIA and create one agency for clandestine human source intelligence collection and another for analysis. Goodman encouraged this step to prevent analysis from being tainted by operational considerations. In reality, it would be better to have the analysts and clandestine operators work more closely together in the interest of making sure that the right data is collected.

General Bill Odom had an even more far-reaching idea. Odom suggested breaking up the analysis directorate of CIA, which he saw as generally irrelevant, and putting more analysts into the National Intelligence Council. He envisioned the creation of National Counterintelligence Service and recommended that more weight be given to the National Security Agency, which he once headed.[14] No one seems to have taken these suggestions seriously.

Larry Kindsvater, a senior analyst at the CIA, writing in the unclassified issue of CIA's professional journal, Studies in Intelligence, suggested that "jointness" could be enhanced with the creation of substantive centers, much like the TTIC, although TTIC had not yet been created when he wrote his article.[15] The centers could be focused on a variety of issues, such as North Korean nuclear proliferation, or other hot topics, and would bring together the combined wisdom of the agencies of the IC. There is a great deal of merit in Mr. Kindsvater's ideas as another way to avoid the "stovepipes" of the current system.

PRESIDENTS AND REFORM

Whatever reform is to come, there is only one way it will take place. It requires the president to initiate the action, with the support of the Congress. The kinds of reforms suggested in the Joint Inquiry or put forward by the rest of us cannot grow, as I have said, from the bottom up. This requires top down action and only the president has the political muscle to start the process. Over the years, presidents have been unwilling to do more than issue Executive Orders ratifying the existing system, rather than seeking change. Unless the White House weighs in on intelligence reform, we are not likely to see it.

As a good first step, the president ought to seek legislation creating the post of Director of National Intelligence, separating the post from the CIA, and giving the DNI the authority to institute the other changes that will make the system function according to the needs of the new era in national and homeland security. Otherwise, we will be fighting the war against terrorism and the other threats with a cold war system that is poorly equipped to deal with the challenges of the twenty-first century.

Liberty and Security

As we remembered the events of 9/11 in September 2003, and the thousands who died in the terrorist attacks, it became clear that Osama bin Laden and his terrorist henchmen did a lot more damage to the United States than the destruction of buildings and the murder of our people. The terrorists had spread terror and fear, as they had hoped, but they had also dealt a serious blow to our economy. Far worse, bin Laden had caused us to set aside some of our precious freedoms in the interest of increasing security and striking back at terrorism. Two years later, Americans are beginning to question the value of security over liberty, and government power over individual privacy. There are no easy answers.

This has happened before. During the Civil War, President Lincoln suspended various civil liberties in the interest of maintaining security, especially when it appeared that Southern sympathizers in the North were cooperating with the rebels. The suspension of legal norms led to abuses by security officials, including rather draconian behavior by Lafayette Baker, the head of the newly created Secret Service. People were jailed without due process, homes were raided without warrants, and surveillance of suspected Southern sympathizers was carried out without court order. These actions may sound familiar to anyone reading about the aftermath of the 9/11 terrorist attack.

After fears of espionage agents and saboteurs grew in World War I, there was again an outcry for increases in homeland security. In 1917, even before the United States entered the war, after German agents blew up the Black Tom ammunition depot, there was a public outcry, even though no one was killed in the blast.[1] President Wilson ordered the Justice Department to "apprehend and detain 'enemy aliens,'" leading the newly established Bureau of Investigation to put not only German agents under surveillance, but also people who opposed U.S. entry into the war.[2]

Among the officials detailed to track enemy aliens was a young lawyer named J. Edgar Hoover, who had been working at the Library of Congress. Hoover took charge of the Enemy Alien Registration Section at the Justice Department and promptly set out to find potential enemy agents. Hoover reportedly jailed people who spoke out against the United States, and in one case, detained a German who had lived in the United States for more than thirty years. It was at this point that Hoover began his practice of keeping records on anyone suspected of being a threat to domestic security.

THE PALMER RAIDS

In 1919, newly appointed Attorney General A. Mitchell Palmer established the General Intelligence Division within the Justice Department to collect information on radicals or revolutionaries.[3] Primary targets included the American Communist Party and leftist elements within organized labor. The leader of this new operation was J. Edgar Hoover.

In June 1919, Palmer became the target of a terrorist bombing at his home in Washington and bombs were placed in eight other cities at about the same time. The attacks were the work of anarchists, but the press blamed Communists for the strikes.[4] Palmer ordered the Secret Service to round up and deport any aliens who might somehow have been connected to the "Palmer Raids," arresting thousands of aliens and U.S. citizens who had attended Communist Party or Communist Labor meetings. Five hundred fifty-six aliens were deported, but most of those arrested were let go; the people who had been responsible for the attack on Palmer were never found.[5]

After the war, the Bureau of Investigation shifted its focus to the fight against crime and in 1924, Hoover became its director. He said that it was time to end the surveillance of radicals and concentrate on organized crime and other threats, but Hoover never ended his practice of keeping files on people he thought might be potential problems. Apparently, he was able to order the collection of information or the placing of people under surveillance without court order or warrant. He merely had to order his agents to do the work.

During World War II, after the surprise attack on Pearl Harbor, persons of Japanese ancestry, even those who had been born in the United States, came under suspicion as potential enemy agents and were rounded up and relocated from the West Coast to concentration camps—the government called them "relocation camps"—east of the Sierra Nevada mountains. The government claimed that this was done to protect the Japanese, but the barbed wire and guard towers were clearly designed to keep people in, not out. Although such steps were not taken against people of German or Italian ancestry, some German and Italian aliens were detained early in the war.

The American people were advised that "loose lips sink ships," mail to and from abroad was censored, and there was a general call to be on the lookout for enemy spies and saboteurs. Since the Soviets had become our allies, anti-Communism was soft-pedaled for the duration of the war. The post–World War II period presented a different picture entirely, as the cold war began and anti-Communism once again became the mantra of domestic security.

HUNTING FOR REDS

During this period, there was another "Red Scare," except this time there was good evidence that Soviet spies had penetrated the U.S. government. Now we know that the Venona intercepts had pinpointed some of these penetrations, although the information was not released to the public until many years later. The House Un-American Activities Committee began a witch hunt for Communists, based on the mistaken belief that Communists (Reds) in Hollywood, aided by Communist sympathizers (Pinks), were polluting American minds through pro-Communist films. The result was the blacklisting of a number of screen writers and directors.

The loyalty of many Americans came into question during this period. Current university students are astonished to learn that I and my fellow high school students back in the 1950s were forced to sign loyalty oaths in order to graduate. Senator Joseph McCarthy, in his zeal to find Communists in government, held hearings in which it became clear that he was attacking the wrong targets. His methods led to calling the witch hunt "McCarthyism," and illustrated how the power of government could be abused in the name of national security.

President Harry Truman was quite correct when he feared that a combination of intelligence and law enforcement had the potential to create a secret police in this country. Thus, the 1947 law creating the CIA specified that the new agency would have no police power, and no role in internal security matters. The firewall created by limiting connections between the CIA and the FBI helped ensure that individual freedom and privacy would not be invaded by the secret services. Nonetheless, the system did break down during the Vietnam War period.

GOING AFTER PROTESTERS

We know from the Church Committee hearings that both the CIA and NSA, as well as the FBI, were targeted against antiwar protesters, ostensibly to make sure that the antiwar movement was not directed by a foreign power. Mail to and from abroad was opened, phone calls were monitored, and people, including some in the government, were put under surveillance. I can remember vividly meeting with the attorney general in the Nixon administration during this period. There was an antiwar demonstration being held on the street just below his office and he went over to the window to see it, muttering that the demonstrators ought to be rounded up and detained. Fortunately, President Nixon did not move in that direction, although he feared that demonstrators might invade the White House. In order to stop them, he ordered the Washington, DC government to surround the White House with buses and garbage trucks as a defensive barrier.

THE FISA RESTRAINTS

When the Foreign Intelligence Surveillance Act was passed in 1978, it offered a measure of control over the indiscriminate use of intelligence and FBI resources in regard to internal security. It required that the FBI seek a warrant from the Foreign Intelligence Surveillance Court before placing someone under surveillance as an agent of a foreign power. The FBI had to demonstrate to the court that there was sufficient evidence—probable cause—to undertake the operation. We believed at the time that the FISA was supposed to reinforce the firewall between intelligence and law enforcement. This was certainly the case in the effort to apprehend Aldrich Ames. After the counterintelligence team pinpointed Ames under an FISA warrant, a criminal team, using a second warrant under the Omnibus Crime laws, then gathered evidence against Ames that could be used in court.

Now, several factors have come together to break down the firewall and close the gap between intelligence and law enforcement, leading to fears that the kind of secret police that Harry Truman sought to scuttle, could become a reality. With the passage of the USA Patriot Act and the strengthening of the FISA, we now have a troubling situation. The Foreign Intelligence Surveillance Court has ruled that the original FISA legislation never intended to create the firewall between intelligence and law enforcement in the first place. In addition, the courts have agreed that the FBI may task the intelligence collection agencies for data gathered abroad for use in criminal investigations. Whether or not such data could be actually used in court has not yet been tested. So far, the government seems reluctant to allow such use, claiming that it might jeopardize intelligence sources and methods. The restrictions on using the IC to target American persons—citizens, resident aliens and U.S. corporations—remain in effect.

ENEMY COMBATANTS

In three cases that we know of in the two years since 9/11, U.S. citizens were declared to be "enemy combatants" and their rights and privileges as citizens were taken away. They were not given the right to counsel and it appeared that they would not be tried in the regular court system, but would face a military tribunal where their right to a fair trial might not be honored. Efforts by civil rights groups to provide legal assistance or even maintain communication with the three had not been successful in the several months after their capture. If a president could declare anyone an enemy combatant and thus remove his or her civil rights, this would be a frightening abuse of constitutional guarantees. For its part, the Bush administration seemed intent on making sure that the enemy combatant cases, or cases involving detainees at the Guantanamo prison camp never saw the light of judicial review so that the president's powers in this regard were not tested. But, the Bush administration made a serious error when it claimed that the federal courts had no jurisdiction in these cases.

In November 2003, the Supreme Court announced that it would hear appeals from people detained in Guantanamo.[6] According to press analysis, the court's decision was as much based on the legal issues involved as it was the challenge to the court's jurisdiction. When the adminstration told the court to "keep out" of the cases, it was a blow to the court's status as the third branch of government, co-equal with the executive and legislative branches. Then, in December, federal courts ruled against the administration in the case of the U.S. citizens held as "enemy combatants." Thus, the courts, perhaps in 2004, will begin to set the limits on how far the White House can go in detaining persons suspected of terrorism, or limiting their access to lawyers and the courts.

GOVERNMENT POWERS

In general, the Patriot Act gives the government the power to invade individual privacy to an extent not seen since the Red Scares of the twentieth century. According to some civil libertarian critics, the Patriot Act gives the government unprecedented access to such things as lawyer–client communications, financial records, and even library use.[7] FBI officials deny that they have either the interest or the manpower to dig away at such materials, but the potential for abuse is certainly there. In my experience, security zealots in government tend to ignore controls and restrictions when it suits them, arguing that national security concerns outweigh personal rights when the country is threatened. Unless there is close supervision and oversight, abuse is inevitable. Further, claims of the need for secrecy might deter oversight or prevent it entirely.

In some ways, FISA does a great deal to protect Americans, since no warrant for surveillance can be issued without seeking approval from the Foreign Intelligence Surveillance Court. This is in marked contrast to the cold war period when FBI surveillance could be ordered by the Director without any such legal moves. According to several sources, the FBI sought

1,228 warrants under the FISA in 2002; the FISA Court rejected none of them. In 2003, the number of approved FISA warrants jumped to 1700, exceeding the number of warrants (1442) requested in criminal cases for the first time. The FBI report on this issue suggested that the rising number of FISA warrant requests were overwhelming the system established to process and approve them.[8] So far, there have been no reported abuses of the FISA process.

PATRIOT ACT REVISIONS

In early 2003, the sentiment in Congress and among the public did not favor strengthening the Patriot Act and most seemed willing to allow the sunset clauses in the law to expire. After touring the country and speaking to carefully selected audiences, Attorney General Ashcroft must have come away with quite the opposite impression. Nonetheless, realizing that the passage of a Patriot Act II was unlikely, President Bush proposed separate legislation in September 2003 to strengthen the government's hand in the war on terrorism. He asked for laws to prevent judges from granting bail in terrorism cases, to impose the death penalty in cases where defendants are found guilty of terrorism, and to provide for the issuance of administrative warrants so that suspected terrorists could be put under surveillance without the need to seek court approval. There were serious problems with each of these requests.

Taking away judicial discretion in granting bail to those suspected of terrorism could cause irreparable harm to those who are eventually found innocent. If the suspects are established members of a community, sending them to jail without the possibility of bail punishes them even before a trial. One of the purposes of having a judge determine if a suspect is a flight risk is to preserve the notion that a person is innocent until proven guilty. Experience shows that some people accused of terrorism will turn out to be innocent; they should not be punished for being suspects.

Demanding the increased imposition of the death penalty demonstrates that the administration has failed to understand the culture of the *jihadis* it seeks to punish. In theory, the death penalty is supposed to deter others from engaging in the same crime as the condemned. But, what if the condemned welcomes the death penalty as a way of becoming a martyr? In cases where Muslim extremists seek martyrdom, imposing a life sentence is a far greater punishment than death. The president's proposal in this regard would be counterproductive.

Finally, taking the courts out of the process of determining whether or not to grant a surveillance warrant destroys the protections the FISA rules have established. Apparently, no requests for FISA warrants have ever been refused. The president seemed to hope that these three measures could be slipped into other legislation in order to gain their passage, a typical ploy in the case of controversial proposals. Even if they pass, they may not provide the tools to stop terrorism.

THE MASTER LIST

Meanwhile, the government announced in September 2003 that it had created a new center to manage what it called a master terror watch list.[9] This move was made in response to complaints that there were as many as a dozen such lists floating about and no one had access to all of them. The new center would be run by the FBI with members from both the CIA and DHS. John Brennan, the CIA officer in charge of the Terrorist Threat Integration Center, said at the time that he expected that there would be about a hundred thousand names on the list. While law enforcement officials said the list would respect privacy and civil rights, they did not say how a person could find out if he or she was on the list, or what to do if an error in compiling the list was made.

It seems to me that the greatest danger to the innocent with such a list is that people who might be listed by mistake would not know it until they were detained. It does not seem possible that a list of the size contemplated would be free of error. People ought to be able to find out if they are suspected of something in the same way as they check their credit. If the private sector can have access to the list, as the government plans, then individuals should have some way of finding out if they are suspects, too. And they should have some way of clearing their names in the same way that they deal with identity theft, or mistaken credit reports.

In one frightening case, a Canadian citizen, Maher Arar, who had been born in Syria, was detained at JFK airport in New York, allegedly because his name had appeared on one of the terrorist lists.[10] Arar was turned over to security officials, and according to one report, was then taken by CIA officers, first to Jordan, and then Syria, where he was turned over to Syrian security officials. Arar claimed later that he had been tortured and kept in an earthen cell, before being released and returned to Canada. The press called the CIA action an "extraordinary rendition," a term not previously used in the agency. It seems to mean the practice of returning low-level terrorist suspects to the security services in their country of origin. There have been cases where persons indicted in the United States have been brought back from overseas to stand trial; the case of Mir Aimal Kansi, the man who assassinated two CIA officers outside its headquarters, was one. The idea of using CIA to return suspects in the United States to their own country would seem to be a violation of the 1947 proscription against the CIA becoming involved in internal security matters. In the matter of

Maher Arar, Secretary of State Colin Powell asked the Justice Department for an explanation, but so far, none has surfaced.

Another terrorist attack on the United States could change attitudes about new legislation very quickly. It took Osama bin Laden and his henchmen eight years to organize the second attack on the World Trade Center after failing to bring down the buildings in 1993. Is bin Laden smart enough to understand that a prolonged period of calm will inevitably erode interest in homeland security and the people's willingness to permit invasions of privacy in the interest of security?

ERODING RIGHTS AND FREEDOMS

The government's efforts to round up, detain, or deport suspected terrorists, illegal aliens, and alleged enemy combatants, without providing them with access to legal aid or due process is troubling indeed. This may be one of the most damaging aspects of the terrorist attack on 9/11. It is understandable that in the first few days after the attack, anger and emotion drove the administration to extreme measures. Over time, however, the erosion of rights and freedoms ought not to be sustained. There is a way to ameliorate this situation, however, although it might not be palatable to the more conservative members of the Bush administration.

What we need is a way to ascertain whether or not detainees are being given fair and legal treatment, while at the same time protecting the secret sources and methods we are using to root out threats to national and homeland security. We should have a nonpartisan go-between, cleared for all the secrets, who can judge the fairness of the government's actions and intervene where abuse is discovered. This is a system that has worked with varying degrees of success in Canada. After concerns were raised about the creation of the Canadian Security Intelligence Service and the possibility of abusing civil rights in Canada, a committee was created to oversee the service and serve as an ombudsman. The Canadian Security Intelligence Review Committee (SIRC), is drawn from former senior members of the government, is nonpartisan, and issues annual reports about its oversight of the CSIS.

CORRECTING ABUSES

We could have a similar kind of ombudsman function to make sure that even the worst of our enemies discovered within the U.S. receives fair treatment, a hallmark of American justice in the modern era. A proposal made by the Gilmore Commission seems to fit the bill nicely. James S. Gilmore III, a former governor of Virginia, chaired a bipartisan federal commission to study responses to terrorism and weapons of mass destruction. The panel, which was set up before 9/11, issued its final report in

December 2003 and included in its report was a recommendation to create a "civil liberties oversight board" that would check into allegations of violations of civil freedoms in the United States.[11] Gilmore's plan would establish a bipartisan board to make sure that increasingly sophisticated technology for surveillance or other intrusive measures do not become excessive or erode protection of privacy or legal rights. If such a panel were created, it could serve as a board of appeals for those who end up on "no-fly" or terrorist lists by mistake.

Secondly, the prison camp that the administration has set up to receive, detain, and interrogate alleged enemy combatants in Cuba ought to have a process for releasing quickly those who have no connection to terrorism, narcotics peddling, or global crime. The idea that the United States can hold these people indefinitely without trial smacks of a concentration camp. We seem to have learned relatively little from the interrogation of the people held in Cuba, although the government claims that useful intelligence has been produced. We are holding these people mostly because we can. The Congress ought to be asking the administration where it is going with this prison policy. Now that the courts have decided to weigh in on the issue, it may be resolved soon.

Toward the end of 2003, stories surfaced in the press that the administration planned to release some of the Guantanamo prisoners, but they would be returned to their country of origin on the condition that the home country put them in prison. In some cases, the Guantanamo prisoners might prefer staying in the U.S. prison because their treatment at home might be far worse.

LIVING WITH DEATH

As the second anniversary of 9/11 approached in September 2003, the press began a low-key review of our situation since that terrible event. Clearly, many who were not touched directly by the event have put it behind them, but others, at least in New York, have a lingering paranoia about the threat of terrorism. Press stories during this anniversary managed to find those who refused to travel, use public transportation, or who had a continuing fear of resuming normal daily life because of the threat that they or their families could be killed by terrorists. Yet, Americans face enormous risks and the threat of death every day from other causes.

The most serious threat to those who fly is not traveling on the airplane, but driving to the airport. In 2002, for example, there were almost 43,000 motor vehicle deaths in the United States. Of those, more than 17,000 were alcohol-related. The leading factor in the motor vehicle deaths, about 59 percent of them, was failure to use a seat belt.[12] Stories circulating in the press suggest that some see seat belts, or motorcycle helmets for bikers, as unnecessary restrictions on their personal freedom. These motorists are quite willing to take risks, even when they know that the odds of surviving a crash are reduced by their behavior. Failure to use a seat belt is illegal in many places but is lightly enforced. Drunk drivers soon return to the highway, licenses intact. How often do we learn that a person has multiple convictions for drunk driving and has been involved in yet another accident?

Even more deadly is the use of tobacco. On average, the United States suffers 400,000 tobacco-related deaths every year. That means that more people die in one year from tobacco use than have died over 20 years from AIDS. Each day, on average, 81 Americans kill themselves, but 1,095 die from tobacco use.[13] Although many jurisdictions have banned indoor smoking, and even a few have tried to ban smoking altogether, American streets are increasingly smoke-filled as tobacco addicts, forced to pursue their habit outside, seek to kill themselves with cigarettes. Tobacco companies have admitted that their products are dangerous and addictive, but nothing has been done to stop tobacco use because sales of tobacco products form a lucrative tax base for the federal and state governments.

While the government cannot stop people from smoking, it certainly could make a better effort to make sure everyone knows about its dangers. We are spending huge sums of money to stop deaths from terrorism, but the number of people killed by terrorists, either at home or abroad, pales in comparison to the number of preventable deaths from other causes. The lesson is clear: Americans take risks every day and the risk of terrorism is far lower than from other causes.

Then there are people who seek ways to tempt death by engaging in such highly risky ventures as mountain climbing, hang gliding, or parachute jumping, sometimes without either proper training or good equipment. When they get into trouble, they expect others to risk serious injury or death to rescue them. How often do we read that someone has tried to scale Mount Ranier in Washington, or Mount McKinley in Alaska without proper clothes, boots, or food? When they become lost or stranded, if they can manage to call for help, then teams from the Park Service have to be organized to go after them. The people who are rescued never seem to recognize either the cost of extracting them from their failed venture, or the risks they impose on others.

PUBLIC INVOLVEMENT

Generally speaking, most people in the United States outside the first responder system or the various offices of Homeland Security, have had little to do with the enormously complex bureaucracy that is being conducted to protect them. There was a brief period when DHS issued vague warnings about terrorism and WMD, driving many people to stock up on supplies including duct tape and plastic sheeting. This was done in the mistaken belief that people could cover up their houses with such materials well enough to prevent penetration of chemical or biological weapons.

After the DHS toned down the warnings, sales of the items returned to normal and interest in protective measures largely went away.

According to informal conversations with first responders, the DHS effort to have people phone in tips about strange or dangerous behavior they might have witnessed, led to people denouncing neighbors they did not like, or wives to turn in ex-husbands, or former boyfriends. According to one source, of the approximately 100,000 tips that were received after the sniper shootings in the Washington area in 2002, only 40,000 had any validity at all. It seems clear that asking the general public to turn into tipsters will waste the resources of the police or security investigators who have to check out the tips.

In fact, there are very few measures the average person can take against terrorism anyway. Perhaps the security checks at airports or the wanding of fans before a major sporting event is a good thing, if for no other reason than to remind people that the fight against terrorism is an ongoing struggle. It would be a good thing if people began to realize that they should be cooperating with security checks and not ignoring their requirements. While some travelers are seeking to wear shoes with plastic instead of metal shanks to avoid setting off alarms, others are causing delays by bringing with them items sure to set off a more stringent security check. One man, arrested when security screeners found a loaded pistol in his carry-on luggage, said he had "forgotten" it was there. Properly trained individuals would never forget where they had put their weapons; firearms should never be left lying around loaded. Ask any policeman or soldier.

According to some sources, millions of potential and real weapons have been confiscated by security screeners since the TSA system was put in place in 2002. People should be reminded, if they really care about stopping terrorists, that putting a strain on screeners by carrying items they have to search out may prevent them from finding the real terrorists when the time comes. People need to be reminded, from time to time, that homeland security is everyone's business; cooperation with security checks, even when they are annoying and intrusive, is the best way to ensure safety for their fellow citizens.

PAYING FOR SECURITY

So far, the American people have not had to pay anything for homeland security. At most, they might have been assessed a small fee at airports to help defray security costs, or have paid slightly higher prices for consumer goods as private firms seek some way to offset the costs of increased security while doing business. The DHS is costing taxpayers about $35 billion in FY 2004, but no one has paid the bill. The federal government has borrowed all the money from our grandchildren, along with funds to sustain the wars in

Iraq and Afghanistan. In moving rapidly from surplus to deficit by borrowing huge sums of money while cutting taxes, the Bush administration has set the government on the path of supply-side economics that failed previously during the Reagan presidency.

The federal government is behaving as if it had a giant credit card with unlimited spending limits, no monthly bill, and no minimum payment requirements. The government manages to do this by printing money, selling treasury notes to foreign investors, and periodically raising the debt ceiling imposed by Congress. State and local governments do not have these options. Instead, they are now in the position of having to beg for money from the federal government, since no state or local government, in today's world, is likely to be successful in trying to raise taxes to finance first responders or other homeland security measures.

Part of the problem with this economic scheme is that U.S. taxpayers have had to pay nothing for homeland security, except perhaps for some airport fees, so they have no financial stake in the system. Those who lost loved ones on 9/11 have had to sacrifice dearly, and surely there have been economic dislocations as the result of the terrorist acts, but for most people homeland security is not a part of their lives. It might have been better policy to have added a homeland security surcharge to federal taxes just to remind people that security does not come free. Just a few dollars might have been enough.

THE NEED FOR TRUTH

It seems pretty clear that the trade-off between liberty and security is not a fixed ratio. If terrorists launch another strike on the United States, those who want stronger measures to put terrorist suspects under surveillance or in detention will receive support in the days following an attack, but as tempers die down, the measures are likely to be questioned and rescinded. In the end, our political system will hear the voices of the people if they bother to speak out. The continuing lack of participation in the electoral process by so many of our citizens is disheartening. The result of this disinterest is that a relatively few citizens out of the total population are choosing the leaders who make policies, including security policies.

People may be losing interest in the political process because they don't know whether or not the government is telling the truth about its policies. This is especially true in regard to intelligence, where most of the information has to remain secret to be useful. In the aftermath of the U.S. attack on Iraq in 2003, it became clear that the Bush administration's claims that Iraq had weapons of mass destruction and was prepared to use them against the United States were distortions of the intelligence the IC had given the White House. No WMD were found in Iraq after the war, so the administration had to fall back on the argument that Saddam Hussein had certainly had the weapons at one time and must have either destroyed them, buried them, or shipped them out of the country. No evidence to support these claims surfaced, however, in spite of pressure on intelligence to find out what had happened.

The White House claimed as well that there were ties before the war and before 9/11 between Saddam Hussein and Osama bin Laden, even though intelligence reports could not confirm this. In fact, the evidence suggested just the opposite, that Osama bin Laden thought that Saddam Hussein was as much an infidel as the Americans. It was only after the conventional war died down in Iraq and the guerrilla war broke out that *jihadis* from around the Middle East moved into Iraq, apparently established ties with Baathists, and began to carry out a terror campaign against U.S. forces. Nonetheless, Vice President Cheney continued to claim that the Osama-Saddam connection predated the war, leading one former intelligence officer to characterize the story as the kind of lie that, told often enough, becomes established truth.

Later, President Bush contradicted Mr. Cheney, admitting that there had been no ties between Osama and Saddam before the Iraq War. Still, polling data showed that a majority of people in the United States believed the ties existed, apparently based on earlier statements by the president. The American people deserve better from the White House.

While it is true that a great deal of intelligence material has to remain secret to protect sources and methods, and to avoid telling our enemies how much (or how little) we know about them, when the White House does see fit to make intelligence information available to the public, it ought to be untainted by a political agenda or partisan philosophy. Intelligence, after all, belongs to all the people, and not just to the officials who happen to inhabit the seat of power.

Good intelligence is the first line of defense in homeland security. Combined with effective law enforcement and the steady and consistent application of the judicial process, Americans can be protected from terrorism, global crime, and industrial espionage. Certainly, the American people are prepared during periods of extreme emergency to cede some of their liberties in exchange for enhanced security, but they are not prepared to give the government a blank check. They expect their freedoms to be restored promptly when the emergency is over and they deserve no less.

Notes

CHAPTER 1

1. Final Report of the Congressional Joint Inquiry into 9/11 (www.fas.org/irp/Congress/2002_rpt).

2. John Solomon, "Sept. 11 plot five years in making, report says," *Boston Globe,* 2 September 2003, p. A1.

3. Good histories of U.S. intelligence include: Stephen F. Knott, *Secret and Sanctioned: Covert Operations and the American Presidency.* New York: Oxford University Press, 1996; George J. A. O'Toole, *Honorable Treachery: A History of of U.S. Intelligence, Espionage, and Covert Action from the American Revolution to the CIA.* New York: Atlantic Monthly Press, 1991; and Rhodri Jeffreys-Jones, *The CIA and American Democracy,* 3rd Edition. New Haven: Yale University Press, 2003.

4. Douglas J. MacEachin, *CIA Assessments of the Soviet Union: The Record vs. the Charges.* Washington, DC: Center for the Study of Intelligence, CIA, 1996.

5. Roberta Wohlstetter, *Pearl Harbor: Warning and Decision.* Stanford, CA: Stanford University Press, 1962.

6. James Bamford, *Body of Secrets: Anatomy of the Ultra-Secret National Security Agency.* New York: Doubleday, 2000; *The Puzzle Palace.* New York: Houghton Mifflin, 1982.

7. John Donnelly, "CIA takes on major new military role," *Boston Globe,* 20 January 2002, p. A1.

8. Ronald Kessler, *The Bureau: The Secret History of the FBI.* New York: St. Martin's Press, 2002; *The FBI.* New York: Pocket Books, 1993.

9. Kessler, *The Bureau,* pp. 299–300.

10. David Wise, *Spy: The Inside Story of How the FBI's Robert Hanssen Betrayed America.* New York: Random House, 2002.

11. John Solomon, "Sept. 11 plot five years in making, report says."

12. Paul R. Pillar, *Terrorism and U.S. Foreign Policy.* Washington, DC: Brookings Institution Press, 2001, pp. 41–72.

CHAPTER 2

1. Richard A. Serrano, "Third Arrest of Staffer at Guantanamo," *Los Angeles Times,* 1 October 2003.

2. Paul Pillar, *Terrorism,* pp. 158–160.

3. Milton Bearden and James Risen, *The Main Enemy: The Inside Story of the CIA's Final Showdown with the KGB.* New York: Random House, 2003, pp. 361–367.

4. Paul Pillar, *Terrorism,* p. 49.

5. Steven Emerson, *American Jihad: The Terrorists Living Among Us.* New York: Free Press, 2002, pp. 30–36.

6. Paul Pillar, *Terrorism,* pp. 50–56.

7. Matthew A. Levitt, "The Political Economy of Middle East Terrorism," *The Middle East Review of International Affairs,* 6 no. 4.

8. Paul Pillar, *Terrorism,* p. 13.

9. James Reston, Jr. *Warriors of God: Richard the Lionheart and Saladin in the Third Crusade.* New York: Doubleday, 2001.

10. Sharon Begley, "Likely Suicide Bombers Include Some Profiles You'd Never Expect," *Wall Street Journal,* 4 April 2003, p. B13.

11. Ibid.

12. Mark Bowden, "The Dark Art of Interrogation," *The Atlantic Monthly,* October 2003, pp. 51–76.

13. Neil MacFarquahar, "Hezbollah Becomes Potent Anti-U.S. Force," *New York Times,* 24 December 2002, p. A1.

14. Amy Waldman, "Masters of Suicide Bombing: Tamil Guerrillas of Sri Lanka," *New York Times,* 4 January 2003, p. A1.

15. Jerry Saper, "Terror Cell on Rise in South America," *Washington Times,* 18 December 2002, p. A6.

16. Bruce Hoffman, *Inside Terrorism.* New York: Columbia University Press, 1998.

17. Jessica Stern, *Terror in the Name of God: Why Religious Militants Kill.* New York: ECCO, 2003, pp. 9–31.

18. Ibid., pp. 147–171.

19. Leila Aboud, "Anti-terrorism's Hidden Costs," *Wall Street Journal,* 26 March 2003, p. A4.

20. John Warrick, "Commercial Devices Could Fuel Dirty Bomb," *Washington Post,* 16 June 2003, p. A14.

21. David Rohde, "$3 Million U.S. Computer Theft, Hatched It Seems in Pakistan," *New York Times,* 20 January 2003, p. A3.

22. Greg Krikorian, "U.S. Drug Rings Probed for Ties to Mideast Terrorists," *Los Angeles Times,* 24 December 2002, p. A7.

23. Paul Kaihla, "Forging Terror," *Business 2.0* (www.business2.com).

24. "America Still Unprepared; America Still in Danger," *Report of an Independent Task Force sponsored by the Council on Foreign Relations,* 2002.

25. Cheryl Thompson, Marcia Slocum, and Sarah Cohen, "INS Moves to Plug Student Visa Leaks," *Washington Post,* 29 January 2003, p. A1.

26. Philip Shenon, "Investigators Entered U.S. With Fake Names and IDs," *New York Times,* 31 January 2003, p. A13.

27. Eric Lichtblau, "Holes Found at INS Checks at Airports," *New York Times,* 24 January 2003, p. A12.

28. Ted C. Dishman, "America's war on terrorism overlooks small-arms trade," *USA Today,* 20 January 2003, p. 13A.

29. Dan Eggen, "Move to Justice Department Brings ATF New Focus," *Washington Post,* 23 January 2003, p. A19.

30. Bob Tedeschi, "E-Commerce Report," *New York Times,* 27 January 2003, p. C4.

31. Kathy Sawyer, "Biowarfare Monitors Are Deployed in the U.S." *Washington Post,* 23 January 2003, p. A6.

CHAPTER 3

1. Dan Eggen and Kimberley Edds, "Ex-FBI Agent, Longtime 'Asset' Arrested in Spy Case," *Washington Post,* 19 April 2003, p. A22.

2. Philip Knightly, *The Second Oldest Profession.* London: Andre Deutsch, 1986.

3. George J. A. O'Toole, *Honorable Treachery.* New York: Atlantic Monthly Press, 1991, pp. 11–16.

4. Ibid., pp. 121–122.

5. Philip Melanson, *The Secret Service.* New York: Carroll and Graf, 2002, p. 5.

6. Jules Witcover, *Sabotage at Black Tom.* Chapel Hill, NC: Algonquin Books of Chapel Hill, 1989.

7. Barbara Tuchman, *The Zimmermann Telegram.* New York: Ballentine Books, 1966, pp. 71–72.

8. Ronald Kessler, *The Bureau,* p. 11.

9. David Kahn, *Hitler's Spies.* New York: Collier Books, 1978, pp. 328–331.

10. Robert L. Benson and Michael Warner, eds. *Venona.* Washington DC: CIA, 1996.

11. Pete Earley, *Family of Spies: Inside the John Walker Spy Ring.* New York, Bantam Books, 1989.

12. Arthur S. Hulnick, "Understanding the Ames Case," *International Journal of Intelligence and CounterIntelligence* 8 no. 2, pp. 133–154.

13. David Wise, *Spy.*

14. Ian Black and Benny Morris, *Israel's Secret Wars.* New York: Grove Weidenfeld, 1991, pp. 416–427.

15. Daniel Benjamin and Steven Simon, *The Age Of Sacred Terror.* New York: Random House, 2002, pp. 123–124.

16. "Intelligence Officer Accused of Spying," *Washington Times,* 9 February 2003, P. A2.

17. "Annual Report," National Counterintelligence Center, 1998.

18. "Technology Collection Trends in the U.S. Defense Industry, 2002," Alexandria, VA: Defense Security Service (www.dss.mil).

19. Del James, "FBI: Spies Cost U.S. Firms \$2 Billion a Month," *USA Today,* 10 February 1999, p. 2B.

20. www.USDOJ/USAO/can/pcs/html/2002_12_4

21. *New York Times,* 26 September 2000, p. A2.

22. Nicholas Eftimiades, *Chinese Intelligence Operations.* Annapolis, MD: Naval Institute Press, 1994.

23. John Fialka, *War By Other Means: Economic Espionage in America.* New York: W.W. Norton, 1997.

24. Edward Robinson, "China's Spies Target America" *Fortune,* 30 March 1998, p. 118.

25. Fialka, *War By Other Means,* p. 23.

26. Ibid., p. 26.

27. Ibid., p. 212.

28. Ibid, p. 29.

29. Yochi J. Dreazen, "McDonnell Douglas to Pay Fine for Problems with Sale to China," *Wall Street Journal,* 15 November 2001, p. A4.

30. Robinson, "China's Spies Target America" *Fortune.*

31. Justin Gillis, "Scientists Accused of Theft," *Washington Post,* 12 May 2001, p. A18.

32. Peter Schweizer, *Friendly Spies.* New York: Atlantic Monthly Press, 1993, pp. 32–45.

33. Ibid., pp. 46–65.

34. William Bulkeley, "IBM, Hitachi Reach Agreement to Combine Disk Drive Units," *Wall Street Journal,* 17 April 2002, p. A3.

35. Schweizer, *Friendly Spies,* p. 13.

36. Ibid., p. 20.

37. Fialka, *War By Other Means,* pp. 88–94.

38. Ibid., pp. 93–94.

39. Ibid., p. 120.

40. Schweizer, *Friendly Spies,* p. 122.

41. Ibid., p. 113.

42. Ibid., p. 221.

43. Ibid., pp. 223–225.

44. Ibid., pp. 236–237.

45. Fialka, *War By Other Means,* p. 182.

CHAPTER 4

1. Stephen F. Knott, *Secret and Sanctioned: Covert Operations and the American Presidency.* New York: Oxford University Press, 1996, pp. 125–126.

2. Robert David Steele, *On Intelligence: Spies and Secrecy in an Open World.* Fairfax, VA: AFCEA International Press, 2000; *The New Craft of Intelligence.* Oakton VA: OSS International Press, 2002.

3. Arthur S. Hulnick, "The Downside of Open Source Intelligence," *International Journal of Intelligence and CounterIntelligence,* 15 no. 4 (Winter 2002–2003), pp. 565–579.

4. David Kahn, *The Codebreakers.* New York: The Macmillan Company, 1967.

5. James Bamford, *Body of Secrets.*

6. Jane Meyer, "The Search for Osama," *The New Yorker,* 4 August 2003.

7. Bamford, *Body of Secrets,* pp. 428–429.

8. Ibid., p. 430.

9. Ibid., pp. 436–440.

10. Gregory W. Pedlow and Donald E. Welzenbach, *CIA and the U-2 Program. 1954–1974.* Washington DC: Center for the Study of Intelligence, CIA, 1998.

11. Jeffrey T. Richelson, *America's Secret Eyes in Space: The U.S. Keyhole Spy Satellite Program.* New York: Harper and Row, 1990.

12. John Donnelly, "CIA," *Boston Globe,* 20 January 2002.

13. Curt Anderson, "FBI Nightstalkers track suspects by flying quietly above U.S." *Associated Press,* 14 March 2003.

14. See, for example, Robert Baer, *See No Evil: The True Story of a Ground Soldier in the CIA's War on Terrorism.* New York: Crown Publishers, 2002; Duane Clarridge, *A Spy for All Seasons: My Life in the CIA.* New York: Scribner, 1997.

15. Bearden and Risen, *The Main Enemy.*

16. Fred Rustmann, Jr. "Debunking the CIA Case Officer Myth," *AFIO Newsletter,* 25 nos. 1 and 2, 2002.

17. Thomas Patrick Carroll, *Middle East Intelligence Bulletin,* 5 no. 4 April, 2003.

18. Benjamin and Simon, *Age of Sacred Terror,* pp. 282–283.

19. Baer, *See No Evil,* pp. 3–7.

CHAPTER 5

1. James Risen, "How Pair's Finding on Terror Led to Clash on Shaping Intelligence." *New York Times* 25 April 2004, p. 171.

2. Stuart A. Cohen, "Myths About Intelligence," *Washington Post,* 28 November 2003, p. A41.

3. *Intelligence in the War of Independence.* Washington DC: Central Intelligence Agency, 1976.

4. Knott, *Secret and Sanctioned,* pp. 129–130.

5. Richard Harris Smith, *OSS: The Secret History of America's First Central Intelligence Agency.* Berkeley, CA: University of California Press, 1972.

6. Nathan Miller, *Spying for America.* New York: Dell Publishing, 1989, p. 279.

7. John Hollister Hedley, ed. *Fifty Years of Informing Policy.* Washington, DC: Central Intelligence Agency, 2002.

8. David Brooks, "The Elephantiasis of Reason," *The Atlantic Monthly,* January–February, 2003.

9. *Global Trends 2015: A Dialogue About the Future with Non-Governmental Experts.* Washington, DC: National Intelligence Council, December, 2000.

10. William Odom, *Fixing Intelligence.* New Haven CT: Yale University Press, 2003.

11. Christopher Andrew, *For the President's Eyes Only*. New York: Harper Collins, 1995.

12. Dean Allen and Brian Shellman, eds. *Defense Intelligence Agency: At the Creation, 1961–1965*. Washington DC: DIA History Office, 2002.

13. Leonard Fuld, *The New Competitor Intelligence*. New York: John Wiley & Sons, 1995.

14. "FY 2004 Budget Fact Sheet" Press release, Department of Homeland Security, 1 October 2003.

CHAPTER 6

1. Edwin Fishel, *The Secret War for the Union*. New York: Houghton Mifflin, 1996, p. 27.

2. Arthur S. Hulnick, "Intelligence and Law Enforcement: The 'Spies Are Not Cops' Problem" *International Journal of Intelligence and CounterIntelligence*, 10 no. 3, pp. 269–286.

3. Kessler, *The Bureau*, p. 99.

4. Hulnick, "Intelligence and Law Enforcement," p. 271.

5. James Adams, *Sellout: Aldrich Ames and the Corruption of the CIA*. New York: Viking, 1995, p. 12.

6. Bearden and Risen, *The Main Enemy*.

7. David Wise, *The Spy Who Got Away*. New York: Random House, 1988.

8. Perhaps the best book on the Ames case is Pete Earley, *Confessions of a Spy: The Real Story of Aldrich Ames*. New York: Putnam, 1997.

9. Bearden and Risen, *The Main Enemy*, pp. 473–474.

10. David Wise, *Spy*.

11. Bearden and Risen, *The Main Enemy*, p. 529.

12. Associated Press, "FBI Planning to Add Officers Overseas," *Washington Post*, 1 April 2003, p. A13.

13. Stewart D. Baker, "Should Spies Be Cops?" *Foreign Policy* 97, Winter 1994–1995, pp. 36–52.

14. Michael Turner, "CIA-FBI Non-Cooperation: Cultural Trait or Bureaucratic Inertia," *International Journal of Intelligence and CounterIntelligence*, 8 no. 3.

15. Benjamin and Simon, *The Age of Sacred Terror*, pp. 226–227.

16. Baker, " Should Spies Be Cops?"

17. Hulnick, "Understanding the Ames Case," p. 282.

18. Clarridge, *A Spy For All Seasons*, pp. 349–359.

19. Hulnick, "Intelligence and Law Enforcement," p. 283.

20. Michael J. Buzomi, "Foreign Intelligence Surveillance Act: Before and After the Patriot Act," *FBI Law Enforcement Bulletin*, June 2003, pp. 25–32.

21. Ibid.

22. Chita Ragavan, "Mueller's Mandate," *U.S. News and World Report*, 26 May 2003.

23. Ibid.

24. Liz Halloran, "Falsely Accused: CIA Agent's Tale," *Hartford Courant*, 11 December 2002.

25. Wise, *Spy*, pp. 205–218.

26. Baer, *See No Evil*, pp. 230–234.

CHAPTER 7

1. Todd Masse, "Domestic Intelligence in the United Kingdom: Applicability of the MI-5 Model to the U.S." Washington, DC: Congressional Research Service, 19 May 2003.

2. Jock Haswell, *Spies and Spymasters*. London: Thames and Hudson, 1977, pp. 110–111.

3. John Sawatsky, *Men in the Shadows: The RCMP Security Service*. Toronto: Doubleday, 1980.

4. Ibid.

5. Reg Whitaker, "The Politics of Security Intelligence Policy in Canada, 1970–1984," *Intelligence and National Security*, 6 no. 4, October 1991, pp. 649–668.

6. Linda Stein, "Terror Info Net Spreads," *The Times* (Princeton, NJ) 2 November 2003, p. A3.

7. Eric Lichtblau, "FBI Is Retailoring to Meet New Threats but Stretched Thin," *New York Times* 19 June 2003, p. A15.

8. David Wise, *Spy*, pp. 220–226.

9. Bearden and Risen, *The Main Enemy*, pp. 25–26.

10. John Mintz and Dan Eggen, "Ashcroft, Ridge Settle Turf Battle," *Washington Post*, 23 May 2003, p. A7.

11. Matthew Purdy and Lowell Bergman, "Unclear Danger: Inside the Lackawanna Terror Case," *New York Times*, 12 October 2003, p. A1.

12. Ibid.

13. Jonathan Eig, "Sounding the Alarm at Shoney's Takes Its Toll On Mrs. Stone," *Wall Street Journal*, 17 June 2003, p. A1.

14. Michael Moss, "False Terrorism Tips to FBI Uproot the Lives of Suspects," *New York Times*, 19 June 2003, p. A1.

15. An extensive discussion of interrogation techniques can be found in Mark Bowden, "The Dark Art of Interrogation," *Atlantic Monthly*, 292 no. 3, October 2003, pp. 51–76.

16. Bearden and Risen, *The Main Enemy*, pp. 20–22.

17. Eric Lichtblau, "Trucker Sentenced to 20 Years in Plot Against Brooklyn Bridge," *New York Times*, 29 October 2003, p. A19.

18. Susan Schmidt, "Suspect Is Named al Qaeda Soldier," *Boston Globe*, 24 June 2003, p. A24.

19. Eric Lichtblau, "U.S. Will Tighten Rules on Holding Terror Suspects," *New York Times*, 13 June 2003, p. A1.

20. Ibid.

21. Curt Anderson, "Few jailed in terror cases, study says," *Boston Globe*, 8 December 2003, p. A2.

22. Eric Lichtblau, "Bush Issues Racial Profiling Ban But Exempts Security Inquiries," *New York Times*, 1 June 2003, p. A1.

23. Charles Doyle, "The USA Patriot Act," *Congressional Research Report*, April 2002.

24. Baer, *See No Evil*, pp. 67–68.

25. Newsletter of the Association of Former Intelligence Officers (AFIO), 21 June 2003.

26. *Wall Street Journal*, 25 June 2003, p. D5.

CHAPTER 8

1. Robin Moore, *The Hunt For Bin Laden*. New York: Random House, 2003, p. 5.

2. Ibid., p. 45.

3. Christopher Ward, *The War of the Revolution*. New York: Macmillan, 1952, pp. 258–259.

4. Stephen Knott, *Secret and Sanctioned*, pp. 94–106.

5. Ibid., p. 136.

6. Ibid., pp. 145–146.

7. H. W. Brands, *TR: The Last Romantic*. New York: Basic Books, 1997, pp. 479–491.

8. Robert R. Kehoe, "1944: An Allied Team with the French Resistance," *CIA Studies in Intelligence,* Winter 1998–1999, pp. 15–50.

9. Richard Harris Smith, *OSS*.

10. See, for example, Gregory Treverton, *Covert Action: The Limits of Intervention in the Postwar World*. New York: Basic Books, 1987; and Theodore Shackley, *The Third Option: An American View of Counterinsurgency*. Pleasantville, NY: Readers Digest, 1981.

11. Jeffreys-Jones, *The CIA and American Democracy,* p. 93.

12. Ibid.

13. Tom Clancy and John Gresham, *Special Forces*. New York: Berkley Books, 2001, p. 11.

14. This view comes through in Jeffreys-Jones, *The CIA and American Democracy,* and in John Prados, *President's Secret Wars: CIA and Pentagon Covert Operations From World War II through Iranscam*. New York: William Morrow, 1986.

15. William M. Leary, ed. *The Central Intelligence Agency: History and Documents*. University, AL: University of Alabama Press, 1984.

16. Uri Bar-Joseph, *Intelligence Intervention in the Politics of Democratic States*. University Park, PA: The Pennsylvania State University Press, 1995.

17. Jeffreys-Jones, *CIA and American Democracy,* p. 192; An inside view is contained in Kristian C. Gustafson, "CIA Machinations in Chile in 1970," *CIA Studies in Intelligence,* 47 no. 3, 2003, pp. 35–49.

18. Antonio J. Mendez, *The Master of Disguise: My Secret Life in the CIA*. New York: William Morrow and Co., 1999.

19. Odom, *Fixing Intelligence,* p. 145.

20. Bearden and Risen, *The Main Enemy,* p. 234.

21. Ibid., p. 180.

22. Baer, *See No Evil,* pp. 191–192.

23. Andrew Koch, "Covert Warriors," *Jane's Defence Weekly,* 19 March 2003.

24. Ibid.

25. Thom Shanker and Eric Schmitt, "Pentagon Says a Covert Force Hunts Hussein," *New York Times,* 7 November 2003, p. A1.

26. Eric Schmitt, "How Army Sleuths Stalked the Adviser Who Led to Hussein," *New York Times,* 20 December 2003, p. A1.

CHAPTER 9

1. David M. McCullough, *Truman.* New York: Simon and Schuster, 1992, pp. 736–741.

2. John Mintz, "Terrorism and Homeland Security: Government's Troubled Giant Homeland Security Is Struggling," *Washington Post,* 7 September 2003, p. A1.

3. Ibid.

4. "Homeland Security," *Special TRAC Report.* Syracuse, NY: Syracuse University, 29 August 2003.

5. Mintz, "Terrorism and Homeland Security."

6. Jason Peckenpaugh, "Homeland border enforcement bureau looks to cross-train agents," *Government Executive Daily Briefing,* 4 August 2003.

7. Syracuse *TRAC* report.

8. Shelley Murphy, "Logan still finding armed travelers," *Boston Globe,* 28 August 2003, p. B1.

9. Bryan Bender, "Flying freight-class reopens debate," *Boston Globe,* 10 September 2003, p. A6.

10. Syracuse *TRAC* report.

11. Mintz, "Terrorism and Homeland Security."

12. See www.usinfo.state.gov.

13. Ibid.

14. DHS Press Release, "FY 2004 Budget Fact Sheet," 1 October 2003.

15. Philip Shenon, "Homeland Security Department Planning 7 Offices Overseas," *New York Times,* 7 October 2003, p. A1.

CHAPTER 10

1. "Emergency Responders: Dramatically Underfunded, Dangerously Unprepared," Report of an Independent Task Force Sponsored by the Council on Foreign Relations, Warren Rudman, Chairman, March, 2003.

2. H. D. S. Greenway, "Is It Safe?" *Boston Globe Sunday Magazine,* 27 July 2003, p. 13.

3. Philip Shenon, "U.S. Widens Checks on Foreign Ports," *New York Times,* 12 June 2003, p. A1.

4. Craig P. Coy, "Air Travelers Deserve Better," *Boston Globe,* 17 November 2003, p. A19.

5. FEMA Press Release R1-03-77, 6 August 2003.

6. Rudman Report.

7. Michael Janofsky, "Intelligence To Be Shared, Ridge Tells Governors," *New York Times,* 19 August 2003.

8. State of Maryland Press Release, June 2003.

9. Sara Michael, "CDC's New Sense of Purpose," *Federal Computer Week,* 7 July 2003.

10. Ibid.

11. Charles P. Connolly, "The Role of Private Security in Combating Terrorism," *Journal of Homeland Security,* July 2003.

12. Richard Brennan, "U.S. Army Finds Its Role At Home Up For Grabs," *Rand Review*, Summer, 2002, pp. 46–47.

13. Mickey McCarter, "Northcom at 1," *Homeland Defense Journal*, 1 no. 7, pp. 38–43.

14. Eric V. Larson, "U.S. Air Force Roles Reach Big in Securing the Skies," *Rand Review*, Summer, 2002, pp. 44–45.

15. Northern Command Fact Sheet, 2002.

16. Ibid.

CHAPTER 11

1. Jeffreys-Jones, *CIA and American Democracy*, pp. 24–25.

2. Ibid.

3. Ibid., p. 36.

4. Larry Kindsvater, "The Need to Reorganize the Intelligence Community," *CIA Studies in Intelligence*, 47 no. 1, 2003, pp. 33–37.

5. Vernon Loeb, "Scowcroft's Vanishing Plan," *Washington Post*, 5 July 2002.

6. James Risen and Thom Shanker, "Rumsfeld Moves to Strengthen His Grip on Military Intelligence," *New York Times*, 3 August 2002, p. A1.

7. Thomas Duffy, "New DoD Intelligence Directorate Will Have Broad Policy, Program Influence," *Inside the Pentagon*, 27 March 2003.

8. Congressional Joint Inquiry on 9/11.

9. Hulnick, *Fixing the Spy Machine*, pp. 191–208.

10. Bruce Berkowitz, "Spying in the Post-September 11 World," *The Hoover Digest*, 13 November 2003.

11. Laura Sullivan, "Amid Criticism, Ashcroft Tours U.S. to Defend the Patriot Act," *Baltimore Sun*, 20 August 2003.

12. Hulnick, *Fixing the Spy Machine*, pp. 96–97.

13. Leigh Strope, "Bush trims federal workers' raises, cites 'national emergency,'" *Boston Globe*, 28 August 2003, p. A13.

14. Odom, *Fixing Intelligence*, pp. 185–193.

15. Larry Kindsvater, "The Need to Reorganize the Intelligence Community."

CHAPTER 12

1. Witcover, *Sabotage at Black Tom*.

2. Kessler, *The Bureau*, p. 11.

3. Ibid.

4. Ibid., p. 14.

5. Ibid., p. 15.

6. Linda Greenhouse, "A Question of Federal Turf," *New York Times*, 12 November 2003, p. A1.

7. Douglas T. Stuart, "Ministry of Fear: The 1947 National Security Act," *Intelligence Studies in Perspective*, 4 no. 3, pp. 293–313.

8. Dan Egger and Susan Schmidt, "Data Show Different Spy Game Since 9/11," *Washington Post*, 1 May 2004, p. A1.

9. Eric Lichtblau, "Administration Creates Center for Master Terror Watch List," *New York Times*, 17 September 2003, p. A18.

10. DiNeen L. Brown and Dana Priest, "Deported Terror Suspect Details Torture in Syria," *Washington Post,* 5 November 2003.

11. Philip Shenon, "Panel on Terror Calls for Board On Protecting Civil Liberties," *New York Times,* 16 December 2003, p. A20.

12. USDOT Highway Fatality Statistics, July 2003.

13. Andrew P. Jenkins, "Annual Smoking Deaths in Perspective," Central Washington University.

Bibliography

Adams, James. *Sellout: Aldrich Ames and the Corruption of the CIA.* New York: Viking, 1995.

Allen, Dean and Brian Shellman, eds. *Defense Intelligence Agency: At the Creation, 1961–1965.* Washington, DC: DIA History Office, 2002.

Andrew, Christopher. *For the President's Eyes Only.* New York: Harper Collins, 1995.

Baer, Robert. *See No Evil: The True Story of a Ground Soldier in the CIA's War on Terrorism.* New York: Crown Publishers, 2002.

Bamford, James. *The Puzzle Palace.* New York: Houghton Mifflin, 1982.

———. *Body of Secrets: Anatomy of the Ultra-Secret National Security Agency.* New York: Doubleday, 2000.

Bar-Joseph, Uri. *Intelligence Intervention in the Politics of Democratic States.* University Park, PA: The Pennsylvania State University Press, 1995.

Bearden, Milton, and James Risen. *The Main Enemy: The Inside Story of the CIA's Final Showdown with the KGB.* New York: Random House, 2003.

Benjamin, Daniel, and Steven Simon. *The Age Of Sacred Terror.* New York: Random House, 2002.

Benson, Robert L., and Michael Warner, eds. *Venona.* Washington, DC: CIA, 1996.

Black, Ian, and Benny Morris. *Israel's Secret Wars.* New York: Grove Weidenfeld, 1991.

Brands, H. W. *TR: The Last Romantic.* New York: Basic Books, 1997.

Clancy, Tom and John Gresham. *Special Forces.* New York: Berkley Books, 2001.

Clarridge, Duane. *A Spy for All Seasons: My Life in the CIA.* New York: Scribner, 1997.

Earley, Pete. *Family of Spies: Inside the John Walker Spy Ring.* New York: Bantam Books, 1989.

———. *Confessions of a Spy: The Real Story of Aldrich Ames.* New York: Putnam, 1997.

Eftimiades, Nicholas. *Chinese Intelligence Operations.* Annapolis, MD: Naval Institute Press, 1994.

Emerson, Steven. *American Jihad: The Terrorists Living Among Us.* New York: Free Press, 2002.

Fialka, John. *War By Other Means: Economic Espionage in America.* New York: W. W. Norton, 1997.

Fishel, Edwin. *The Secret War for the Union.* New York: Houghton Mifflin, 1996.

Fuld, Leonard. *The New Competitor Intelligence.* New York: John Wiley & Sons, 1995.

Global Trends 2015: A Dialogue About the Future with Non-Governmental Experts. Washington, DC: National Intelligence Council, December, 2000.

Haswell, Jock. *Spies and Spymasters.* London: Thames and Hudson, 1977.

Hedley, John Hollister, ed. *Fifty Years of Informing Policy.* Washington DC: Central Intelligence Agency, 2002.

Hoffman, Bruce. *Inside Terrorism.* New York: Columbia University Press, 1998.

Hulnick, Arthur S. *Fixing the Spy Machine.* Westport, CT: Praeger, 1999.

Intelligence in the War of Independence. Washington, DC: Central Intelligence Agency, 1976.

Jeffreys-Jones, Rhodri. *The CIA and American Democracy,* 3rd ed. New Haven: Yale University Press, 2003.

Kahn, David. *The Codebreakers.* New York: The Macmillan Company, 1967.

———. *Hitler's Spies.* New York: Collier Books, 1978.

Kessler, Ronald. *The FBI.* New York: Pocket Books, 1993.

———. *The Bureau: The Secret History of the FBI.* New York: St. Martin's Press, 2002.

Knightly, Philip. *The Second Oldest Profession.* London: Andre Deutsch, 1986.

Knott, Stephen F. *Secret and Sanctioned: Covert Operations and the American Presidency.* New York: Oxford University Press, 1996.

Leary, William M., ed. *The Central Intelligence Agency: History and Documents.* University, AL: University of Alabama Press, 1984.

MacEachin, Douglas J. *CIA Assessments of the Soviet Union: The Record vs. the Charges.* Washington, DC: Center for the Study of Intelligence, CIA, 1996.

McCullough, David M. *Truman.* New York: Simon and Schuster, 1992.

Melanson, Philip. *The Secret Service.* New York: Carroll and Graf, 2002.

Mendez, Antonio J. *The Master of Disguise: My Secret Life in the CIA.* New York: William Morrow and Co., 1999.

Miller, Nathan. *Spying for America.* New York: Dell Publishing, 1989.

Moore, Robin. *The Hunt for Bin Laden.* New York: Random House, 2003.

Odom, William. *Fixing Intelligence.* New Haven: Yale University Press, 2003.

O'Toole, George J. A. *Honorable Treachery.* New York: Atlantic Monthly Press, 1991.

Pedlow, Gregory W., and Donald E. Welzenbach. *CIA and the U-2 Program 1954-1974.* Washington, DC: Center for the Study of Intelligence, CIA, 1998.

Pillar, Paul R. *Terrorism and U.S. Foreign Policy*. Washington, DC: Brookings Institution Press, 2001.

Prados, John. *President's Secret Wars: CIA and Pentagon Covert Operations from World War II through Iranscam*. New York: William Morrow, 1986.

Reston, James, Jr. *Warriors of God: Richard the Lionheart and Saladin in the Third Crusade*. New York: Doubleday, 2001.

Richelson, Jeffrey T. *America's Secret Eyes in Space: The U.S. Keyhole Spy Satellite Program*. New York: Harper and Row, 1990.

Sawatsky, John. *Men in the Shadows: The RCMP Security Service*. Toronto: Doubleday, 1980.

Shackley, Theodore. *The Third Option: An American View of Counterinsurgency*. Pleasantville, NY: Readers Digest, 1981.

Shulsky, Abram N. *Silent Warfare: Understanding the World of Intelligence*. New York: Brassey's, 1991.

Smith, Richard Harris. *OSS: The Secret History of America's First Central Intelligence Agency*. Berkeley: University of California Press, 1972.

Steele, Robert David. *On Intelligence: Spies and Secrecy in an Open World*. Fairfax, VA: AFCEA International Press, 2000.

———. *The New Craft of Intelligence*. Oakton, VA: OSS International Press, 2002.

Stern, Jessica. *Terror in the Name of God: Why Religious Militants Kill*. New York: ECCO, 2003.

Treverton, Gregory. *Covert Action: the Limits of Intervention in the Postwar World*. New York: Basic Books, 1987.

Tuchman, Barbara. *The Zimmermann Telegram*. New York: Ballentine Books, 1966.

Ward, Christopher. *The War of the Revolution*. New York: Macmillan, 1952.

Wise, David. *Spy: The Inside Story of How the FBI's Robert Hanssen Betrayed America*. New York: Random House, 2002.

Wise, David. *The Spy Who Got Away*. New York: Random House, 1988.

Witcover, Jules. *Sabotage at Black Tom*. Chapel Hill, NC: Algonquin Books of Chapel Hill, 1989.

Wohlstetter, Roberta. *Pearl Harbor: Warning and Decision*. Stanford, CA: Stanford University Press, 1962.

Index

About the Author

ARTHUR S. HULNICK is Associate Professor of International Relations at Boston University and a veteran of 35 years as an intelligence professional. He began his service as an intelligence officer in the U.S. Air Force and joined the CIA in 1965. He served in a variety of assignments in the U.S. and overseas before becoming the CIA Officer-in-Residence at Boston University in 1989, where he created and taught courses on aspects of intelligence. After retiring from the CIA in 1992, he continued to teach at BU and, in 1999, published his first book *Fixing the Spy Machine* (Praeger). In 2003 he taught one of the first courses in the U.S. on Intelligence and Homeland Security.